Wiltshire Record Society

(formerly the Records Branch of the Wiltshire Archaeological and Natural History Society)

VOLUME XXVIII
FOR THE YEAR 1972

Impression of 400 copies

WILTSHIRE EXTENTS FOR DEBTS EDWARD I—ELIZABETH I

EDITED BY

ANGELA CONYERS

DEVIZES
1973

ISBN: 0 901333 05 0

Set in Times New Roman 10/11pt.

PRINTED IN GREAT BRITAIN BY
GLEVUM PRESS LTD.,
GLOUCESTER

CONTENTS

PREFACE

The plan to prepare an edition of Wiltshire extents for debts was contrived in the late 1940s by Professor R. B. Pugh, now President of the Society, who noticed the absence of an edition of that class of documents for any county and resolved to supply the deficiency. The work, however, made little progress until it was resumed by the present editor, Mrs. Angela Conyers, in 1968.

Mrs. Conyers wishes to thank Professor Pugh for making a number of suggestions during the course of editing. For help and encouragement in other directions she is no less grateful to Dr. Patricia M. Barnes, an Assistant Keeper of the Public Records, and to Mr. William Kellaway, Secretary and Librarian of the Institute of Historical Research. The Society is indebted to Dr. G. D. Ramsay, Fellow of St. Edmund Hall, Oxford, for reading the introduction in draft and helpfully commenting upon it.

January 1973 DOUGLAS CROWLEY

ABBREVIATIONS

Cal. Inq. Misc.	*Calendar of Inquisitions Miscellaneous* (H.M.S.O.)
C.C.R.	*Calendar of Close Rolls* (H.M.S.O.)
L.C. 4	Public Record Office: Lord Chamberlain's Department, Recognizances
oct.	octave
quin.	quindene
Rec. Com.	Record Commission
S.J.B.	the feast of the nativity of St. John the Baptist
V.C.H. Wilts.	*Victoria History of Wiltshire*

INTRODUCTION

The 'extents' abstracted in this volume are descriptions, with valuations, of the lands and goods of defaulting debtors who held property in Wiltshire.[1] They are the outcome of various writs issuing out of Chancery to the sheriff of that county, especially the writs of *capias* and *elegit*. The first of these writs originated in the Statute of Acton Burnell, 1283, the second in the Statute of Westminster II, 1285. Both are therefore legal innovations attributable to Edward I's reforming zeal.

Nearly all the extents and their accompanying writs are drawn from two classes, C 131 and C 239, in the Public Record Office, London. They cover the period from 1306, the date of the earliest known Wiltshire extent of this character, to the end of Elizabeth I's reign. For that period all known extents have been abstracted, though there are many more for later years, running up to 1774–5. No collection of such abstracts has been published for any county before. Indeed this type of document has been but little studied,[2] partly no doubt because, until 1970, many examples of it were inaccessible to the public.[3]

ACKNOWLEDGEMENT OF DEBTS UNDER STATUTES MERCHANT AND STAPLE AND THE WRIT OF *CAPIAS*

The statute made at Acton Burnell, in Shropshire,[4] was introduced to provide a quick means for merchants to recover their debts. It supplemented but did not supersede older methods of procedure by the action of debt-detinue, by writs of *fieri facias* and *levari facias* (described below),[5] and by the law merchant. It made provision for the acknowledgement and registration of debts before the mayors of certain towns at the time at which the debts were contracted. Such acknowledgements were called recognizances. The original towns were London, York, and Bristol, but several more were added later. Among these additions was Salisbury, authorized in 1351,[6] before whose mayor one debt in this volume **(16)** was acknowledged in 1356. The mayors were aided by royal clerks, each furnished with a special seal and all subsequent legislation made provision for such clerks and seals. Recognizances were to

1 See pp. 13-16 for their classification and archival history and pp. 9-10 for the meaning of 'debt'.

2 The best discourse on statute merchant and staple procedure is perhaps that by E. E. Rich in the introduction to *The Staple Court Books of Bristol* (Bristol Rec. Soc. v). *Select Cases in the Law Merchant*, III, ed. H. Hall (Selden Soc. xlix) is also useful. Neither makes much use of the extents grounded upon procedure.

3 As Professor L. Stone notes: 'The extents . . . are widely scattered, incompletely listed, entirely unindexed and consequently impossible to use for comprehensive statistical purposes': 'The Elizabethan aristocracy', *Economic History Review*, 2nd ser. iv. 317 n.

4 Statute of Merchants, 11 Edw. I, *Statutes of the Realm* (Rec. Com.), i. 53–4.

5 See pp. 5-6.

6 *V.C.H. Wilts*. vi. 176.

be entered upon a roll and also upon bonds sealed with the debtor's seal and the special royal seal above referred to.[1] If the debtor defaulted, the creditor could report the default to the mayor, who would order the sale of the debtor's goods and devisable burgage tenements, which were likewise deemed to be goods. If the debtor owned goods and such burgages outside the mayor's jurisdiction, the mayor would send the recognizances into Chancery whence a writ would be issued to the sheriff of the county where the goods and burgages were to be found. If there were no goods or burgages there, the debtor was to be sent to prison until a settlement had been reached. If necessary he was to be maintained at the creditor's expense, but then only on bread and water.

Merchants complained that sheriffs misinterpreted the statute and so delayed the procedure that it laid down. Accordingly, two years later, the statute was re-enacted in a revised form, commonly called the Statute of Merchants (1285),[2] though at times it still retained the name of Acton Burnell.[3] Under this a fee was to be collected by the Crown on each recognizance. A debtor defaulting on a recognizance was to be at once imprisoned at his own expense. If the mayor could not find him within his jurisdiction, he was to send the recognizance into Chancery, which would issue a writ of *capias*, whose form is prescribed in the statute, to the sheriff to take and imprison him. During the first three months of imprisonment the debtor's goods were supposed to be sent to him so that he could discharge the debt himself. If he failed to do so, not only his goods but his lands were to be delivered to the merchant, who as 'tenant by statute merchant' would have possession of the lands that the debtor held on the day of recognizance until the debt had been repaid from their profits and could no more lawfully be disturbed than if he had acquired them otherwise. The sheriff was to make his return by a certain day,[4] at which time the merchant was able to sue for the debt if no settlement had been reached. If the sheriff made a return of *non est inventus*, as frequently happened, the creditor could secure a *capias* to the sheriff of any county in which the debtor was believed to hold land and goods. The *capias* against Robert Lok in 1347 **(9)** was issued under this procedure and the wording of the statute is reproduced in the abstract. The case of William Huloun in 1306 **(1)** provides an example of alleged failure by the sheriff to disclose all the debtor's lands and goods and carried a warning to the sheriff that he would be amerced if he failed to carry out his orders. In both these cases the recognizances were made before the mayor of London.

The Ordainers took exception to some provisions of the statute and the Ordinances of 1311 include some measures for amending it.[5] In particular the procedure that it established was to be limited to recognizances between

[1] For a fragment of a statute merchant roll of much later date see *The Statute Merchant Roll of Coventry* 1392–1416, ed. Alice Beardwood (Dugdale Soc. xvii).

[2] Statute of Merchants, 13 Edw. I, *Statutes of the Realm* (Rec. Com.), i. 98–100.

[3] *Staple Ct. Bks. of Bristol*, ed. Rich (Bristol Rec. Soc.), p. 44 and n.

[4] The writ of *capias* as indeed of *elegit* was in general returnable to Chancery, less commonly to other courts. See p. 15.

[5] Ordinances, c. 33, *Statutes of the Realm* (Rec. Com.), i. 165.

merchants and land was once again to be confined to burgages. With the rest of the Ordinances this was repealed in 1322.[1]

From Edward I's reign Englishmen began to grow familiar with the concept of a staple town—a trading centre at which merchants, both native and foreign, were exclusively authorized to deal in England's 'staple' (or principal) exports of wool, hides, woolfells, and tin. These staple towns were at first fixed in foreign parts but from 1326 attempts, never lasting, were made to transfer them to home ground. The Ordinance of the Staple of 1353,[2] confirmed by Parliament in 1354,[3] whereby the foreign staples were replaced by domestic ones in 15 different English, Welsh, and Irish towns, represents the last attempt.[4] The statute incidentally extended the benefits of the Statute of Merchants by stipulating that recognizances of debt could be entered into before the officers of a staple, who should collect fees thereon, and by omitting in such cases the three-months' delay in execution of the debt which the earlier statute required. It is not clear whether the advantages of the new statute could from the outset be enjoyed by non-merchants, but in 1362 it was expressly extended to them.[5] For the next 170 years the *capias* writ, whether prosecuted under a statute merchant or statute staple recognizance, became, for merchants and non-merchants alike, the most popular means of exacting payment.

In the period from 1353–4 until the Act of 1532 (described below) most of the recognizances in this volume were taken before the 'mayors' or chief officers of the Staple of Westminster, and of Winchester **(11–12, 15, 19, 21, 60, 151).** In **50** and **53** John Thacham acknowledged the same debt to John Romsey on the same date before the mayor of Southampton and the mayor of the Southampton staple. Clearly Romsey felt the need to be doubly sure of repayment. The incident also well illustrates the concurrence of the two systems of acknowledgement: by statute merchant and by statute staple. In **74** the debt was acknowledged before the mayor of Bristol and (the same man) the mayor of the staple there, together with the constables of the staple, in **85** before the mayor and constables of the Staple of Exeter.

In 1532 a new Act sought to re-emphasize the distinction between private and trade debts by instituting a separate but parallel procedure for the former.[6] While the power of the mayors and constables of the staple to take recognizances made between those who were genuinely merchants of the staple for genuine merchandise of the staple was preserved, other people were required to make such acknowledgements before the chief justices of the Common Pleas or King's Bench, or, out of term, before the mayor of the Staple of Westminster and the recorder of London together. Obligations were to be enrolled

[1] Ibid. 189.
[2] 27 Edw. III, Stat. II, c. 9, ibid. 336–7.
[3] 28 Edw. III, c. 13, ibid. 348–9.
[4] The only records of an English staple court known to have been published are those edited by Professor Rich (see above, p. 1, n. 2).
[5] 36 Edw. III, Stat. I, c. 7, *Statutes of the Realm* (Rec. Com.), i. 373. See Hall, *Select Cases*, p. xxviii.
[6] 23 Hen. VIII, c. 6, *Statutes of the Realm* (Rec. Com.), iii. 372–3.

on duplicate rolls in a set form prescribed by the Act, one roll to remain with a chief justice or the mayor, as the case might be, and the other with a clerk of the recognizances appointed by the Crown.[1] The first example of the new procedure in this volume is **71.** Anthony White, a haberdasher, made such a recognizance 'in the nature of a statute staple' in 1571 to John Conyers **(104)** before the chief justice of Common Pleas and a recognizance under the statute staple before the mayor of the Staple of Westminster and the recorder of London in the same year to Thomas Browne **(105).**

Why did Parliament pass the Act of 1532 prohibiting in intention the mayors of the staple from taking recognizances from non-merchants? Why did that Act disingenuously ignore the statute of 1362 and seek to restore the *status quo* of 1353–4? In part the measure was directed against the old staple jurisdictions which had long been out of favour with the Crown and whose activities the Crown sought to curtail by the setting up of new royal procedures.[2] The chief justices of the senior courts of common law and the civic powers of London and Westminster, who stood to gain from the fees collected by the clerk of the recognizances, presumably supported the Crown and were strong enough to prevail against provincial interests represented in the staple courts. It is probable that the Act was also provoked by an increase in financial dealings between individuals and was part of an attempt to clarify and make more secure the registration of the debts they contracted. The large and imperfectly investigated problem of debt collection, however, remained, to say the least, no less complex after 1532, and only part of it is illuminated by this volume.[3]

Recognizances in the nature of a statute staple were not only enrolled on the recognizance rolls but were also entered in entry books[4] belonging to the office of the clerk of the recognizances. For the years covered all recognizances in this volume are in the entry books. Most, but not all,[5] entries have the note '*cert. in canc.*' with the date. This signifies that the creditor had obtained his certificate from the clerk of the recognizances and returned it into Chancery. Chancery would then issue the *capias* writ which initiated the procedure under the Statute Staple by ordering the sheriff to imprison the debtor and make an extent of his lands and goods for delivery to the king. As comparison with the entry book shows, the *capias* was generally issued within a few days of certification. It was often necessary for the *capias* to be issued more than once. Several entries in the entry books (e.g. **79, 81)** record

[1] The recognizances were also recorded in entry books. See below and n. 4.

[2] Rich, op. cit. 62. The new procedures were, of course, liable to be evaded: ibid.

[3] For the history of negotiable instruments see J. M. Holden, *History of Negotiable Instruments in English Law.*

[4] There are entry books from 32 Hen. VIII to 32 Geo. II. For the period covered by this volume there are nine volumes (P.R.O., L.C. 4/187–195) and four indexes ([L.C. 4/207–10] Ind. 8950, 8951A, 8951B, 8952). There are no indexes for the years 3–36 Eliz. I and no entry books for 16–32 Eliz. I. For reasons never satisfactorily explained the rolls, entry books, and indexes form part of the records of the Lord Chamberlain's Department.

[5] Omission must have been accidental, as certification was necessary before action could be taken.

a second or even third certification, though only one *capias* has survived. In other instances both *capias* writs are in the volume; **102** and **131** both relate to the same case and similarly **110** and **118.**

When an extent was received in Chancery, a writ of *liberate* was issued instructing the sheriff to release the lands and goods to the creditor. A number of *liberates* have survived, though often separated from the original writ of *capias*, and they provide a useful check on the wording of the extent itself as they repeat its contents verbatim.

If a debtor was believed to hold land within a liberty, the sheriff on receipt of the *capias* passed it to the bailiff, who might make the extent himself, as in **42,** where both the sheriff and the bailiff did so, or in **64, 80,** and **107.** If the sheriff reported to Chancery that he had had no answer from the bailiff a *non omittas* was issued instructing him to ignore the liberty and proceed with the extent himself. Nos. **1, 8, 10,** and **25** are examples, the last after *elegit.*

If a debtor died, his heirs were liable for his debt but not liable to imprisonment. If the heir was a minor, his lands were to remain with him until he came of age (see **90**). If the sheriff reported the debtor's death, a writ of extent (*extendi facias*) was issued ordering the sheriff to make the extent, e.g. **45, 50, 90, 99, 119, 160,** and **167.** In **41, 45, 50, 53,** and **168-9** no *extendi facias* or extent follows and it may perhaps be assumed that the case was allowed to drop. No action seems to have been taken in 1572 against the estate of William, Lord Stourton, on the sheriff's return that Stourton was dead **(102),** since fourteen years later the case was reopened and a further writ of *capias* issued **(131).** Land held by a debtor's tenants was also liable; in **117** a *scire facias* was issued to the tenants of the late John Michell and a moiety of the yearly value of their lands was delivered to the creditors by *elegit.*

THE ACKNOWLEDGEMENT OF DEBTS IN CHANCERY AND THE WRIT OF *ELEGIT*

It must be emphasized that debts might very well be acknowledged in other courts or before other officials than those described above. Such an acknowledgement might be made in open court after the inception of an action, or enrolled, as in the case of statute merchant recognizances, at the time of contract. Recognizances were certainly being made in Chancery by 1273 and from about that time they appear on the Close Rolls with growing frequency.[1] To those to whom the acknowledgements were made, the conusees, the common law writs of *fieri facias* and *levari facias* were available. In the form that they eventually assumed these directed the sheriff to 'make' the sum from the debtor's goods or to levy it from the profits of his lands. From 1285, the year of the Statute of Merchants, a new remedy for this type of creditor was provided under the Statute of Westminster II.[2] This gave him power to 'choose' a different writ, hence called *elegit*, by which the sheriff was to deliver to the creditor all the debtor's chattels, except his oxen and plough-

[1] See R. B. Pugh, 'Some Medieval Moneylenders', *Speculum*, xliii. 274–5.

[2] 13 Edw. I, c. 18, *Statutes of the Realm* (Rec. Com.), i. 82.

beasts, and half his lands. The lands to be seized were those held at the date of judgment and not, as with the Statute Staple, the date of the recognizance. If a year or more had elapsed from the date of acknowledgement of debt, a writ of *scire facias* had to be issued before the *elegit*, informing the debtor that action was to be taken against him, as in **5, 6,** and **18** where the *scire facias* was issued to the debtor's heirs who had become responsible for the debt on his death. By Elizabeth I's time it appears to have become standard practice, when debts were acknowledged in London, to sue out the *scire facias* to the sheriffs of London or Middlesex, and to issue the *elegit* into other counties when those sheriffs reported that the debtor held no lands within their bailiwicks. In all the Elizabethan cases the debtor failed to appear to answer such writs of *scire facias*, except in **146** where a debtor did in fact appear but could not deny the creditors' allegations. In the case of William Aylmer **(5)** the heirs appeared in Chancery and gave no reason why judgment should not go against them, while in **6** the heirs failed to appear and in **8** the heirs were able to show that only half the original debt was still outstanding.

There are in this volume only two examples of the *levari facias* procedure; in **98** Anthony Hungerford acknowledged his debt in Chancery and a writ of *levari facias* was sued out against him, and in **96** a *capias* was issued upon a *levari facias* to John Hamlyn. In **165,** a complicated case, a *fieri facias* was issued against an elder and a younger John Toppe for the sheriff to 'make' a specified amount from their goods, being the rents and profits they had enjoyed from certain lands wrongly assigned to them.[1] In the Wiltshire examples *elegit* was commonly used before 1362[2] **(2–8, 10)** and continued to be used throughout the period covered by this volume, examples occurring in 1383 **(26),** 1386 **(27),** 1437 **(46),** and ten times between 1568 and 1598 **(94–5, 97, 100, 117, 129, 132, 142, 146, 159).** The comparative smallness of the sums involved in these cases suggests that *elegit* was preferred for smaller debts. In **100** the creditor is a grocer, which shows that the process originally intended for private debts was used on occasion by tradesmen also. The tenant by *elegit* was protected in his occupancy of land in the same way as the tenant by statutes merchant and staple. It is strange that of the 36 known cases on the common law side of the Chancery ('Placita in Cancellaria')[3] which appear to be proceedings on recognizances of debt in Wiltshire only two **(137** and **138)** relate directly to extents abstracted in this volume and in both these cases we have no knowledge of a writ of *elegit*. Since the cases were instigated by writs of *scire facias* to the sheriffs of London or Middlesex are we to assume that the *elegits* were for some reason never sent to the sheriff of Wiltshire, or alternatively that the writs were filed separately and have not yet come to light?

Just as a creditor might secure an acknowledgement before the chief justice of the Common Pleas and the mayor of the staple, so he might require the debtor to acknowledge his debt both before a person authorized to take it by

[1] See p. 11.
[2] For the statute of 1362 see p. 3.
[3] P.R.O., C 43.

the 1532 Act and also in Chancery. Lancelot Stokker thus acknowledged his debt to Matthew King both in Chancery and in the Common Pleas **(82)**.[1]

THE DEBTORS AND CREDITORS

That the statute staple and *elegit* procedures were extensively used by many classes of society is clear from the variety in the occupations and social standing of both debtors and creditors. In about a third of the cases in this volume the creditors are called merchants or tradesmen. Several trades are represented,[2] the cloth trade in particular. 'Merchants' occur slightly less frequently as debtors.

At the top level there are three peers among the debtors, Lords Cobham, Stourton, and Mountjoy, and 17 knights. Certain family names recur: Sir John Blount was sued for 120*l*. in 1376 **(18)** and 60*l*. in 1383 **(26)** and his descendant William Blount, Lord Mountjoy, was involved in no fewer than 4 suits between 1585 and 1588,[3] having acknowledged either alone or with others a total of 1,200*l*. John, Lord Stourton, was joint debtor for 200*l*. in 1494 **(54)**, and William, Lord Stourton, was sued for 300*l*. in 1570 **(99)**, for 2,000*l*. in 1572 **(102)**, and for the same sum in 1586 **(131)**. Cases involving the Chatterton family of Lydiard Millicent shed light on the complexities of the statute staple procedure.[4] *Elegits* were sued out against Thomas Chatterton, 'gentleman', for 200*l*. in 1569 **(45)** and against Thomas Chatterton, 'esquire', for 120*l*. in 1585 **(129)**. Debts of 1,000*l*. and 600*l*. respectively were also acknowledged to James Altham[5] by the second Thomas **(108)** and by William and Henry Chatterton **(107)**. The entry books also show that at the time the recognizances in **107–8** were recorded Thomas, William, and Henry Chatterton together acknowledged 800*l*. to Thomas Bowyer of London. The purposes of the Chattertons in borrowing money at this time, like those of other borrowers, are, however, at present unknown.

Others involved in more than one case include John Calley **(158, 167)**, Thomas Goddard **(94, 149)**, William Latnar or Latiwere **(101, 111)**, James Lovell **(154, 171)**, and John Michell **(100, 117, 139)**. Edward Essex acknowledged to Hugh Stucley debts of 1,000 marks **(116)** and 500 marks **(127)**. Stucley also appears in **121** as the administrator of the estate of Sir William Essex who sued for 800*l*. from Edward Darrell, perhaps suggesting that the statute staple procedure was here being used for a complex family settlement.

Professional persons often appear to have had large sums of money at their disposal: a doctor of civil law sued for 500*l*. in 1568 **(93)**, John Fowell of the Middle Temple and William Carnsew 'of the University of Oxford' were joint creditors for 2,000*l*. in 1598 **(157)**. The second was at the time M.P. for

[1] C 43/6 no. 53.

[2] Subject index, s.v. trades and occupations.

[3] Lord Mountjoy was saved by James I from total ruin through the excesses of grandfather, father, and brother: L. Stone, 'Anatomy of the Elizabethan aristocracy', *Economic History Review*, 1st ser. xviii. 53. But see below, p. 8.

[4] See pp. 3-5.

[5] For Altham see p. 8.

Camelford.[1] The four members of the Tyndall family who were creditors in 1601 **(167)** included a doctor of theology. In ten cases knights appear as creditors. Professor Trevor-Roper[2] suggests that the same loan might be renewed by a different lender, so that when a man appears twice as debtor he may in fact have renegotiated his original loan. There is insufficient evidence here to show how far this was the case in Wiltshire.

We have only one early example **(5)** of a clerk as debtor, the rector of Deddington, Oxon. Two bishops appear among the creditors. Two separate Edmund Daunteseys acknowledged 1,000 marks to the bishop of London in 1398 **(38)** and William Rede and Anthony St. Amand (Sayntmond) acknowledged 1,000*l.* to the bishop of Rochester and the archdeacon of York in 1519 **(69).** The prior of the hospital of St. John of Jerusalem sued for the much smaller sum of 13*l.* 12*s.* in 1498 **(55)** and the vicar of Willesden, Mdx., for 50*l.* in 1570 **(96).** An impressive group of creditors headed by the earl of Warwick and a canon of St. Paul's sued for 400*l.* acknowledged by the brothers John and Edmund Bernard in 1363 **(14).** Clerks also appear among the creditors in **35** and **42–4.** The Royal Household is represented by John Slegh, king's butler, in 1391 **(31).**

In one case **(52)** the debtor was a woman; Margaret Chaworth acknowledged 100*l.* to Elizabeth Barbour and the writ was sued out by Elizabeth and her husband. In four other cases **(44, 89, 114, 152)** a woman's name appears among the creditors, in the last three in association with her husband, though the sum was due to the wife. More frequently the writ was sued out by the woman acting as executrix of her husband's estate.

It is rare for the same man to appear as both debtor and creditor. Indeed, there is only one definite example of this. Henry Ferrers of the Middle Temple was sued for 80*l.* **(142)** and 200*l.* **(146)** and on his death his administrator sued for repayment of 500*l.* which had been owed to him for many years. This makes it unlikely that hardship drove Ferrers to borrow those relatively small sums; otherwise why did he not demand repayment of the debt sooner?

The same man may appear as creditor in two or more cases. James Altham, who lent substantial sums to the Chattertons **(107–8),** has already been mentioned. He also lent 200*l.* to Edward Morgan and Thomas Stafford **(103).** A rich London alderman and clothworker, sheriff in 1557, he was discharged from the aldermanry in 1561 after 'contemptuous disobedience'[3] and was subsequently to become sheriff of Essex. One wonders whether such a man, who clearly had large sums at his disposal, was among other things a professional moneylender. In an earlier period Laurence Andevere, merchant of the Staple of Winchester, is also creditor twice **(12, 15),** as are George Ayliffe **(169–70),** Richard Hurst **(156, 171),** and the executors of Alexander Staples **(144, 165)** later on. From such a small sample, however, it is impossible to show that these men regularly lent money at interest.

[1] J. Foster, *Alumni Oxonienses.*

[2] H. R. Trevor-Roper, 'The Elizabethan aristocracy: an anatomy anatomized', *Economic History Review*, 2nd ser. iii. 286.

[3] A. B. Beaven, *Aldermen of the City of London*, ii. 172; P. Morant, *History and Antiquities of Essex*, ii. 488.

THE NATURE OF THE 'DEBTS'

Both conusors and conusees, therefore, were varied in their economic and social standing. Otherwise the analysis tells us very little, because no recognizance bears upon its face an explanation of its true intent. Only where collateral evidence exists do we know the conditions in which the debt was contracted or indeed whether it was a true debt, a security for the repayment of a debt, or a security for some other purpose such as the performance of an agreement. Often, too, we know nothing about the cancellation of the debt.[1] When Roger Walton acknowledged 9½ marks to a London tailor in 1379 **(23)** and a Hertfordshire yeoman acknowledged 61*l.* 2*s.* 10*d.* to a London fishmonger in 1462 **(48)**, it is perhaps reasonable to assume that the sums were genuine trade debts already incurred by the debtors. About a fifth of the cases in this volume arise from an individual or individuals being sued by a merchant or merchants and while some simply represent debts already run up, others involving larger and rounder sums surely suggest that a customer was obliged to pledge himself in a certain sum before he could receive credit from the tradesman. The tradesman had to allow for his interest and expenses and it is logical that he should have asked for a pledge of a greater amount than the credit he was prepared to give. A significant number of the extents arise from debts between merchants and a number of these are also likely to represent not actual sums handed over but securities.

Professor Trevor-Roper[2] has shown that sums named in 16th-century recognizances generally represented a figure a little less than twice that actually borrowed and that the debtor would only be obliged to pay this sum if he failed to fulfil the condition of the loan, which was generally repayment of the principal and interest by a fixed date. Unfortunately these conditions are only rarely recorded in the entry books so the precise nature of each transaction must be uncertain. Of 45 Wiltshire recognizances so recorded only two have conditions for repayment[3] and both bear out Professor Trevor-Roper's contention. The record of Gabriel Pledell's[4] acknowledgement of 200*l.* to Robert Colman on 20 June 1564 **(91)** has a condition that the bond would be void if he paid 124*l.* by 4 July 1565. In this case the original loan was probably in the region of 100*l.* and interest 24*l.* and the security demanded was thus double the original loan. The other case is very similar; the condition attached to Anthony White's[5] acknowledgement of 240*l.* to Thomas Browne on 9 July 1571 was that he should repay 122*l.* 4*s.* by 25 July 1572 between the

[1] Professor L. Stone, in 'The Elizabethan aristocracy', *Economic History Review*, 1st ser. xviii, put forward a theory that the aristocratic class was 'on the brink of financial ruin' and heavily in debt, a view disputed by Professor H. R. Trevor-Roper in 'The Elizabethan aristocracy: an anatomy anatomized', *Economic History Review*, 2nd ser. iii. 279 *et seq*. Professor Stone answered the criticism in 2nd ser. iv. 302 *et seq*.

[2] Trevor-Roper, op. cit. 283.

[3] The conditions of two loans made to the Chattertons relate to repayment of other debts they had contracted: L.C. 4/190, pp. 126, 203.

[4] L.C. 4/189 p. 308.

[5] L.C. 4/191 p. 222.

hours of 1 and 3 p.m. In an earlier example **(18)** the *liberate* is endorsed to the effect that the creditor was to hold the lands until 40*l.* of an acknowledged debt of 120*l.* was paid. Payment by instalments is specified in **6,** and, as the total sum equals the debt acknowledged, that probably represents a genuine debt. In **44** the extent is endorsed that the lands were delivered to the creditor's executors to hold until 52*l.* 12*s.* 8*d.* had been paid out of a debt of 400*l.* acknowledged 16 years earlier. Perhaps part of the debt had already been repaid or had been levied from property elsewhere, since the amount of security seems high in proportion to the sum repaid.

Of all debts those between non-merchants are least likely to be the simple transactions they appear to be. There may have been a family arrangement, as in two cases where a son acknowledged 1,000*l.* to his father **(3, 130),** and one where a father acknowledged 1,000*l.* to his son **(115).** Nos. **35** and **168** are probably family transactions too, and **161** was possibly both a family and a business transaction, since Francis Shute, a goldsmith, lent 2,000*l.* to William Shute, an embroiderer. Evidence from the entry books[1] shows that in many instances the debt mentioned in the extents formed part of a series of transactions involving the debtor. For example, on the same day as the recognizances in **107-8** were entered into, Thomas, William, and Henry Chatterton acknowledged 800*l.* to Thomas Bowyer and the recognizance was twice certified into Chancery,[2] although no *capias* survives. On the same day as **114** Sir William Kelwaye, with Francis Kelwaye of Burstall, Yorks., acknowledged to Thomas Essex of Childrey, Berks., 1,000*l.* with provision for defeasance if Essex would make a recognizance in an identical sum with one Edward Poole.[3] On the same day as **115** James Mores acknowledged to Edward Dauntsey and William Buttyll 1,000*l.* and Francis Mores also acknowledged 1,000*l.* to James Mores.[4]

There could be three or even four co-debtors. Members of the same family might have acknowledged a debt together (e.g. **14, 38–9, 79, 99, 106, 123, 163, 165).** One of the debtors might have acted as backer[5] for the other, a pledge that he would provide the money if the debtor defaulted. Sureties were proceeded against as debtors, but as long as the debt could be levied from the debtor's goods they went unharmed.[6]

The date given for repayment of a debt was invariably within a year or so of the recognizance and judgment usually followed soon after the appointed day, although there are several instances of long delays, 23 years in 1341 **(6),** 40 years in 1484 **(51),** 30 years in 1570 **(99),** and, the longest gap, 72 years in 1596 **(151).** It seems possible that, when the writ was issued soon after the recognizance, no money was actually advanced until judgment had been awarded to the creditor. It was clearly in the creditor's best interests to specify an early date for repayment so as to keep the loan as liquid as possible.

[1] See pp. 4-5.
[2] L.C. 4/190 p. 203.
[3] L.C. 4/190 p. 25.
[4] L.C. 4/191 p. 58.
[5] Hall, op. cit., p. xxix.
[6] Tomlins' Law Dictionary, s.v. statute merchant.

In theory repayment of debts in the nature of statute staple was noted in the entry books and in three cases there is a note that the debtor was exonerated **(91, 114, 162)** and the name in the margin of the entry book has been crossed out. The borrower had no pressing reason to have the fact of his repayment recorded so that this low percentage cannot prove how many debts were in fact repaid.[1] Yet disputes over repayment clearly took place and some evidence of them exists. Acknowledgement of the receipt of a debt is recorded in the Close Rolls[2] upon a *capias* issued by Peter Curteys in 1485 against John Stourton and John Heynes, but a further writ of *capias* was sued out in 1494 **(54)** for the same debt. Perhaps the debt was taken up again at a later date or the creditors refused to acknowledge the repayment. There is one early case when it was alleged that the creditors prosecuted the debtor for a debt already repaid and a writ of *scire facias* was issued for the creditors to appear in Chancery and acknowledge receipt, which they subsequently did **(22)**. A *supersedeas* in 1397 **(33)** ordered a debtor's release from prison because the creditor had earlier released him from all his obligations.

If a debtor was aggrieved, he had a remedy in the writ of *audita querela*. In **165** there is an example of its use: George Blount and others were in debt to Henry Ughtred and their lands in Staffordshire were surrendered to Ughtred on their failure to pay. Ughtred assigned these lands to the elder and the younger John Toppe. Roland Lacon, however, claimed that the lands had belonged to him and not to Blount at the time of the recognizance. He brought a writ of *audita querela* against the Toppes by which he recovered the annual profits, which they had received from the lands, to be levied from their property in Wiltshire.

ACTION BY THE SHERIFF ON RECEIPT OF THE WRIT

There are many instances in this volume of writs which do not appear to have an accompanying extent. The dispersal of the documents into several classes[3] makes it hard to be certain that, where there is no extent, no extent was made. We have already seen that in many cases where the debtor had died no further action appears to have been taken, and there are numerous instances of sheriffs employing delaying tactics which may or may not have been successful. The conventional return *adeo tarde*,[4] i.e. that the writ arrived too late for execution, is fairly common in the volume (e.g. **35, 36, 38–9, 48, 95, 167**). In **39** a *capias sicut alias* was issued, and perhaps no further action was taken in the other cases. On one occasion **(70)** the creditor appeared in Chancery and asserted that the writ of *capias* had been accidentally lost.

Allegations that the sheriff had failed to make a full extent were also fairly common and resulted in the issuing of a writ of extent or a *capias sicut alias* followed by further extents. Such an allegation is recorded in the first extent.

[1] Trevor-Roper, op. cit. 282.
[2] *C.C.R.* 1476–85, no. 1414.
[3] See pp. 14-15.
[4] Hall, op. cit., p. xxvi.

It is also recorded in **25,** where the extent implies that the debtor held only goods, but where two writs of extent alleging that lands were also held, were followed by further extents before different juries denying it. In **42** it was also alleged that lands were held, but that was again denied. In **107** the writ of extent resulted in the production of a long list of ordinary household goods held in addition to the crops and goods already listed. Delaying tactics seem to have been employed in **166** where the sheriff stated that as the jury had not been charged to extend lands held at the time of the recognizance, as distinct from the time of the inquisition, they had not done so. This is strange, since under the Statute Staple it was lands held at the time of the recognizance that were to be extended. Nevertheless it gave the debtor a few months' grace which perhaps enabled him to raise the money for repayment.

The *liberate* was frequently endorsed with a note that the land had been handed over to the creditor. The sheriff was not always able to secure such a surrender easily, for in **108** there is a lively account of the attempts of Thomas Chatterton to use force to prevent the sheriff and his party from seizing the manor-house of Lydiard Millicent.

Other sources provide evidence of changes in tenure of some of the lands mentioned in extents. In 1438 John Hertwell, for example, was said to have disposed of a third of the manor of Hardenhuish[1] surrendered to him 2½ years earlier **(46).** Henry Ferrers was said to hold the same rents and reversions in 1592 **(146)** as he held in 1590 **(142),** yet the later inquisition shows that, as a moiety of the rents had been handed to the previous creditors by *elegit*, the then creditors were only entitled to half the moiety still held by Ferrers. Anthony St. Amand was debtor in three cases between 1529 and 1531 **(67, 69, 70)** and in all three it was reported that his lands in Allington were handed to the creditors. He must in each case have recovered possession quickly to enable the same lands to pass to his successive creditors.

IMPRISONMENT

Both the Statute of Merchants and the Statute of the Staple prescribed imprisonment for the debtor, yet in only eight instances **(30, 33–4, 49, 56–7, 72, 104)** is imprisonment actually recorded. Three of those imprisoned were 'gentlemen', the others tradesmen. Most commonly, however, the sheriff returned *non est inventus*. Anthony White, reported to be in prison on 8 August 1572 **(104),** could not be found by the sheriff when he received another *capias* writ dated 27 August **(105).** Either he had been released quickly or the sheriff was giving the stock answer of *non est inventus* without investigating the facts. There are no instances of peers being imprisoned and indeed there is some doubt whether they were liable to imprisonment. In the case of Harris v. Mountjoy in 1587, quoted by Professor Trevor-Roper,[2] the judges of the Common Pleas gave the opinion that peers were liable, but there is no

[1] *C.C.R.* 1435–41, 169.
[2] Trevor-Roper, op. cit. 280.

evidence to show that peers were ever imprisoned as a result. Clerks were exempt from arrest and the phrase *si laicus sit* was incorporated in the wording of the *capias* writ.[1]

THE EXTENTS

The form taken by the extent is the same whether the case was brought under the statute merchant, statute staple, or *elegit* procedure. The sheriff made the extent in a town or village close to the debtor's property with the aid of a local jury composed of at least twelve men, occasionally more. When he was instructed to make more than one extent a different jury was empanelled, though some of its members may have been the same, as in the three extents of **42.** In four instances **(42, 64, 80, 107)** the bailiff of a liberty made the extent at the request of the sheriff.[2]

Most of the extents are concerned only with lands as then understood. Presumably it was not generally thought necessary to list the household goods of a debtor who had lands enough to cover the debt, though an *elegit* of 1571 **(100)** lists first the goods of John Michell and then his lands, because the value of the goods was not sufficient to cover the debt.

Under the statute staple procedure all lands held at the time of the recognizance were liable to be surrendered to the creditor. In **81** John Cryppes held lands in Castle Eaton at that time and although he had granted them to Richard Verney some months before the issue of the *capias* they were still listed among his property. When several years stood between the recognizance and the *capias* it was probably difficult for the jury to discover what property the debtor had owned. John Care acknowledged his debt in 1532 **(85)** but the *capias* was issued 31 years later. In 1541 he sold his land and the jury could only ascertain that he was seised of it a few days before the sale. Details were sometimes given of land held before or after the recognizance; the Bernard brothers **(14)** were said to have held no land at the time of the recognizance but the land they held a few months previously was described and valued. Richard Talbot was said to hold no lands in Wiltshire, since two years before the recognizance he granted them to two others who held them to the use of his son.

There are instances where the debtor was said to hold no lands or goods[3] **(23, 37, 84, 91,** *etc.*) and just as the debtors came from many ranks of society so the value of their property varied, from the yearly quit-rent of a rose **(28)** to the manors, lands, and rents of knights such as Edward Darrell **(121),** worth over 100*l.* yearly. In 1558 William Latnar demised his lands in Wiltshire to Brian Lec for 61 years and was at the time of the recognizance in 1572 seised of the reversion worth only a farthing a year **(111).**[4]

[1] See Appendix, p. 127.

[2] See p. 5.

[3] He may of course have had property in other counties.

[4] This fact seems not to have been uncovered by an earlier jury **(100)** when Latnar was sued for payment of another debt.

When an extent included both lands and goods,[1] the goods are generally described in both English and Latin, as in **82** and **107.** In five cases the extent of lands is followed by a separate inventory of goods in English; **61** gives the contents of the house and shop of the mercer Nicholas Chaffyn; **73,** the longest inventory, concerns Thomas Hele, merchant, whose shop was stocked with groceries and spices and a wide range of textiles. The contents of Hele's house and the tavern next door are also listed, the total value being almost 100*l.* An insight into the fittings of a typical Elizabethan inn is given in **156** (in both English and Latin), the inventory of John Maskeleyn, keeper of the Bear, Marlborough. Silverware worth 10*l.* was the most expensive item. The inventories at **158** and **167** both relate to John Calley, gentleman, the former being compiled specially for the extent, the latter extracted from the Prerogative Court of Canterbury wills and giving far more detail and including a wider range of goods. These and other extents of goods portray a gentleman's household, its furniture, bedding, and kitchen utensils. Equipment for brewing and butter- and cheese-making occurs in several inventories. Among the more unusual items were a mirror with studded case **(82),** a hawking glove **(107),** and a pair of virginals **(167).** John Danvers **(167)** had a book of Common Prayer and 'sondrye sortes of bookes' and Henry Chatterton **(107)** a copy of Chaucer. Bibles are frequently mentioned. Crops and animals are included with household goods as chattels and form a substantial part of the total value. In **166** animals accounted for 114*l.* 10*s.* of a total value of 323*l.* 10*s.* 7*d.* and crops for 73*l.* of the total

DEFINITION OF MANUSCRIPTS

The pre-17th-century documents generically known as 'extents for debts' are to be found mainly in two Chancery classes each bearing that title and distinguished as series I (C 131) and II (C 239).[2] Both these series have emerged from the files of the Chancery, but by different routes.

Those files were at first an undifferentiated mass of returned writs and returns to writs and formed one of the main subdivisions of the Chancery records. In course of time they were segregated into a small number of different subject categories. This segregation, which in the case of inquisitions post mortem had begun by Edward III's reign, was continued and intensified, but neither early 'methodizers' nor later record-keepers ever completed it. It follows that though by the early 1900s a segregated class of 'extents for debts' had been formed and made available to the public, a large residuum of documents of the same nature remained on undifferentiated Chancery files which were not so available. To make up the former series (C 131) some documents were withdrawn from files of inquisitions post mortem. Possibly

[1] See F. W. Steer, *Farm and Cottage Inventories of Mid-Essex 1635–1749*. Although for a later period, it provides detailed descriptions of many of the items listed in this volume.

[2] See introduction to P.R.O. List of Extents for Debts (TS.) and introduction of *Calendar of Inquisitions Miscellaneous*, Vol. I. Much help in compiling this section has been given by Dr. R. F. Hunnisett of the P.R.O.

the class called 'Inquisitions Miscellaneous' (C 146) was similarly raided, but, if so, not thoroughly, for the extent of Nicholas St. Lo's property (**27**) is still in that class and has been already published in abstract in the *Calendar of Inquisitions Miscellaneous*. Other extents may yet be found in C 146.

Inquisitions of various kinds running at least to the end of Richard III's reign and possibly for a much longer period were formerly kept in the record office in the Tower of London, those mainly of later date in the Rolls Chapel record office. It was originally intended that C 131 should contain only documents formerly kept in the Tower; a separate class, 'Certificates and Recognizances of Statute Staple (Rolls Chapel Office)' (C 152), comprised those kept in the Rolls Chapel. Rolls Chapel series documents, however, were added to C 131 because it came to be recognized that C 152 was faultily entitled. There thus arose a considerable overlap in the dates covered by the two series, which fails to reflect any difference between the documents themselves.

The two classes C 131 and C 152 were brought together in 1970 to form 'extents for debts' series I and II, though no C 152 document was placed in C 131 unless it was clear that it should have been associated with a document already there. Additions were made from unsorted Chancery material formerly in 'Chancery Files, Tower and Rolls Chapel Series' (C 202) and in 'Miscellanea of the Chancery' (C 47). Series I is itself divided into two main numerical sequences, files 1–162 covering the period 10 Edward II–20 Charles I and files 171–270 the period 10 Edward II–20 Henry VIII. The former sequence consists very largely of the writs and returns in the old class 'Extents for Debts' (C 131), and several writs found among previously unsorted material in Chancery files have been reunited with their extents here. Detached writs whose returns have not been found and writs returned unexecuted comprise the second sequence. The unsorted writs, formerly C 131/163–170, have now been placed in their chronological sequence in C 131/171–270. There are in addition three files (C 131/271–3) of *capias* writs to imprison such debtors as could not be found in their own counties. They cover the period from Edward II to the Interregnum. File 274 consists of loose inventories and file 275 is an original file covering the period 39 Elizabeth I–11 James I.

The abolished class C 152 is the basis of series II (C 239). This consists of 111 files covering the years 21 Henry VIII–24 Charles I. The abolished class bore some traces of an earlier alphabetical arrangement by county. For the years 21–29 Elizabeth I all the Wiltshire extents abstracted in the volume were found in C 131, since the extents for those years in C 152 include none for any county that comes after Sussex in alphabetical order.

In many instances *capias* writs were returnable not into Chancery but into the King's Bench, the Common Pleas, or other courts; three such writs to the sheriff of Wiltshire (**2**, **9**, and **16**), returned into the Common Pleas, were found in the class called 'Writs and Returns (Selected)' (C.P. 51). Since no systematic search was made in the records of the Common Pleas, others may yet come to light from this source.

As has been said,[1] this volume covers all known Wiltshire extents for

[1] See p. 1.

debts to the end of Elizabeth I's reign, that is, in series I, C 131/1–141 and /171–275, and, in series II, C 239/1–69. There are later extents in the later files of series I and II and also in 'Proceedings on the Statute Staple (Petty Bag Office)' (C 228), which covers the period from 15 James I to 15 George III, the end of the series.

EDITORIAL METHOD

Specimens of all the writs on which the extents are grounded are printed in full in the Appendix. This has made it possible to reduce the abstracts of the writs themselves to a minimum. Any deviations from or additions to the forms shown in the specimens are noted in the abstracts. Where the acknowledgement of the debt in Chancery has been found in the *Calendar of Close Rolls*, the appropriate reference has been given in square brackets in the text.

That part of the extent which repeats the terms of the writ is omitted, except when the writ itself has not survived. The sheriffs before whom the extents were taken have been named but after the names of Wiltshire sheriffs the words 'sheriff of Wiltshire' (or the equivalent) have been omitted. The words 'the oath of' have been omitted between 'by' and the names of jurors.

The description of the lands and goods extended is, in general, translated directly from the original, although longer entries have been condensed to avoid repetition, e.g. where the description of the lands and goods is followed by a separate valuation of each item. Round brackets are used in long passages to denote the yearly values or rents of the lands extended, instead of the phrase 'worth . . . yearly'. The phrase '*in tenura sive occupacione*' is translated as 'held by' and '*per estimacionem*', used of land measurement, as '*c.*' The inventories in English are reproduced in full and English words or phrases occurring in the extents are given in inverted commas. Household articles are often described in both English and Latin, and in the abstracts the Latin word has been appended in brackets after the English, except in the cases of *candelabrum*, *cathedra*, and *olla*, which in the inventories are invariably the words used for candlestick, chair, and pot. Endorsements upon the writs and extents have been noted only when they provide information not to be found elsewhere in the abstract.

The original spelling of place and personal names has been retained, except that Latin prefixes or suffixes, such as 'Episcopi' in Cannings Episcopi, have been translated, and modern forms have been used for the staple towns of Bristol, Exeter, and Winchester and for London, Westminster, and Salisbury.

A tear or blindness in a manuscript has generally been noted on the first occurrence of a gap in the abstract and subsequent omissions have been indicated by dots. It has often proved possible to supply gaps in the extents by reference to a *liberate* and square brackets have been used in such cases.

WILTSHIRE EXTENTS FOR DEBTS

1 William Huloun, merchant, of Salisbury

14 June 34 Edw. I [1306]. *Non omittas, sicut alias* returnable in quin. of Mich. next [13 Oct.], on account of the bishop of Salisbury's liberty, upon a *capias* sued out by John Fraunceys the elder, burgess of Bristol, to whom William acknowledged 100*l.* before John le Blound, mayor of London, and Henry de Leyc', king's clerk, payable in oct. of Mich. 33 Edw. I [6 Oct. 1305]; as the sheriff returned 3 weeks from Eas. [24 Apr.] that he had delivered all William's goods and lands to John, but it has been testified in Chancery on John's behalf that William holds more lands and goods than were delivered. Unless the sheriff carries out the instruction he will be heavily amerced.

Thurs. after St. Peter's chains 34 Edw. I [4 Aug. 1306]. Appraisement at New Salisbury before John Gereberd by Thomas le Batyere, Alexander le Ku, Nicholas de Stratford, Philip de Devyses, William le Hattere, Peter le Cartere, John Wytfot, Roger Upewel, Ellis le Bakere, Thomas de Wynterburn, and John de Frytham.

The following goods: a bed worth 6*s.* with linen cloths (*pannis lineis*) worth 20*s.*; 3 forms (*formulas*) worth 9*d.*; a 'haketon' and a case (*mala*) with towel (*manitergio*) worth 8*s.*; 2 chests (*coffr'*) and a table (*tabulam mensalem*) with 3 trestles worth 40*s.*; a brass pot worth 18*d.*; 2 brass candlesticks worth 6*d.*; 2 pewter dishes (*disc' de peutre*) worth 12*d.*; an overcoat (*supertunicam*) worth 2*s.*; a cloth (*mappa*) worth 6*d.*; a cask (*doleum*) worth 12*d.*; an 'ippere' and 2 axes (*secur'*) worth 18*d.*; 2 shovels (*scope*) and a chair with 2 trestles worth 7*d.*; a 'caundel' with a candlestick worth 4*d.*; 2 vats (*vette*) worth 6*d.* Total 4*l.* 4*s.* 2*d.*
C 131/1 no. 3

2 Alan Plukenet

8 Feb. 6 Edw. II [1313]. *Elegit* returnable at Westminster in 3 weeks from Eas. next [6 May], sued out by Hugh le Despencer the elder, for 53*l.* 6*s.* 8*d.* and 10*l.* in expenses which he recovered against Alan at Westminster.
Endorsed. All Alan's goods and half his lands have been delivered to Hugh.

22 Apr. 6 Edw. II [1313]. Extent of the manors of Langeford and Waddene belonging to Alan Plukenet before Adam Walraund by William Warde, Nicholas de Wyly, Thomas le Eyr, John Donebredan, Peter Wyppe, John de Netheravene, John Huloun, Stephen Huloun, Hugh Shereman, William de Wyly, Thomas Daubeny, Richard Mancornoys, and Ralph of the mill.

The manor-house of Langeford Plukenet with gardens and curtilage, vineyards and ditches, worth 3*s.* 4*d.* yearly; a water-mill worth 10*s.* yearly; from the town of Nounton for a path beyond (*ultra*) the said tenements, 15*d.* Total 14*s.* 7*d.*

Free tenants. 9 free tenements there: Walter de Langeford holds a messuage and ⅔ virgate of land and pays 8*s.* 1*d.* yearly; John Aynel holds a messuage and 5 a. of land (12*d.*); the heirs of Adam de Kynggesmille hold a plot of pasture in common (6*d.*); John le Warde holds a messuage and a virgate of land (10*s.*); John atte Mille holds a messuage and 5 a. of land (3*s.*); William le Diyon holds 5 a. of land (12*d.*); Walter Thomas holds a messuage and 9 a. of land and pays 1 lb. pepper yearly, worth 6*s.*; Maurice le Botiller holds 15½ a. of land and pays 1½ lb. cumin, worth 2¼*d.* Total 24*s.* 4¼*d.*

Customary tenants. John le Kyng holds a messuage and 8 a. of land in villeinage (5*s.*); his services are to cut down the lord's crops for as long as necessary to provide the lord's food, of no yearly value; to manure the lord's meadow for 3 days, worth 6*d.*; to harvest and stack the lord's corn, worth 3*d.*; to dig for 2 half-days, worth 1*d.* a day; to mete out or perform labour-service for a month from the gule of Aug. to Mich., worth 2*s.*; to pay church-scot of a hen and a cock, worth 5½*d.* Aur' le Knygh, William Knygh, William Bernard, and Roger Bernard hold the same amount of land and perform the same services. Simon le Taillur holds a messuage (3*s.*); Walter le Holt holds a messuage and 1 a. (22*d.*); Agnes le Mont holds a messuage and 1 a. of land . . . [*MS. torn*]; Richard le Chepman holds a messuage and 1½ a. of land; . . . [Robert] Shepburde holds a messuage and 1 a. . . . messuage and 1 a. of land . . . ; . . . messuage and 3 a. of land (2*s.*); . . . (12*d.*). Each has to perform services except Robert de Shepburde who has to mow for a day . . . with 1 man and the service is worth 1*d.* . . . and has to dig for 2 . . . [to pay] church-scot of 3 hens and a cock, worth 5½*d.* . . . Total of the customs with church-scot 43*s.* 5*d.*

. . . worth 22*s.* 1½*d.* yearly (. . . an a.) . . . crops worth 72*s.* 6¾*d.*, of which 21½ a. are sown with barley . . . worth 2*s.* 4*d.* an a.; . . . worth 21*d.* an a.; . . . worth 8*s.* 9*d.* . . . an a.; 31 a. 1 r. of meadow worth 75*s.* yearly . . . ; pasture in common for oxen and avers worth . . . ; . . . worth 3*s.* 4*d.* yearly; 1 weak . . . 107*s.* 9*d.* . . . ; 7*l.* 5*s.* . . . ; 9*l.* 10s. 1¼*d.* yearly.

Wadden: easements for houses with gardens and curtilages worth 2*s.* yearly; perquisites of court worth 2*s.* yearly. Total 4*s.*

Free tenants: Roger le Rous, John Tropynel, Roger Tropynel, William Lovecok, John Kylabat, Alexander le Tayllur, and Richard de Worton pay in rents of assize 10*s.* and 1 lb. pepper worth 6*d.* Total 10*s.* 6*d.*

Customary tenants: Nicholas atte Grene holds a messuage [and] ½ virgate (5*s.*). His services are to manure the lord's fields and to make hay, worth 2*d.*; to reap and . . . a twentieth of sheaves, worth 1*d.*; to perform carrying-service three times yearly, worth . . . ; to plough 2 a., worth 8*d.*; . . . bz. barley, 4 bz. corn, 1 qr. oats, comprising a 'reek', worth nothing. John le Kyng, William Gurop, Cecily Wille, Adam Kyng, and Richard the reeve hold the same lands for the same services. Robert Gorlewey holds a messuage [and] 10 a. of land and pays 2*s.* 6*d.* in rent; his services are as Nicholas atte Grene's, except that he has to perform carrying-service . . . worth 6*d.*; he is to pay church-scot of 3 hens and a cock, worth 5*d.* William Tabour, Margaret Glace, John Hobbes, Agnes atte Church, Walter . . . , David Isabele hold the same lands for the same services. Total of customary rents 47*s.* 6*d.* Total of customary rents with church-scot 30*s.* 11½*d.*

Cottars: Margaret Duke holds a cottage (12*d*.); her services are . . . ; William Cacheray holds a cottage and an a. of land (3*s*.) . . . ; Robert . . . holds a cottage . . . and pays 3*s*. Total . . .

In demesne: 17½ a. . . . 2*d*. an a. . . . of which 34 a. are sown . . . 2*s*. an a.; 3 a. sown . . . 16*d*. an a.; 21½ a. 1 r. . . . 22*d*. an a.; . . . 6½ a. . . . 14*d*. an a.; 2½ a. . . . 22*d*. an a.; . . . 18*d*. an a.; . . . 8*d*. . . . an a.; . . . worth 19*s*. 4*d*. . . . 46*s*. yearly, 2*s*. an a.; . . . pasture and close with pasture in common. Total of the extent of the manor of Waddene . . .

C.P. 51/1 no. 50

3 Peter son of James de Norton

16 Feb. 18 Edw. II [1325]. *Elegit* returnable in quin. of Eas. next [21 Apr.], sued out by James de Norton, knight, of Hants, to whom Peter acknowledged 80*l*. in Chancery on 3 Aug. last [*C.C.R.* 1323–7, 305], payable at Mich. then next.

Endorsed. The sheriff has delivered to James half of Peter's lands worth 31*s*. 8½*d*. yearly.

Sat. after Lady Day 18 Edw. II [18 May 1325]. Extent and appraisement at Fischerton by Babeton' before Adam Walrond by Philip le Cok, Ralph Dalewey, John de Haselholte, John Carpenter, Adam le Foghel, Roger le Porter, Reynold Warfton, John Adam, William le Frye, John the clerk, William Faukes, and Ellis Attemulle.

No goods in Wilts. At Fischerton: ⅓ messuage worth 12*d*. yearly; 60 a. of arable land worth 3*d*. an a.; 2 a. of meadow in Babbemed by Norton and ½ a. of meadow worth 12*d*. an a.; pasture in severalty for 4 oxen and an aver from Holy Cross [3 May] to St. Peter's chains [1 Aug.] worth 15*d*. yearly; pasture for 150 sheep worth 6*s*. 3*d*. yearly (½*d*. a head); 2¾*d*. and ⅓ lb. pepper in rent from a free tenant and 42*s*. assessed rent of villeins' rent. Total 63*s*. 5½*d*., moiety 31*s*. 8¾*d*.

C 131/2 no. 3

4 Thomas de Harpeden and William de Lusteshull

4 Mar. 18 Edw. II [1325]. *Elegit* returnable in 1 month from Eas. next [5 May], sued out by master John Walewayn, to whom Thomas and William acknowledged 45*l*. 19*s*. in Chancery on 27 May last [*C.C.R.* 1323–7, 189].

C 131/172 no. 30

5 William Aylmer, of Sevenhampton, late parson of Dadington, now deceased[1]

20 Oct. 3 Edw. III [1329]. *Elegit* returnable in quin. of Martinmas next [25 Nov.], sued out by Robert de Staunton, knight, and William de Ingewardeby, to whom William acknowledged 60*l*. in Chancery on 14 May 2 Edw. III [1328] [*C.C.R.* 1327–30, 386], payable at Eas. then next [23 Apr.]; upon a *scire facias* to the heirs and tenants of William at the time of the recognizance, to which the sheriff returned that half William's lands and tenements were in

[1]Abstract previously printed in *Wilts. Inq. p.m. 1242–1326* ed. E. A. Fry (Index Libr. xxxvii), 49-50.

the hands of Queen Isabel by escheat and the other half in the hands of Walter de Hungerford, to whom the sheriff issued the writ of *scire facias;* Walter appeared in Chancery and asserted that Robert de Hungerford was his co-feoffee; *scire facias* for the appearance of Robert in Chancery in quin. of Mich. last [13 Oct.], on which day Walter and Robert appeared and showed no cause to be quit of the debt.
Endorsed. Philip de la Beche, sheriff, has delivered half the lands.

5 Nov. 3 Edw. III [1329]. Extent at Heighwrth before William de Rameshulle, bailiff of Queen Isabel's liberty of Heighwrth hundred, by Walter de Canynges, William Page, John James, Richard son of Hugh, Henry Stanford, Richard le Cok, Matthew Picot, William Saundre, Walter Hubert, Robert James, William le Scrywein, and John Pikard.

At Sevenhampton: a capital messuage with a garden and the whole close worth 13*s.* 4*d.* yearly; in the south field 31 a. of arable land worth 12*d.* an a. (31*s.*); 5 a. of meadow in 'Merdych' worth 3*s.* an a. (15*s.*); a 'hamme' of meadow at 'Hackornesbrygg' (12*s.*); meadows at 'Langeham' (15*s.*), 'Smezeham' (3*s.*), 'Greneweysham' (12*s.*), 'Shepeswaisch' within and without (6*s.*), 'Crokewell' (18*d.*), and 'Povyham' (12*d.*); in the east field 40 a. of arable land worth 8*d.* an a. (6*s.* 8*d.*); 5 a. of meadow in 'Merdych' (15*s.*); a 'hamme' of meadow at 'Hackornesbrygg' (12*s.*) and at 'Wheles' (20*s.*); 1 a. of meadow (3*s.*); 2 plots of meadow at 'Swanesneste' (4*s.*); ½ a. of meadow at 'Combes' (12*d.*); a plot of meadow at 'Wopoul' (5*s.*); a cottage (2*s.*); a close called 'Dauwes' (2*s.*); the meadow of 'Chichewesham' (6*s.* 8*d.*).

At Estrop: a messuage formerly of William atte Pounde (2*s.*); a void plot at 'Emmewell' (6*d.*); the meadows of 'Sondermed', 'Oldelond', 'Rowenden', and 'Langemorre' (14*d.*); 1 a. of meadow in 'Estmed' (2*s.*); a messuage formerly of Ellis Spontyng (3*s.*); in the various fields in Estrop 49½ a. of arable land worth 8*d.* an a. (33*s.*); pasture for 4 oxen (16*d.*).

At Hampton: ½ messuage with a curtilage (12*d.*); ⅔ of 2 virgates of meadow in 'Estmed' (4*s.*); the meadow of 'Porsfen' (16*d.*); in the various fields 26 a. 1 r. 1 'morwedole' of arable land worth 10*d.* an a. (21*s.* 11*d.*); pasture for 4 oxen (20*d.*); pasture for cows and bullocks (5*d.*); pasture for sheep (12*d.*).

Total 14*l.* 0*s.* 18*d.*, moiety 7*l.* 0*s.* 9*d.*

C 131/3 no. 18

6 Ralph de Farleye and John le Chamberlayn, of la Rugg

26 Oct. 15 Edw. III [1341]. *Elegit, sicut alias* returnable in oct. of Hil. next [20 Jan.], sued out by Ellis de Hungerford, to whom Ralph and John acknowledged 200*l.* in Chancery on 14 [Jan.] 11 Edw. II [1318] [*C.C.R.* 1313–18, 601] payable in instalments of 50*l.* at quins. of Mich. and Eas. and oct. of the Purification then next and of 25*l.* at the quins. of Mich. and Eas. following; upon a *scire facias* for the appearance of Ralph and John in Chancery in oct. of the Purification [9 Feb.], to which the sheriff returned that both were dead, and a like writ for the appearance of their heirs and tenants at the time of the recognizance in 1 month from Eas. [6 May], to which the sheriff returned that he sent the writ to Nicholas Homedieu, bailiff of the earl of Gloucester's

liberty of Kynwardeston hundred, who returned no answer; *non omittas* for the issue of a *scire facias* for the appearance of the heirs and tenants in oct. of Trin. [10 June], to which the sheriff returned that he had informed [John], Ralph's [son and] heir, and William le Chamberlayn, brother and heir of John; on which day John and William failed to appear.
Endorsed. The sheriff has delivered half the lands to Ellis in the presence of William Chamberlayn. John, son and heir of Ralph, was not present, nor could he be forewarned of the extent as he had no lands in the bailiwick, William having recovered by a writ of novel disseisin against John all the lands and tenements held by John from the lands of his father Ralph.

. . . [*MS. torn*] after Hil. . . . Edw. III . . . Extent at . . . before [John Mauduyt] by John Homedieu, Reynold de Hamp . . . , Ellis Haynes, John Farmer, John Jakemyn, Thomas Cotes . . .
William Chamberlayne holds at la R[ugge] . . . worth 10*s*. yearly; 100 a. of land . . . 48 a. of arable land lying in common . . . At Somerfeld: 22 a. . . . in the common fields worth . . . an a. . . . worth 2*s*. an a. yearly.
C 131/6 no. 29

7 Ellis Farman, of Hungerford
25 June 16 Edw. III [1342]. *Elegit* returnable in quin. of Mich. next [13 Oct.] for 20 marks, sued out by William de Burton, 'chivaler', to whom Ellis acknowledged 20*l*. in Chancery on 17 Oct. last [*C.C.R.* 1341–3, 340], payable at Whitsun then next [19 May]. The sheriff of Berks. is to levy the residue.

. . . [*MS. torn*] 16 Edw. III [1342]. Inquisition at New Salisbury before John Mauduyt by Adam R . . . , . . . de Langeford, Edmund Kydenot, Nicholas Wellibaund, John . . .
At . . . corn worth 33*s*. 4*d*.; 17 . . . ; 4 a. of land sown with peas and . . . worth 32*s*.; 60 a. of arable land worth . . . an a.; winter pasture in the 'Parkmede' worth 6*l*. 2*s*. 2*d*. yearly; the services of Robert Stede the smith, his tenant.
C 131/6 no. 16

8 Ralph de Sharpenham
. . . [*MS. blind*] Dec. 20 Edw. III [1346]. *Non omittas* returnable in oct. of the Purification next [9 Feb.], on account of the liberty of the honor of Walyngford, upon a *liberate* returnable in quin. of Mich. next [13 Oct.], which was delivered to Thomas de Oadeford, bailiff of the liberty, for Gilbert de Berewyk, to whom Ralph acknowledged 40*l*. in Chancery on 27 July [14] Edw. II [1320] [*C.C.R.* 1318–23, 317], payable in moieties at Mich. and Christmas then next; as Gilbert has sued out an *elegit* with *scire facias* for Ralph's appearance in Chancery on the morrow of the Assumption 19 Edw. III [16 Aug. 1345], to which the sheriff has returned that Ralph is dead; whereupon he had sued out a *scire facias* for the appearance of Ralph's heirs and tenants in Chancery, to which the sheriff has returned that through Alexander Botild and Walter le Whyte he has instructed Ralph's son, John, and Ralph's tenants, James de Mouns and his wife, Edith, to appear. On the

appointed day, Gilbert, through his attorney, Robert de Burcant, and John, James, and Edith through their attorney, Thomas de Hoddeston, appeared in court. Gilbert sought payment of the 40*l.* and John, James, and Edith alleged that Gilbert had received satisfaction for half that amount, testifying to the payment of 20*l.* This Gilbert did not deny. John, James, and Edith showed no cause why the case should not be judged against them. Therefore it was decided that Gilbert should be paid the remaining 20*l.*
Endorsed. Half the lands have been delivered.

Sat. after St. Peter and St. Paul 21 Edw. III [30 June 1347]. Inquisition at Draycote Folyet before John de Roches by John de Chilton, Robert de Moncketon, William Gyboun, Alexander Botyld, John [?Dyer], . . . , Robert . . . , Philip [?Paul], Walter Scolas, John le Ferour, Thomas de Hoddeston, and John Phaon.

At Draycote Folyet 100 a. of arable land . . . In the north field: in the furlong called 'Netherelangelond' . . . in the east; at 'Stanlynches' ½ a. 1 r. in the east; in 'Blecchesdon' 2 a. . . . 1 r. in the east; at the 'Gore' 1½ a. in the east; in the 'Brech' ½ a. in the south; . . . south; in 'Eldelegh' ½ a. 1 r. in the south; at 'the windmill' (*molend' ventric'*) 1½ a. . . . ; at the 'Harpath' 1½ a. in the south; in 'Woostycch' ½ a. 1 r. in the south. In the south field: . . . the 'Redelond'; at the 'Tounesende' 1 a. in the south; in 'Middelredelond' 1½ a. 1 r. in the south; on the . . . 1 a. in the south; . . . at 'Chonghput' 1 a. 1 r. in the south; in 'Thornhull' 1 a. 1 r. in the east; in Thornhull 2 a. 1 r. in the east; in 'Pathforlang' 1 a. in the east, 1 a. in the east; at the 'Meere' ½ a. in the east; in 'Northforlang' 1½ a. in the east; in 'Pridemosteforlang' 1 a. 1 r. in the east; in 'Onemosteforlang' ½ a. 1 r. in the east; in 'Borslad' 6 a. in the south; in 'Hevedlondes' 2½ a. in the east; in 'Deenlondes' ½ a. 1 r. in the south; in 'Dereforlong' 2 a. ½ r. in the south; in 'Byestechedoune' ½ a. in the south; on the 'doune' 3 a. in the east; at the 'Choeryle' 2½ a. in the east; at 'Coppedlynch' ½ a. in the south; at the 'Berghere' 2 a. 1 r. in the south. Each acre worth 12*d.* yearly.

C 131/7 no. 7

9 Robert Lok, of Berkshire

7 May 21 Edw. III [1347]. *Capias, sicut alias* returnable at Westminster in oct. of Mich. next [6 Oct.], sued out by Walter atte Borgh, to whom Robert acknowledged 76*l.* 13*s.* 4*d.* on 13 Feb. 20 Edw. III [1346] before Richard Lacer, late mayor of London, and Thomas Colle, clerk, payable at Whitsun then next [4 June]; upon a *capias* returnable in quin. of Eas. next [15 Apr.], to which the sheriff has returned that Robert has not been found; for the first 3 months after his taking, Robert is to dwell in prison at his own expense and all his goods and chattels are to be brought to him so that he may discharge his debt; if he does not do so within the first 3 months, the sheriff is to deliver to Walter all lands and goods held by Robert at the time of the recognizance and Robert is to remain in prison on bread and water at Walter's expense; Robert is to be allowed to sell his lands and so discharge his debt, with expenses; if Robert is not found in the bailiwick or if he is a clerk

the sheriff is to deliver to Walter all lands and goods held by Robert at the time of the recognizance or after.
Endorsed. Robert has not been found.

Sat. after St. Margaret 21 Edw. III [21 July 1347]. Inquisition at Alvedeston before Thomas de Seymour by Richard Alwyne, Thomas Tidoleshyde, Richard de Perham, Nicholas le Haytour, Thomas Warde, Thomas Gurardeston, John Wake, William Danialys, John Petyt, Richard de Ferne, Peter Redleg, and Stephen Somet'.

In Eblesbourn' Wake: 20 a. sown with corn worth 4*s.* an a.; 50 a. sown with corn worth 2*s.* 6*d.* an a.; 46 a. sown with barley worth 2*s.* an a.; 20 a. sown with oats worth 18*d.* an a.; 25 a. sown with peas and beans worth 12*d.* an a. Total 17*l.* 12*s.*

At Alvedeston: 3 avers worth 15*s.*; an old cart worth 6*s.* 8*d.*; 21 oxen worth 8*s.* each; 6 rams worth 14*d.* each; 279 ewes worth 14*d.* each; 4 lambs worth 6*d.* each; 20 pigs of over a year worth 12*d.* each; 10 piglets worth 10*d.* each; parcels of wool in a room, weighing 14 stone, worth 40*s.*; 82 a. sown with corn worth 3*s.* an a.; 46 a. sown with barley worth 2*s.* an a.; 29 a. sown with peas, beans, and dredge, worth 18*d.* an a. Total 47*l.* 17*s.* 4*d.* Hay worth 66*s.* 8*d.* Total 68*l.* 16*s.*

C.P. 51/1 no. 64

10 Nicholas Homedieu, of Westbedewynde

10 June 25 Edw. III [1351]. *Non omittas, sicut alias* returnable in oct. of S.J.B. next [30 June], on account of the earl of Stafford's liberty of Kynewardeston hundred, upon an *elegit* sued out by Robert de Perham, to whom Nicholas acknowledged 40*l.* in Chancery on 4 Mar. 17 Edw. III [1343] [*C.C.R.* 1343–6, 105], payable at Mich. then next; as William Homedieu, bailiff of the liberty, has returned no answer.

Thurs. after S.J.B. 25 Edw. III [30 June 1351]. Extent and appraisement at Bediwynde before Thomas de la Ryvere by Robert Louf, William Chamberlayn, John Baldameshale, Ellis Haynes, Henry Lyveden, Robert Tabletier, Richard Salesbury, William Rud, William Kyng, William Cok', Robert Totere, and Richard Nyweman.

No goods in Wilts.

At la Rigge: a messuage worth nothing beyond reprises; 56 a. of arable land, of which 20 a. lie in severalty and are worth 40*d.* yearly (2*d.* an a.) and 36 lie in common and are worth 3*s.* yearly (1*d.* an a.); 2 a. of pasture worth 12*d.* yearly; 3 a. of wood and underwood worth 6*d.* yearly; all held of William Chamberlayn at 1*d.* rent yearly. The bailiwick of the bedelry of Kynewardeston hundred in fee worth 6*s.* 8*d.* yearly. Total 14*s.* 5*d.*

C 131/8 no. 25

11 William de Wyke, merchant, of Westgrafton

12 July 32 Edw. III [1358]. *Capias* returnable on the morrow of the Assumption next [16 Aug.], sued out by John Maleweyn, merchant of

London, to whom William acknowledged 200*l.* on 27 Sept. last before Stephen Haym, mayor of the Staple of Winchester, payable at Eas. then next [1 Apr.]. *Endorsed.* William has not been found.

Tues. the eve of the Assumption 32 Edw. III [14 Aug. 1358]. Extent and appraisement at Westgrafton before Thomas de Hungerford by John de Flor', Walter de Litelcote, William Chamberlayn, Thomas de Stock', John Waryn, James de Stoundene, Adam Burgolon, Hubert Corderay, William Savage, Thomas Forstebury, John Chavyn, and John de Kepenhulle.

At Westgrafton: ⅔ messuage and garden and a vineyard surrounding the messuage worth 26*s.* 8*d.* yearly; 70 a. of arable land of which 35 a. can be sown each year, worth 52*s.* 6*d.* (18*d.* an a.) and the other 35 a. at 'Wrect' are worth nothing because they lie in common; 4 a. of meadow in severalty worth 32*s.* 4*d.* yearly with winter pasture (8*s.* 4*d.* an a.); a green worth 12*d.* yearly; from rents 2*s.* 6*d.*; 2 crofts next to the pasture of which the ⅔ held by William are worth 4*s.* yearly; 1 r. of pasture in severalty belonging to John Malewayn and William of which William's ⅔ of half a pasture is worth 3*s.* Total 6*l.* 3*s.*

The following goods there: 14½ a. of grain worth 7*l.* 5*s.* (10*s.* an a.); 14½ a. of dredge of which 7 a. are worth 46*s.* 8*d.* (6*s.* 8*d.* an a.) and the other 7½ a. 25*s.* (3*s.* 4*d.* an a.); 1 a. of green peas worth 10*s.* In the house: 2 tables with trestles, a form and chair worth 10*s.*; a basin (*pelvem*) with ewer (*lavatorio*) worth 5*s.*; in the pantry 2 cloths (*mappe*) and a towel (*manutergium*) worth 5*s.*; brass vessels (*vasa enea*), a pot, a posnet (*pocinettum*), 2 small dishes (*patell'*) and an oven (*fornax*) worth 14*s.* 6*d.*; wooden vessels (*vasa lingnea*), a vat, a kimnel (*cumulinum*), a cask (*tinam*), and 2 barrels, worth 6*s.* 8*d.* Total 13*l.* 7*s.* 10*d.*

18 Aug. 32 Edw. III [1358]. *Liberate* returnable in quin. of Mich. next [13 Oct.]; with *capias* against William's body.

Sat. the feast of Mich. 32 Edw. III [29 Sept. 1358]. An indenture testifies that the sheriff has delivered to John Malwayn the aforesaid lands and goods.

C 131/11 no. 8

12 William Wyke, of Westgrafton, and Thomas atte Stocke, of Wiltshire

14 May 36 Edw. III [1362]. *Capias* returnable on the morrow of Trin. next [13 June], sued out by Laurence de Andevere, merchant of the Staple of Winchester, to whom William and Thomas acknowledged 10*l.* on Wed. the feast of the Purification last [2 Feb.] before Hugh le Cran, mayor of the Staple of Winchester, payable on Sun. in mid Lent then next [20 Mar.].
Endorsed. Henry Sturmy, sheriff, has sent the writ to William de Wyke, bailiff of Ralph earl of Stafford's liberty of Kynewardeston hundred, who has returned no answer.

C 131/183 no. 18

13 John de Cottelegh, of Cherdestoke parish, Dorset

30 Jan. 37 Edw. III [1363]. *Capias* returnable in quin. of Eas. next [16 Apr.], sued out by Gilbert le Despencer, 'chivaler', to whom John acknowledged 500*l.* on 9 Mar. 35 Edw. III [1361] before John Pyel, late mayor of the Staple of Westminster, payable on 2 May 35 Edw. III [1361].

4 Mar. 37 Edw. III [1363]. Extent and appraisement at Marlebergh before Henry Sturmy by John Auncel, John Mallewayn, Robert Loof, Richard Beydon, Walter Carbonel, John atte Prevendre, John atte Gristmille, Peter Botillot, Richard Tommes, Thomas Pilton, John Frankeleyn, and William Weston.

At Hiwyssh: the manor with advowson of the church; a house with 2 rooms, a kitchen, . . . [*MS. blind*] and a ruined dovecote, worth nothing yearly beyond reprises; another dovecote (6*s.* 8*d.*); 240 a. of arable land worth 3*d.* an a. (60*s.*); 6 a. of meadow (12*s.*); pasture in severalty for 18 oxen and 6 avers and pasture in common (10*s.*); rents from various free life tenants (. . . *l.* 9*s.*), payable on the quarter days; the perquisites of the manor court with the fines, amercements, and other profits from the court (26*s.* 8*d.*). Total 9*l.* 8*s.* 4*d.* Twenty a. sown with grain worth 40*s.* (2*s.* an a.). C 131/14 no. 2

14 John Bernard, of Woubourn on Thames, and Edmund, his brother

10 Nov. 37 Edw. III [1363]. *Non omittas* returnable on Sat. after St. Andrew next [2 Dec.], on account of Queen Philippa's liberty, upon a *capias* returnable in oct. of All Saints [8 Nov.], sued out by Thomas, earl of Warwyk, Richard de Piriton, canon of St. Paul's church, London, and William de Wenlok, clerk, to whom John and Edmund acknowledged 400*l.* on 12 Feb. 36 Edw. III [1362] before John Pyel, then mayor of the Staple of Westminster, payable at Eas. then next [17 Apr.], as John Whitsyde, bailiff of the liberty, has returned no answer.

Thurs. the feast of St. Andrew 37 Edw. III [30 Nov. 1363]. Extent and appraisement at Marlebergh before Henry Sturmy by Simon de Berewyk, Thomas Crouk, Peter Harald, William Trotewik, Henry le Walsshe, John Tockenham, William Wolewey, Nicholas le Frye, William Roser, John Wade, Roger Tarente, and John Perham.

No goods or lands in Wilts. within or without the liberty now or on the day of the recognizance. On All Saints Day 36 Edw. III [1 Nov. 1362] John Bernard held the following lands at Brodeblountesdon within the liberty: a messuage with house, rooms, kitchen, barn, stable, and garden, worth nothing beyond reprises; 60 a. of arable land lying in common, worth 20*s.* yearly (4*d.* an a.); 10½ a. of meadow worth 14*s.* yearly (16*d.* an a.); in the said messuage, rents from various tenants worth 60*s.* yearly; a messuage called the 'Hyde' worth nothing beyond reprises; in the said messuage 100 a. of pasture in severalty worth 25*s.* yearly (3*d.* an a.). All these lands John granted to William de Riborgh who is now seised in fee. Total value 119*s.* yearly.

C 131/14 no. 8

15 Richard de Perham, knight

16 Feb. 39 Edw. III [1365]. *Capias* returnable in one month from Eas. next [11 May], sued out by Laurence de Andevere, merchant, to whom Richard acknowledged 32*l.* on 4 Mar. 36 Edw. III [1362] before Hugh le Cran, mayor of the Staple of Winchester, payable at Mich. then next.
Endorsed. Henry Sturmy, sheriff, has sent the writ to Walter atte Burghe, bailiff of the bishop of Salisbury's liberty, who has returned no answer. The writ was delivered to the sheriff too late for execution.

C 131/185 no. 8

16 Walter de Coumbe, of Wiltshire

12 May 39 Edw. III [1365]. *Liberate sicut pluries* returnable at Westminster in oct. of Trin. next [15 June], for John de Ware and Thomas Cole, executors of John de Wynton, knight, of Hants, to whom Walter acknowledged 40*l.* on 15 July 30 Edw. III [1356] before Henry . . . , late mayor of Salisbury, and Nicholas Chaunterel, clerk, payable at Lady Day then next.

. . . [*MS. torn*] 39 Edw. III . . . Extent at Ambresbury before Henry Sturmy by Edmund Godewyne, William de Harnham, John Bartour, John Gowyne, Richard Loukeharm, . . . , John Hat, John Gyn, Robert Alesaundre, and John Harwedoune.

At Milder: a toft with curtilage worth 12*d.* yearly; 60 a. of arable land . . . (30*s.*) yearly; 4 a. of meadow with the 'ware' adjoining (13*s.*); . . . water-mill (13*s.* 4*d.*); . . . pasture for sheep (40*s.*); . . . mill now in the hands of John le Thorp and his wife Katherine, late wife of Thomas de Berkele, knight.

At Compton by Enford: . . . water-mill (100*s.*) . . . in the hands of John Litelcote who is of age, by the grant of Walter, Walter's son and heir.

C.P. 51/1 no. 131

17 Robert atte Slade, of Bromham

30 Oct. 49 Edw. III [1375]. *Capias* returnable in quin. of Hil. next [27 Jan.], sued out by John Wecche, to whom Robert acknowledged 40*l.* on 1 July last before William de Walleworth, mayor of the Staple of Westminster, payable at Mich. then next.
Endorsed. Hugh Cheyne, sheriff, has taken Robert and put him in prison. As for the extent he has sent the writ to Nicholas Houke, bailiff of the abbot of Battle's liberty, who has returned no answer. Robert was taken outside the liberty.

C 131/193 no. 36

18 John Blount, knight

3 Feb. 50 Edw. III [1376]. *Capias* returnable in quin. of Eas. next [27 Apr.], sued out by Robert Pikerell, citizen and saddler of London, to whom John acknowledged 120*l.* on 20 Oct. last before William de Walleworth, mayor of the Staple of Westminster, payable at Martinmas then next [10 Nov.]. Like writs to the sheriffs of Lond. and Essex.
Endorsed. John has not been found.

16 Apr. 50 Edw. III [1376]. Extent and appraisement at Devyses before

Hugh Cheyne by John Stodlegh, William Wichampton, John atte Halle, Thomas Felawe, William atte Grene, Richard Roude, Nicholas Sage, Richard Gobet, William Ryngeborn, William Spicer, William Cray, anp Thomas Luffewyk.

No chattels in Wilts. At Beveresbrouk: the manor, with lands, tenements, and rents in Calston' belonging to it, except for a rent of 1 lb. pepper which Richard Myblank formerly gave to John yearly at Mich., in lieu of all services, for a messuage and a virgate of land at Beveresbrouk. This rent John granted by deed to Henry Spelly and other feoffees whose names are not known in fee. Yearly value of the manor 106*s*. 8*d*. beyond the said pepper rent and 40*s*. yearly rent from the said manor, lands, and tenements which John granted by deed to his brother, Henry Blount, and his assigns for Henry's life.

At Devyses, Roude, and Parklond by Devyses: rents from various free life tenants by the grant of John worth 60*s*. yearly. Long before the recognizance John granted this rent of 60*s*. by deed to Henry Spelly and the others for the lifetime of the tenants, with reversion to them in fee on condition that if John Blount paid to Ellis Spelly, burgess of Bristol, a sum of money at Bristol on Ascension Day next [22 May], Henry and the others should not enjoy the rent or the reversion. This sum the jury cannot specify.

8 Dec. 50 Edw. III [1376]. *Liberate*[1] returnable in oct. of the Purification [9 Feb.]; with *capias* against John's body.
Endorsed. On 8 May 2 Ric. II [1379] the manor was delivered to Robert Pykerell by a writ returnable in oct. of Trin. [12 June]. On 8 Dec. then next the writ was corrected and was then returnable in oct. of the Purification [9 Feb.]. It was returned to Chancery with seal unbroken. On 3 July 2 Ric. II [1378] the manor was delivered to Robert to hold until 40*l*. of the debt was paid. This writ was returnable on the morrow of the Nativity [9 Sept.].

C 131/24 no. 11

19 Reynold Love, merchant of London

14 Feb. 51 Edw. III [1377]. *Liberate* returnable in quin. of Eas. next [12 Apr.], for Henry Jurdan, merchant, of Winchester, to whom Reynold acknowledged 95*l*. on 16 Aug. last before Stephen Hayme, mayor of the Staple of Winchester, payable on St. Matthew then next [21 Sept.] of (i) the following lands outside the bishop of Salisbury's liberty: a messuage with curtilage adjacent, a cottage, ½ a., 1 r., and 3 'hamlets' of meadow, and 30 a. of arable land at Bymerton'; a curtilage at Quydhampton'; 16 a. of arable land, 2½ a., 2 plots of meadow, and 23*s*. 4*d*. yearly rent from 13 cottages, a dovecote, and a croft at Fissherton which John Mercer, of Fyssherton, his wife Margaret, and his son Stephen hold for life by the grant of Reynold, with reversion on their deaths to Reynold in fee; and (ii) the following lands within the liberty in the city of New Salisbury: a messuage next to the tenement of John Ferneborgh on the one side and the stile of the graveyard of St. Thomas's church on the other, formerly of Thomas de Hereford, which

[1] Writ printed in full in Appendix, p. 127.

Reynold held jointly with William Wilde, chaplain; a tenement called the 'Nyweyn' between the tenement of Nicholas Taillour and that formerly of Thomas Huchones, which he held jointly with William Wilde; 2 shops in the 'Potrewe' between the shop formerly of John Talbot and that of William Wilton, 'bocher'; 20*s.* yearly rent for the life of Christine Styntes from a tenement outside the bars between the tenements of John Vole and John Mildenhale. Total, excluding the rent, 11*l.* 16*s.* yearly; with *capias* against Reynold's body; as Henry had sued out a *capias* returnable in oct. of the Purification [9 Feb.], to which the sheriff in respect of (i) and Thomas Hungerford, bailiff of the liberty, in respect of (ii) have severally returned that Reynold has not been found.
Endorsed. Reynold has not been found. The sheriff has delivered the aforesaid lands. Regarding the lands within the bishop of Salisbury's liberty, he has sent the writ to Thomas Hungerford, bailiff, whose answer is annexed.

The bailiff has delivered the lands within the liberty. Reynold has not been found. C 131/16 no. 6

20 John Husee, of Berton Sacy, Hampshire

18 Aug. 1 Ric. II [1377]. *Capias* returnable in quin. of Mich. next [13 Oct.], sued out by Hugh Craan, citizen and merchant of Winchester, to whom John acknowledged 400*l.* on 11 Nov. 41 Edw. III [1367] before Fulk de Horwod, late mayor of the Staple of Westminster, payable at Christmas then next. Like writs to the sheriffs of Hants and Dors.

Sat. after St. Matthew 1 Ric. II [26 Sept. 1377]. Extent and appraisement at New Salisbury before Ralph Cheyne by Henry Haversham, Thomas le Rede, Thomas Pycot, Thomas Cuttyng, John Gilbard, John Alewyne, John Trowe, Vincent Perham, John Raundes, Roger Pychard, Ralph Cuwell, and Richard Lambard.

The manor of Bridemere, from which is paid yearly to the abbess of Wilton 70*s.* 11*d.*, 192 fleeces of wool, 16 qr. 2½ bz. of wheat, 11 qr. 3½ bz. of barley, and 11 qr. 2½ bz. of flax (*lineum*). Beyond this payment the manor is worth 6*s.* 8*d.* yearly. The manor of Northyngton worth 10*l.* yearly.
C 131/25 no. 4

21 William fitz William, of Wiltshire

16 May 2 Ric. II [1379]. *Capias* returnable in oct. of Trin. next [19 June], sued out by John atte Yerd and William Worston, merchants of the Staple of Winchester, to whom William acknowledged 60*l.* on 17 Nov. 47 Edw. III [1373] before Stephen Haym, then mayor of the Staple of Winchester, payable at Lady Day then next.
Endorsed. William has not been found.

10 June 2 Ric. II [1379]. Extent and appraisement at Chippenham before William Worston by John Bremelham, William Kaynesham, John Halle,

John Huberd, Robert Heigheweye, William Eyr, Ralph Bluet, Robert Perham, John atte Brugge, Robert Eyton, John Jogel, and Richard Pundfold.

A messuage and a carucate in Wambergh, with meadows, feeding, and pasture belonging, worth 4 marks yearly.

Endorsed. The lands were delivered on 14 June according to the writ returnable the morrow of St. Peter's chains [2 Aug.].

C 131/26 no. 4

22 Thomas West, knight

8 June 3 Ric. II [1380]. *Capias* returnable in oct. of Mich. next [6 Oct.], sued out by John Chaunflour, merchant, and by John Romesye, of Warldham, and Richard Wetham, executors of Stephen Welewyk, merchant, to whom Thomas acknowledged 400*l.* on 10 Apr. 49 Edw. III [1375] before Stephen Haym, then mayor of the Staple of Winchester, payable at Midsummer then next. Like writ to the sheriff of Hants.

Endorsed. Thomas has not been found. On 12 Oct. 4 Ric. II [1380] John Chaunflour and Stephen's executors came into Chancery and acknowledged that they had received satisfaction for the debt. They asked that Thomas's lands and chattels be restored to him.

Mon. after St. Mary Magdalene 4 Ric. II [23 July 1380]. Extent and appraisement at Tissebury before Ralph de Norton by William Scammel, Henry le Bartour, Peter Whiton, Robert Wichford, John Hat, Vincent Perham, John Lyngynere, John Drynkewater, John Trowe, Roger Niwe, Stephen Davy, and Robert Wallebroun.

At Bridemere: the manor worth 6*l.* 13*s.* 4*d.* yearly; 9 oxen worth 4*l.* 10*s.* (10*s.* a head); 2 avers worth 20*s.* (10*s.* a head); 160 sheep worth 8*l.* (12*d.* a head); 30 a. of corn worth 100*s.* (3*s.* 4*d.* an a.); 20 a. of barley worth 50*s.* (2*s.* 6*d.* an a.); 19 a. of dredge and oats worth 23*s.* 9*d.* (15*d.* an a.); 3 a. of peas and 4 a. of vetch worth 7*s.* (12*d.* an a.); a weak cart with iron tires in poor condition worth 3*s.* 4*d.*; a plough with all its gear and a harrow with iron teeth (*herciam ferro dentatam*) worth 3*s.* 4*d.*; a sow with 6 hogs worth 6*s.* 8*d.*

At Swaleweclyve: 3 avers worth 20*s.* (6*s.* 8*d.* a head); 2 foals worth 4*s.* (2*s.* a head); 20 oxen worth 10*l.* (10*s.* a head); 2 bulls worth 13*s.* 4*d.* (6*s.* 8*d.* a head); 5 cows worth 33*s.* 4*d.* (6*s.* 8*d.* a head); 250 sheep worth 18*l.* 15*s.* (18*d.* a head); 30 pigs worth 30*s.* (12*d.* a head); a plough and wagon worth 26*s.* 8*d.*

At Wyke: 3 avers worth 20*s.* (6*s.* 8*d.* a head); 16 oxen worth 8*l.* (10*s.* a head); 10 cows worth 66*s.* 8*d.* (6s. 8*d.* a head); 2 heifers worth 6*s.* 8*d.* (3*s.* 4*d.* a head); 7 bullocks worth 17*s.* 6*d.* (2*s.* 6*d.* a head); 5 yearlings worth 7*s.* 6*d.* (15*d.* a head); 11 calves worth 14*s.* 8*d.* (16*d.* a head); 240 sheep worth 16*l.* (16*d.* a head); 15 piglets worth 15*s.* (12*d.* a head); a weak cart with iron tires in poor condition worth 3*s.* 4*d.*; a wagon with iron tires worth 10*s.*

Total yearly value of all the above lands 6*l.* 13*s.* 4*d.* Total value of all the above goods 90*l.* 7*s.* 9*d.* C 131/27 no. 20

28 July 4 Ric. II [1380]. *Scire facias* for the appearance of John and Stephen's executors in Chancery in oct. of Mich. next [6 Oct.] to show why Thomas's bond should not be annulled and execution of the writs stayed; as, by a deed in Thomas's possession, John and Stephen granted that if Thomas discharged their own debt of 400*l.* by a bond issued according to the Statute Staple to William Venour, citizen and merchant of London, then Thomas's bond for 400*l.* would be suspended and annulled; although Thomas correctly discharged John and Stephen's debt of 400*l.*, John and Stephen's executors are continuing illegally to sue out writs of *capias* and *extendi facias* against Thomas to the sheriff of Wilts. and others.
Endorsed. John and Stephen's executors have not been found.

C 131/198 no. 8

23 Roger Walton, of Somerset

10 Feb. 4 Ric. II [1381]. *Capias* returnable in quin. of Eas. next [28 Apr.], sued out by Richard de Burton, citizen and tailor of London, to whom Roger acknowledged 6*l.* 6*s.* 8*d.* on 23 Sept. 3 Ric. II [1379] before William de Walleworth, mayor of the Staple of Westminster, payable at Eas. last [25 Mar.].

9 Apr. 4 Ric. II [1381]. Extent and appraisement at Wereminster before Laurence of St. Martin by Richard Halle, Nicholas Bradford, John Leverich, Walter Colston, John Pilton, William Lynedene, John Cherk, of Codeford, John Casy, Robert Waite, Edward Payn, William Ceresy, and William Ballard.

No goods or lands in Wilts. C 131/28 no. 8

24 Richard Clyvedon, of Somerset

6 May 4 Ric. II [1381]. *Capias* returnable in oct. of S.J.B. next [30 June], sued out by Peter de Courtenay, knight, to whom Richard acknowledged 333*l.* 6*s.* 8*d.* on 23 Oct. last before William de Walleworth, mayor of the Staple of Westminster, payable at Christmas then next. Like writs to the sheriffs of Glos. and Som.
Endorsed. Richard has not been found.

Sat. before S.J.B. 4 Ric. II [22 June 1381]. Extent and appraisement at Cryckelade before Hugh Cheyne by John Andrew, Richard Wade, John Dygher, Robert Chaumbre, James Wade, John Jacob, John atte Court, Adam Symondes, David Crook, Roger Saundres, John Duke, and John Robyns.

At Westrop by Heyworth: 2 carucates of land worth 26*s.* 8*d.* yearly; 53*s.* 4*d.* yearly rent from various tenants, payable quarterly; 30 a. of meadow worth 16*d.* an a.; 50 a. of pasture worth 3½*d.* an a. Total 6*l.* 14*s.* 7*d.*
Endorsed. The lands were delivered on 20 Oct. 5 Ric. II [1381].

[The property listed above is also given in tabular form, together with the

property in Som., whose total value was 6*l.* 13*s.* 4*d.* The land in Wilts. was to be held until 166*l.* 13*s.* 8*d.* of the debt had been paid, that in Som. until 166*l.* 10*s.*]
C 131/28 no. 4

25 Robert Redyng, of New Salisbury

28 Feb. 5 Ric. II [1382]. *Non omittas*[1] returnable in quin. of Eas. next [20 Apr.], on account of the bishop of Salisbury's liberty, upon a *capias* returnable in oct. of Hil. last [20 Jan.], sued out by Adam Fermer, citizen and cutler of London, to whom Robert acknowledged 80*l.* on 26 Feb. 1 Ric. II [1378] before William de Walleworth, mayor of the Staple of Westminster, payable at Midsummer then next; since Thomas Hungerford, bailiff of the liberty, has returned no answer.
Endorsed. The sheriff has taken Robert and put him in custody.

Wed. in Eas. week 5 Ric. II [9 Apr. 1382]. Extent and appraisement at New Salisbury before Nicholas Wodhull by John Wychford, Robert Deverell, John Kyngbrugge, Hugh Goudy, Edward Fonteigne, Robert Weyer, Gilbert Oword, Adam Countewell, John Harnham, Richard Ludde, William le Northerner, and John Scammel.

No lands in Wilts. At New Salisbury the following goods: a 'dosser', a 'banker', a table (*tabulam mensalem*), 2 stools (*stolos*), a sanap (*saunapa*), 5 seats (*salles*) worth 3*s.*; a long chair (*cathedram*) worth 20*d.*; 2 chests (*cistas*) worth 7*s.*; a coverlet (*cooptorium*), 2 linen sheets (*lintheam*') with other equipment worth 2*s.*; an old iron pot (*ferrum*) worth 4*d.*; a towel worth 2*d.*; 4 barrels worth 10*d.*; 2 'vatez' worth 16*d.*; a wooden bushel worth 4*d.*; a large lead seal (*plumbum*) worth 40*s.*; a pig of lead worth 12*d.*; a vat (*cuve*) with 15 hoops (*cuvar*') worth 9*s.* 6*d.*; a 'clausyngfane' with 'gaderere' worth 4*d.*; a table (12*d.*); 4 chests worth 3*s.* 4*d.*; a seat (*sellam*); 4 'kivierez' worth 6*d.*; 2 pairs of crystals worth 8*d.* Total 72*s.* 4*d.* C 131/28 no. 24

20 May 5 Ric. II [1382]. *Extendi facias* returnable in oct. of S.J.B. next [30 June], as it is understood that Robert held lands in Wilts., and held other goods not included in the previous extent.

Sat. the eve of St. Peter and St. Paul 6 Ric. II [28 June 1382]. Inquisition at New Salisbury before Nicholas Wodhull by William de Godmeston, Robert Sexhampcote, Richard Whiteparissh, Richard Hakeleston, William Hele the elder, John Harnham, John Canynges, John Portman, Gilbert Skynnere, John Grene, Thomas Radenham, and Roger Skynnere.

No goods or lands in Wilts. except those goods formerly appraised.
C 131/28 no. 27

10 Feb. 6 Ric. II [1383]. *Extendi facias* returnable in quin. of Eas. next [26 Apr.], for all Robert's lands in Wilts. and all goods not included in the previous return.

3 Apr. 6 Ric. II [1383]. Inquisition at New Salisbury before Bernard Brocas

[1] Writ printed in full in Appendix, p. 128.

by Richard Stilly . . . , Simon Bont, John Nedlere the younger, John Ondel, Robert Bady, John Chaundeler the elder, John Preston, John Drewer, John Nyweman, Robert Pope, Hugh Hore, and Reynold Druwery.

No lands in Wilts. No goods except those recently appraised before Nicholas Wodhull, the former sheriff.

C 131/30 no. 13

26 John Blount, knight

14 July 7 Ric. II [1383]. *Elegit* returnable in oct. of Mich. next [6 Oct.], upon John's nonappearance in Chancery to answer Thomas Dryffeld, to whom he acknowledged 66*l*. in Chancery on 7 Nov. 1 Ric. II [1377] [*C.C.R.* 1377–81, 103], payable at Whitsun then next [6 June]; as Thomas has sued out an *elegit* with *scire facias*, which was delivered to and executed by Roger Bailly, bailiff of William la Zouche of Haryngworth's liberty of his hundred of Calne.

Endorsed. The sheriff has delivered half the lands to Thomas through his attorney, John Orchard.

Wed. after St. Matthew 7 Ric. II [23 Sept. 1383]. Extent and appraisement at New Salisbury before Bernard Brocas by Thomas Cuttyng, John Nicholas, William Weston, Thomas Ryngesborn, Robert Devenyssh, William Bryght, Roger Warde, William Arnold, John le Eyr, John Wardes, John Fallyngworth, and John Staunford.

The manor of Beveresbrouk not built upon worth 40*s*. yearly, moiety 20*s*. At Calston the rents of various free life tenants worth 26*s*. 8*d*. yearly, moiety 13*s*. 4*d*. Total value of the moiety 33*s*. 4*d*.

C 131/31 no. 4

27 Nicholas Seynloo[1]

26 Sept. 10 Ric. II [1386]. *Elegit* returnable in oct. of Martinmas next [18 Nov.], sued out by William Bayford, to whom Nicholas acknowledged 100*l*. in Chancery on 4 Dec. last [*C.C.R.* 1385–9, 98], payable at Mich. then next.

Endorsed. The sheriff has delivered half the lands to Henry Littone, William's attorney. The extent could not be made in the presence of Nicholas as he had died long before the receipt of the writ.

Wed. the morrow of St. Leonard, 10 Ric. II [7 Nov. 1386]. Extent and appraisement at Fisherton Aucher before John Salesbury by Thomas Pycot, John Meriot, William Moone, Adam Hordere, Thomas Guyn, Philip Wyndhulle, Thomas Tonnere, Thomas Felawe, John Bacon, Walter Moody, Walter Gomeldon, and Walter Sawiere.

Four messuages built, 2 tofts, 8 a. of arable land, and 2½ a. of meadow in Fissherton Aucher and 2 cottages and 22 a. of arable land in Bymerton, worth 40*s*. yearly.

C 145/236 no. 7

[1] Abstract previously printed in *Cal. Inq. Misc.* iv, no. 360.

28 Edmund de Tettesworth, of Wiltshire

20 Feb. 10 Ric. II [1387]. *Capias* returnable in 3 weeks from Eas. next [28 Apr.], sued out by Thomas Restwold to whom Edmund acknowledged 60*l.* on 3 Apr. 4 Ric. II [1381] before William de Walworth, late mayor of the Staple of Westminster, payable at Mich. 5 Ric. II [1381].

Endorsed. The sheriff has sent the writ to Thomas Hungerford, bailiff of the bishop of Salisbury's liberty, who has returned no answer.

C 131/203 no. 44

12 July 11 Ric. II [1387]. *Non omittas* returnable in oct. of Mich. next [6 Oct.].

Endorsed. Edmund has not been found.

Sat. before Mich. 11 Ric. II [28 Sept. 1387]. Extent and appraisement at New Salisbury before John [Salesbury] by William Gys, William Lord, John Steshall, Thomas Deverell, John atte Hethe, William Don, William Harleston, Thomas Pycot, Richard Love[dy], John Borham, Nicholas Wodeford, and Thomas Goyn.

No goods or lands in Wilts., except the yearly rent of a rose from a tenement lately given to Robert Borham in Wynchestrestret in New Salisbury between the tenements of John atte Heth' on the east and Richard Lathe on the west. This yearly rent Robert's wife Agnes gave to Edmund during her life and she is now dead.

C 131/35 no. 28

29 Nicholas Woodhull, merchant, of Derneford and Thomas Lainer, citizen and merchant of London

25 July 13 Ric. II [1389]. *Capias* returnable in quin. of Mich. next [13 Oct.], sued out by William More, citizen and vintner of London, to whom Nicholas and Thomas acknowledged 104*l.* on 9 July 12 Ric. II [1388] before Nicholas Exton, mayor of the Staple of Westminster, payable at Christmas then next. Like writs to the sheriffs of Hants and Northants.

Endorsed. Nicholas and Thomas have not been found.

C 131/37 no. 2

2 Aug. 13 Ric. II [1389]. Extent and appraisement at Ambresbury before Ralph Cheyne by John Madyngton, Thomas Spaldyng, John Harwedoune, Nicholas Petyt, Robert Alisaundre, Thomas Goyn of Lake, Roger Boltford, William Symond, Hugh Vyvas, Edward Lake, Thomas Gyn, and Richard Loukeharm.

Nicholas holds the manor at Little Derneford by Great Derneford worth 10*l.* 13*s.* 4*d.* yearly, including the water-mill; another manor at Little Derneford by Wodeford worth 8*l.* yearly; the manor of Tuderlegh worth 66*s.* 8*d.* No goods in Wilts.

Thomas has no lands or goods in Wilts.

C 131/11 no. 9

30 Matthew Sampson, of Miere

18 July 14 Ric. II [1390]. *Capias, sicut alias* returnable in oct. of Mich. next [6 Oct.], sued out by John Claydych, citizen and 'peuterer' of London, to whom Matthew acknowledged 12*l.* on 4 July 13 Ric. II [1389] before Nicholas Exton, mayor of the Staple of Westminster, payable at Christmas then next; or else the sheriff is to show cause why he has not carried out the instruction.
Endorsed. Matthew has been taken and put in custody.

4 Aug. 14 Ric. II [1390]. Extent at Mere before Richard Mawardyn by John Perys, William Hikkes, John Hutche, John Forward, John Immere, Thomas Ferour, John Aubrey, William Noteben, John Holte, William Boveclyve, John in the Combe, and Bennet Dounynge.
No lands or goods in Wilts. C 131/39 no. 14

31 Robert Hampton

5 Feb. 14 Ric. II [1391]. *Capias, sicut alias* returnable in quin. of Eas. next [9 Apr.], sued out by John Slegh, king's butler, to whom Robert acknowledged 200*l.* on 20 Feb. 12 Ric. II [1389] before Nicholas Exton, mayor of the Staple of Westminster, payable at Mich. then next. Like writ to the sheriff of Berks.
Endorsed. Robert has not been found.

Mon. before St. Gregory 14 Ric. II [6 Mar. 1391]. Inquisition at Marlebergh before John Roches by Thomas Canynges, John Wydyhull, Laurence Horder, William atte Halle, James Gore, John Banak, Walter Bayly, John Haytfeld, John Appelman, Thomas Penne, Richard Foxelegh, and William Wykelescote.
The manor of Brodeblundesdon which is called 'Orchardesplace', held in fee for himself and his heirs worth 10*l.* yearly.
Endorsed. The manor was delivered on 20 Apr. 14 Ric. II [1391].

20 Apr. 14 Ric. II [1391]. *Liberate* returnable in oct. of Trin. next [28 May]; with *capias* against Robert's body.
C 131/39 no. 1

32 Richard Talbot, knight, of Hyrchenfeld

20 Jan. 15 Ric. II [1392]. *Capias* returnable on the morrow of St. Gregory next [13 Mar.], sued out by William Heron, knight, and John Trygge, citizen and fishmonger of London, to whom Richard acknowledged 5,000 marks on 17 July last, before John Hale, mayor of the Staple of Westminster, payable at Christmas then next. Like writs to the sheriffs of Glos., Hants, Oxon., Berks., and Herefs.
Endorsed. Richard has not been found.

Wed. before St. Gregory 15 Ric. II [6 Mar. 1392]. Inquisition at Hyswyndon before Robert Dynley by John Palmere, Thomas Canynges, John Ferour, James Gore, Sampson Horput, William Kene, Robert Perham, Walter

Gylemyn, Robert Rademore, William Shigtman, William Vitel, and John Debenham.

No lands in Wilts., as at or about Martinmas 13 Ric. II [10 Nov. 1389] Richard granted by charter all his lands to William Spark and John Hunt to hold in fee. By this enfeoffment William and John were seised at Martinmas of all lands and held them to the use of Richard's son and heir, Gilbert, his wife Joan, and Thomas, duke of Gloucester. No goods in Wilts.

C 131/42 no. 3

33 Thomas Salford, merchant, of Bristol

20 May 20 Ric. II [1397]. *Capias* returnable in quin. of S.J.B. next [8 July], sued out by Hugh Plommer, merchant, of Bristol, to whom Thomas acknowledged 35*l.* on 4 June 13 Ric. II [1390] before John Vyell, then mayor of the Staple of Bristol, payable at Christmas then next. Like writ to the sheriff of Som.

Endorsed. The sheriff has taken Thomas and put him in prison. Later, because of another writ, he has released him.

Wed. before the Translation of St. Thomas the Martyr 21 Ric. II [4 July 1397]. Extent and appraisement at Wermestre before Richard Mawardyn by Peter Frankeleyn, Robert Ennok, Thomas Eyr, William Tommes, Roger Wyther, Thomas Gore the younger, John Grenyng, John Grenhull, John Tabour, John Goule, John Wacche, and John Gay.

A cottage at Westbury worth 3*s.* 4*d.* yearly; 2 cottages at Bradeford worth 6*s.* 8*d* yearly; 2 cottages at Rode worth 10*s.* yearly. At Lavyngton: 4 oxen worth 10*s.* each; 3 horses worth 6*s.* 8*d.* each; a plough with all its gear and 2 harrows (*hercias*) worth 6*s.* 8*d.*

2 July 21 Ric. II [1397].[1] *Supersedeas*, with order for the release of Thomas from prison; as Hugh, after the recognizance of debt, made a general release to Thomas in the name of Thomas Salforde, merchant, of Roode, Som., of all actions, plaints, and demands both real and personal which he had or could have against him by reason of trespass, contract, debt, account, or otherwise, as appears from writing under Hugh's seal produced in Chancery. Hugh, however, demands execution of the 35*l.* by various writs of *capias* to the sheriffs of Wilts. and Som. and Thomas is being kept in prison unlawfully by the sheriff of Wilts.

Writ of *scire facias* has been sent to the sheriff of Bristol for the appearance of Hugh in Chancery in quin. of S.J.B. next [8 July] to show cause why the execution of the said writs should not be stayed and to accept the judgment of Chancery. John Skyllyng and Richard Habervyle of Wilts. have mainprised in Chancery to have Thomas there on the said day, under pain of 40*l.* each to be levied from their lands and chattels if Thomas does not appear.

C 131/46 no. 11

[1] Abstract printed in *C.C.R.* 1396–9, 200.

34 John Asshele, merchant, of New Salisbury

27 June 21 Ric. II [1397]. *Capias* returnable in oct. of Mich. next [6 Oct.], sued out by John Nyweman, merchant, of Salisbury, to whom John acknowledged 40*l.* on Wed. the eve of St. Andrew 20 Ric. II [29 Nov. 1396] before William Mapill, then mayor of the Staple of Southampton, payable at Christmas last.

Endorsed. The sheriff has sent the writ to Oliver de Harnham, bailiff of the bishop of Salisbury's liberty, whose answer is annexed. John holds no lands outside the liberty.

The bailiff has taken John and kept him in prison because he is so sick that he could not bring him on the appointed day for fear of his death.

C 131/47 no. 5

35 Robert Waryner, of Marleburgh

18 Jan. 22 Ric. II [1399]. *Capias* returnable in 15 days from Eas. next [13 Apr.], sued out by Richard Waryner, of Marleburgh, and William North, clerk, of Marleburgh, to whom Robert acknowledged 40*l.* on 16 July 7 Ric. II [1383] before William Walworth, late mayor of the Staple of Westminster, payable at Eas. then next [22 Mar.].

Endorsed. The writ was delivered to Richard Mawardyn, sheriff, too late for execution.

C 131/214 no. 45

36 Thomas Canynges, of Stratton, William atte Halle, of Heyworth, Walter Bayly, of Heyworth, and John Henton, of Brodebluntesdon

10 Feb. 22 Ric. II [1399]. *Capias* returnable in oct. of Trin. next [1 June], sued out by John Spencer, Henry Somer, and Richard Hatton, executors of John Sligh, esquire, to whom Thomas, William, Walter, and John acknowledged 100*l.* on 7 June 14 Ric. II [1391] before John Hadelee, mayor of the Staple of Westminster, payable at Mich. then next.

Endorsed. The writ was delivered to Richard Mawardyn, sheriff, too late for execution.

C 131/214 no. 52

37 John Roche, knight

16 Feb. 1 Hen. IV [1400]. *Capias* returnable in quin. of Eas. next [2 May], sued out by Simon Barber, citizen and vintner of London, to whom John acknowledged 100*l.* on 15 Jan. 22 Ric. II [1399] before William Brampton, mayor of the Staple of Westminster, payable at All Saints then next [1 Nov.].

Endorsed. John has not been found.

Wed. after Lady Day 1 Hen. IV [31 Mar. 1400]. Extent and appraisement at Fissherton Aucher before John Daunteseye by Robert Reyner, Thomas Eyr, Richard Homyngton, John Nicholas the elder, John Nicholas the younger, John Madyngton, Thomas Spaldyng, William Upton, William Duyk, Simon Cherlton, William Peyracourt, and John Coof.

No lands or chattels in Wilts.

C 131/49 no. 10

38 Edmund Dauntesey, clerk, and Edmund Dauntesey, esquire, of Wiltshire

10 Dec. 3 Hen. IV [1401]. *Capias* returnable in quin. of Eas. next [9 Apr.], sued out by Robert Braybrook, bishop of London, and Nicholas Braybrook to whom Edmund and Edmund acknowledged 1,000 marks on 24 Jan. 21 Ric. II [1398] before William Brampton, mayor of the Staple of Westminster, payable at St. Gregory the pope then next [12 Mar.]. Like writ to the sheriff of Devon.
Endorsed. The writ was delivered to John Gaweyn, sheriff, too late for execution. C 131/216 no. 2

39 John Gilbard the elder and John Gilbard the younger, merchants, of la Vyse

8 Feb. 3 Hen. IV [1402]. *Capias* returnable in quin. of Eas. next [9 Apr.], sued out by William Wermynstre, merchant, of Bristol, to whom John and John acknowledged 40*l.* on 3 July 21 Ric. II [1397] before Thomas Knap, then mayor of the Staple of Bristol, payable at Mich. then next.
Endorsed. The writ was delivered to John Gaweyn, sheriff, too late for execution.

1 July 3 Hen. IV [1402]. *Capias, sicut alias* returnable in oct. of Mich. next [6 Oct.].
Endorsed. John Gaweyn, sheriff, has taken John Gilbard the elder and put him in prison and has sent the writ to John Wylmyndon, bailiff of the bishop of Salisbury's liberty, who has returned no answer.
C 131/216 no. 5

40 [William] Bagot, 'chivaler', and John Wyndesore, esquire

Wed. before S.J.B. 4 Hen. IV [20 June 1403]. Inquisition at Fennysotton before William Cheyne by William Upton, of Wermestre, John Osebern, John Mulle, William Pole, Thomas Spencer, William Wir, John Botiller the elder, John Wade, William atte Nasshe, John Colles, David Taillour, and John atte Rigge.

No lands or chattels which can be delivered to Edmund Brudenell.
C 131/51 no. 13

41 John Richard, of Berewyk St. James

11 Feb. 6 Hen. IV [1405]. *Capias* returnable in quin. of Eas. next [3 May], sued out by William Trendelere, 'coupere' of London, to whom John acknowledged 16*l.* on 25 Jan. 5 Hen. IV [1404] before William Askham, mayor of the Staple of Westminster, payable at Mich. then next.
Endorsed. John is dead and therefore John Lisle of Wodyton, knight, sheriff, has not executed the writ.
C 131/219 no. 25

42 Hugh de la Lynde, of Wiltshire

3 Sept. 2 Hen. V [1414]. *Capias* returnable on Mon. after Mich. next

[1 Oct.], sued out by Walter Lynton, of Leics. and [Thomas Bailley], clerk, of London, to whom Hugh acknowledged 300*l.* on 7 Sept. 10 Hen. IV [1409] before Richard Whityngton, mayor of the Staple of Westminster, payable at Christmas then next.
Endorsed. The sheriff has made an extent of Hugh's lands outside the bishop of Salisbury's liberty of the hundreds of Poterne and Canynges and has sent the writ to Richard Osborne, bailiff of the liberty, who has given no answer. Hugh has not been found.

Mon. before St. Matthew 2 Hen. V [17 Sept. 1414]. Extent of Hugh's lands outside the bishop of Salisbury's liberty of the hundreds of [Potterne] and Canynges at Wilton before Ellis de la Mare by Robert Cuttyng, Thomas Stabbe, John Battere the elder, Richard Fairsong, William Peracourt, John Spencer, Walter Plomer, James . . . [*MS. torn*], John Wanney, Henry Goldyng, Peter Gurold, and John Turpyn.
In Wynterbourne Cherborgh outside the hundred 2 messuages, 2 tofts, and 30 a. of land, with advowson of the church, held for life by the grant of John atte Mersshe the elder worth 20*s.* yearly. In Bisshopestrowe a messuage and 12 a. of land held for life by the grant of Thomas Felawe, of no yearly value.

2 Oct. 2 Hen. V [1414]. *Non omittas* returnable on Sat. after the Conception [8 Dec.].

Wed. after the feast of . . . [*MS. torn*] 2 [Hen. V] [1414–15]. Extent of Hugh's lands within the liberty of the hundreds of Potterne and Canynges at Wermestre before Ellis de la Mare by . . . Devises, John Hethowolf, Robert Cuttyng, Thomas Stabbe, Thomas Biston, William Spende, . . . , and Thomas Laffull.
[By the grant of] John atte Mershe the elder in Borton and Bishop's Canynges 4 [messuages, 100 a. of land, 12 a. of meadow], and 200 a. of pasture, which Hugh later, on Wed. after the feast of St. Vincent 11 Hen. IV [26 Feb. 1410], gave to Robert Best and his wife Agnes, to hold [for the life of] Hugh; in Rendwey $1\frac{1}{2}$ virgate of land; in Poterne, Worton, and Mershton 3 cottages, 28 [a. of land, and 4 a. of meadow]; in Horton, Southbrome, and Chittowe 3 messuages, 12 a. of land, 3 a. of meadow, and 20 a. of pasture worth 10 marks yearly; in Lavyngton 2 carucates of land, 10 a. of meadow, and 300 a. of pasture, which Hugh, with all the lands in Wynterborne Cherborgh, on the feast of St. Margaret the Virgin before the day of the recognizance [20 July] recovered by assize of novel disseisin from [John] Skyllyng and others named in that assize. Total value of the lands 10 marks yearly.

5 Nov. 2 Hen. V [1414]. *Extendi facias* returnable on Sat. after the feast of . . . , as it is understood that the lands in Bisshopestrowe can be valued and that Hugh held other lands in Wilts. not included in the previous extent.

Wed. after the feast of . . . [*MS. torn*] 2 Hen. V [1414–15]. Extent of a messuage and 12 a. of land which Hugh held in Bisshopestrowe made at

Wermestre before Ellis de la Mare by . . . , John Lupyat, John Gilberd, John Hethowolf, Robert Cuttyng, Thomas Stabbe, Thomas . . . , Thomas Upton, John Malet, Edward Dier, and Thomas Laffull.

The lands in Bisshopestrowe are worth 12*d.* yearly. No other lands in Wilts. outside the liberty.

[*Undated*]. *Liberate;* with *capias* against Hugh's body.
Endorsed. The lands have been delivered. Hugh has not been found.
C 131/59 no. 5

43 Thomas Wyfold, gentleman, of Scheperygg

18 May 9 Hen. V [1421]. *Capias* returnable in quin. of Martinmas next [25 Nov.], sued out by master Walter Cook, clerk, to whom Thomas acknowledged 52*l.* 10*s.* on 21 May 6 Hen. V [1418] before Richard Whityngton, mayor of the Staple of Westminster, payable at All Saints then next [1 Nov.].
Endorsed. Thomas has not been found.

Wed. Martinmas 9 Hen. V [11 Nov. 1421]. Extent and appraisement at Marleburgh before William Darell by John Ingram, John Benger the elder, Robert Turney, Edward Waryn, William Turney, Richard Child, John Laneford, John Lydyate, Richard Mildenhale, Thomas Baldewyn, William Beek, and John Gore.

In Great and Little Sheperygge: 2 messuages with gardens and closes adjoining worth 4*d.* yearly; a dovecote within the boundaries of those messuages and closes worth 12*d.* yearly; 300 a. of arable land worth 1*d.* an a. yearly; 1,000 a. of meadow in 'Great and Little Huggemershe' and 'Brodemede' worth 3*d.* an a. yearly; 1,000 a. of underwood worth 1*d.* an a. yearly.
C 131/60 no. 18

44 John Kirkeby, esquire

[*Undated*]. *Capias* returnable in oct. of Mich. next [6 Oct.], sued out by Robert Shotesbrok, knight, John Frank, clerk, John Pecche, and John Radewell, executors of Eleanor of St. Amand, to whom John acknowledged 400*l.* on 8 Nov. 13 Hen. IV [1411] before Richard Whityngton, then mayor of the Staple of Westminster, payable on 23 Nov. then next. Like writ to the sheriff of Hants.
Endorsed. John is dead.

Wed. after the Assumption 5 Hen. VI [20 Aug. 1427]. Extent at Ambresbury before John Stourton the younger by Thomas Sawer, John Carre, John Madyngton, William Sampson, Richard Whytewey, Richard Gover, John Appelby, Thomas Babestoke, William Marleburgh, Richard Towker, William Felpott, and Thomas Hobbes.

In Westharnham seised in fee of 6 messuages, 120 a. of pasture worth 4*l.* yearly. In Estharnham seised in fee of 9 messuages, 50 a. of land, and 10 a. of meadow, with a well for burning lime, worth 4*l.* yearly.

Endorsed. The sheriff delivered the lands to the executors on 4 Feb. 6 Hen. VI [1428], to hold until 52*l.* 12*s.* 8*d.* of the debt has been paid.

C 131/61 no. 21

45 John Reynes, knight, of Buckinghamshire

22 June 13 Hen. VI [1435]. *Extendi facias* returnable in quin. of S.J.B. next [8 July], for John Hertwell, esquire, the elder, and John Hertwell, the younger, citizen and mercer of London, to whom Reynes acknowledged 1,000*l.* on 10 Feb. 3 Hen. V [1416] before Richard Whityngton, then mayor of the Staple of Westminster, payable at Christmas then next; as John and John had sued out a *capias* to which the sheriff has returned that John is dead.

28 June 13 Hen. VI [1435]. Inquisition at Troubrugge before Stephen Popham, knight, by Roger Trwbody, Thomas Hubberd, Robert Galbard, John Gybbes, John Cannyng, John Gayell, William Newman, John Taunton, Thomas Loveday, John Geffray, Peter Talman, and Thomas Taunton.

Seised in his demesne as of fee of: the manor of Upton Escudemore, otherwise called Skydmorisupton, worth 24*l.* yearly; 6 messuages and 1 carucate and 6 virgates in Wermyster, Norrigge, and Tholeston worth 4*l.* 2*s.* 6*d.* yearly; $\frac{1}{3}$ of the manor of Hardenhuwyssh worth 4*l.* 6*s.* yearly.
Endorsed. The lands were delivered on 11 July 13 Hen. VI [1435].

C 131/63 no. 23

11 July 13 Hen. VI [1435]. *Liberate* returnable in quin. of Mich. next [13 Oct.].
Endorsed. The manors and lands have been delivered. C 131/229 no. 38

46 Henry Perpoynt, 'chivaler', Roger Bernardeston, esquire, of Kedyngton', Suffolk, and Robert Eland, esquire, of Ratheby

18 May 15 Hen. VI [1437]. *Elegit*[1] against Roger returnable in quin. of Mich. next [13 Oct.], upon Roger's nonappearance in Chancery to answer John Wynter, Roger Wynter, John Breghton, and Adam Lovelord, to whom Roger, Henry, and Robert acknowledged 23*l.* 6*s.* 8*d.* in Chancery on 7 Nov. 12 Hen VI [1433], payable at Christmas 1434; as John, Roger, John, and Adam had sued out a *scire facias* to which the sheriff has returned that he has executed the writ in respect of Roger through William Smythe and John Randolf and had no means of executing it against Henry and Robert.

C 131/64 no. 5

47 Edmund Stradlyng, esquire, of Dauntesey

10 Dec. 14 Edw. IV [1474]. *Capias* returnable in oct. of Hil. next [20 Jan.], sued out by Edward Langford, esquire, to whom Edmund acknowledged 2,000*l.* on 13 Feb. 38 Hen. VI [1460] before Godfrey Feldyng, then mayor of the Staple of Westminster, payable at Eas. then next [13 Apr.].
Endorsed. Edmund has not been found.

[1] Writ printed in full in Appendix, pp. 128-9.

11 Jan. [14] Edw. IV [1475]. Inquisition at Marleburgh before [Walter Bonham], esquire, by William St . . . [*MS. torn*], John Weston, Robert Foster, Robert Somerfeld, William Gyfford, Thomas Bowyer, John Haclyet, Richard Croke . . .

Seised solely of: the manors of Dauntesey . . . , Smythecote . . . , Bremylham (10 marks), Wyntreborne Dauntesey (100*s*.), Wyvellesford (9*l*.), Me . . . (20 marks); . . . [messuages], 100 a. of land, 20 a. of meadow, 40 a. of pasture called 'Pertonhales' . . . ; 6 messuages, 100 a. of land, 30 a. of meadow, and 100 a. of pasture called . . . (10 marks).

C 131/77 no. 14

48 William Bestney, 'yoman', of Hitchyn, Hertfordshire

9 Feb. 14 Edw. IV [1475]. *Capias* returnable in quin. of Eas. next [9 Apr.], sued out by Laurence Blyton, citizen and fishmonger of London, to whom William acknowledged 61*l*. 2*s*. 10*d*. on 10 Feb. 1 Edw. IV [1462] before Godfrey Feldyng, then mayor of the Staple of Westminster, payable at Christmas then next. Like writs to the sheriffs of Surr. and Herts.

Endorsed. William has not been found. The writ was delivered to Henry Longe, esquire, sheriff, too late for execution.

C 131/243 no. 22

49 John Crekelade, Thomas Halle, and William Walrond

The sheriff has taken John and put him in prison. Thomas and William have not been found.

20 Oct. 18 Edw. IV [1478]. Extent at Stipleaissheton before John Mounpesson by Robert Styleman, John Fortheware, John Crouche, Peter Crouche, John Wise, Thomas Mastall, Andrew Taunton, Thomas Bowier, John Alcombe, Patrick Vaughan, John Alyn, and John White.

The following chattels have been delivered to the king: 6 oxen and a bull belonging to John worth 66*s*. 8*d*.; 6 oxen belonging to Thomas worth 60*s*.

The following lands belonging to Thomas have been delivered to the king: a capital messuage and 60 a. of land in Henton by Stipleaissheton and a messuage with land adjoining in Semyton by Stipleaissheton worth 4*s*. 4*d*. yearly; a capital messuage with land adjoining with a close of pasture held by Robert Ballard (26*s*. 8*d*); a messuage with land adjoining held by Robert Long in Stipleaisheton (13*s*. 4*d*.); a toft of a messuage there with land adjoining held by Thomas Hancok (4*s*.); a messuage there with land adjoining held by Richard Wynsele (5*s*.); a toft of a messuage with close adjoining and arable land held by Agnes Husee (1*s*. 8*d*.); a close of pasture in Westaissheton held by Walter Alcombe (16*s*. 8*d*.); a messuage with land adjoining in Stipleaissheton held by Walter Lucas (6*s*. 8*d*.); a close of pasture in severalty called 'Pynnokes' in Westaissheton held by John Palmere (10*s*.).

C 131/78 no. 14

50 John Thacheham, gentleman, of Idmoston

18 [Nov.] 21 [Edw. IV] [1481]. *Extendi facias* returnable in . . . [*MS. torn*]

for John Romesey, esquire, of Bycketon, Hants, to whom John acknowledged 100*l.* on 8 Mar. 15 Edw. IV [1475] before Robert Bagworth, then mayor of the town of Southampton, payable at Midsummer then next; as John Romesey had sued out a *capias* to which William Colynborne, late sheriff, returned that John is dead.

9 Mar. 22 Edw. IV [1482]. Inquisition at Wilton before John [Mounpesson], esquire, by Thomas Gilbert, Robert Burley, John Chancy, John Perham, Thomas Gomeldon, John South, John White, of Stokton, John Wyxhale, Thomas Andrewe, William Mortymer, Simon Swafyng, and Robert Byrd.
No lands or chattels in Wilts. C 131/80 no. 3

51 William Stantor, gentleman, of Wiltshire

10 July 2 Ric. III [1484]. *Capias* returnable in quin. of Mich. next [13 Oct.], sued out by John Touke, to whom William acknowledged 26*l.* 13*s.* 4*d.* on 6 Nov. 23 Hen. VI [1444] before William Estfeld, knight, then mayor of the Staple of Westminster, payable at Midsummer then next.
Endorsed. William is dead. C 131/246 no. 8

16 Oct. 2 Ric. III [1484]. *Extendi facias* returnable on the morrow of All Souls next [3 Nov.].

23 Oct. 2 Ric. III [1484]. Inquisition at Wilton before Edward Haregill by Thomas Burton, esquire, John Gullok, John Grene the elder, William Frye, Stephen Haye, John Pliser, Thomas atte Nelme, Roger Crede, John Broune, John Grene the younger, Reynold Valeys, and Thomas Thryng.
Seised in his demesne as of fee of: a capital messuage, a dovecote, 4 a. of meadow, and 60 a. of arable land in the fields in Fouleston in the suburbs of Wilton, worth 20*s.* yearly; a toft of a messuage with 3 closes of pasture and 40 a. of arable land in Rigge, worth 13*s.* 4*d.* yearly C 131/81 no. 15

4 Nov. 4 Hen. VII [1488]. *Liberate* returnable in quin. of Hil. next [27 Jan.].

10 Nov. 4 Hen. VII [1488]. The lands have been delivered.
C 131/247 no. 25

52 Margaret Chaworth, relict of John Chaworth, esquire, of Kyrklyngton, Nottinghamshire

11 Feb. 1 Hen. VII [1486]. *Capias* returnable in quin. of Eas. next [9 Apr.], sued out by John Hanley and his wife Elizabeth Barbour, gentlewoman, as Margaret acknowledged 100*l.* to Elizabeth on 1 Dec. 6 Edw. IV [1468] before Ralph Verney, then mayor of the Staple of Westminster, payable at Eas. then next [29 Mar.]. Like writs to the sheriffs of Yorks. and Hants.
Endorsed. Margaret is dead.

30 Jan. 4 Hen. VII [1489]. *Extendi facias* returnable in quin of S.J.B. next [8 July].

Wed. in Eas. week 4 Hen. VII [22 Apr. 1489].[1] Inquisition at Brencheburgh before Thomas Unwyn by John Wyse, of Tailside, Richard Popyngay, George Ploughman, John Makerell the younger, John Kyngman, John Bukke, Richard Frankelyn, William Pery, William Palmer, John Kyng, Robert Haye, and John Makerell the elder.

Seised in her demesne as of fee of: a messuage called 'Countes Courte' in Ambresbury, worth 6*l.* 13*s.* 4*d.* yearly; a mill and 6 other messuages in Ambresbury, worth 6*l.* 13*s.* 4*d.* yearly. C 131/82 no. 21

53 John Thatcheham, gentleman, of Idmoston

24 June 3 Hen. VII [1488]. *Capias* returnable in oct. of Mich. next [6 Oct.], sued out by John Romesey, esquire, of Bicketon, Hants, to whom John acknowledged 100*l.* on 8 Mar. 15 Edw. IV [1475] before Lewis Eynes, mayor of the Staple of Southampton, and William Erneley, clerk, payable at Midsummer then next.

Endorsed. John is dead. C 131/247 no. 20

54 John Stourton, knight, Lord Stourton, and John Heynes, gentleman, of London

21 Nov. 10 Hen. VII [1494]. *Capias* returnable in quin. of Eas. next [3 May 1495], sued out by Peter Curteys, gentleman, of London, to whom John and John acknowledged 200*l.* on 28 Mar. 2 Ric. III [1485] before John Broun, knight, then mayor of the Staple of Westminster, payable on 26 Apr. then next. Like writs to the sheriffs of Lond., Mdx., Som., Dors., Glos., and Hants.

Endorsed. John Stourton is dead and John Heynes has not been found.

4 May 10 Hen. VII [1495]. Inquisition at Crekelade before Richard Pudsey, esquire, by John Stone, gentleman, Richard Aleyn, Nicholas Olyver, Thomas Frise, John Winchecombe, John Clerk, John Jenkyns, William Hindon, William Reve, Thomas Gefferes, Robert Carter, John Rassheley, and John Raves.

John Stourton was seised in his demesne as of fee of: the manor of Penley worth 20*s.* yearly; in Westassheton, Stepulassheton, Henton, and Bulkyngton 7 messuages, 4 carucates of land, 20 a. of meadow, and 40 a. of pasture (40*s.*); in New Salisbury, Old Salisbury, and Stratford-sub-Castle (*subtus castrum*) 12 cottages, 21 a. of land, 10 a. of meadow, 6 a. of pasture (4*l.*); the manor of Bakehampton (10*l.*); the manors of Ablyngton and Madyngton (8*l.*); the manor of Alton (4*l.*); in Stoford, Newton, and Quedhampton 5 messuages, 50 a. of land, and 5 a. of meadow (13*s.* 4*d.*).

John Heynes has no lands or goods in Wilts. C 131/83 no. 25

[1] At the top of the extent is written 'Lib' fuit cur' 11 July 4 Hen. VII [1489] per manus Humphrey Conyngesby.'

6 July 10 Hen. VII [1495]. *Liberate* returnable in quin. of Mich. next [13 Oct.]; with *capias* against John Heynes's body. Like writs to the sheriffs of Mdx., Glos., Som., Dors., and Hants in respect of John Stourton.

The lands were delivered on 5 Sept. 11 Hen. VII [1495]. John Heynes has not been found.

C 131/248 nos. 16–17

55 William Temse, gentleman, late of Netheravon

21 July 13 Hen. VII [1498]. *Capias* returnable on the morrow of the Purification next [3 Feb.], sued out by John Kendall, prior of the hospital of St. John of Jerusalem in England, to whom William acknowledged 13*l*. 12*s*. on 3 June 8 Hen. VII [1493] before John Broun, knight, mayor of the Staple of Westminster, payable at Midsummer then next. Like writs to the sheriffs of Lond. and Mdx.
Endorsed. William has not been found.

11 Jan. 14 Hen. VII [1499]. Inquisition at Fyssherton Auger before John Seymour, knight, by John Aport, Richard Popyngay the elder, Robert Packer, Robert Heyward, Richard Amberlesley, William Wolfe, Richard Wode, John Popyngay the younger, Thomas Langston, William Crosse, Guy Penye, and Laurence Dabeney.

Seised in his demesne as of fee of: the manor of Trenchfoyle and 8 messuages, 5 tofts, 50 a. of land, 40 a. of meadow, and 40 a. of pasture in Netherhavyn; a messuage, 50 a. of land, 4 a. of meadow, and 4 a. of pasture in Beydon worth 10 marks yearly.

The above were delivered to the king on 11 Jan. 14 Hen. VII [1499].

C 131/84 no. 15

56 Thomas Escourt, gentleman, of Fysshertowne Dalamere

6 July 18 Hen. VII [1503]. *Capias* returnable in quin. of Hil. next [27 Jan.], sued out by William Isaac, citizen and alderman of London, to whom Thomas acknowledged 300 marks on 7 Dec. 15 Hen. VII [1499] before Henry Colet, knight, mayor of the Staple of Westminster, payable at Christmas last. Like writs to the sheriffs of Lond., Dors., Som., Hants, Oxon., Mdx., and Glos.
Endorsed. The sheriff has taken Thomas and put him in the prison at Fyssherton within the city of New Salisbury in the custody of Henry Uvedale, esquire, keeper of the prison. William Kayleway, knight, former sheriff, has sent the writ to John Danvers, knight, sheriff.

6 Nov. 19 Hen. VII [1503]. Inquisition at New Salisbury before William Kayleway, knight, by John Botsilion, Henry Andrewes, Thomas Gaunt, William Score, John at Chamber, Robert Godwyn, William Lyte, John Rowde, John Tyngcok, John Bokebynder, Richard Strognell, Robert Thayne, John Cosyn, and John Bekar.

Seised in his demesne as of fee of: 2 messuages, 20 a. of meadow, and 12 a. of pasture in Newton worth 30*s*. yearly; 6 messuages, 100 a. of land, 120 a. of pasture, and 6 a. of wood in Whiteparyssh (40*s.*); a messuage and 4 a. of land and pasture in Wyly (4*s.*); a messuage in Stockton (3*s.* 4*d.*); 4 messuages, 26 a. of land, 4 a. of meadow, and 12 a. of pasture in Babton and Scheryngton (25*s.*); a messuage in Tisbery (16*d.*).

The following goods: a horse, saddle, and bridle worth 7*s.*

C 131/86 no. 32

11 Feb. 19 Hen. VII [1504]. *Liberate* returnable in quin. of Eas. next [21 Apr.].

Endorsed. The lands have been delivered. C 131/252 no. 5

57 Thomas Arney, gentleman, of London, son and heir of John Arney, gentleman, late of Chalbury, Dorset

10 Feb. 20 Hen. VII [1505]. *Capias* returnable in quin. of Trin. next [1 June], sued out by Henry Paunscefote, gentleman, to whom Thomas acknowledged 16*l.* on 19 June last before Henry Colet, knight, then mayor of the Staple of Westminster, payable at Mich. then next. Like writ to the sheriff of Dors.

Endorsed. The sheriff has sent the writ to the bailiff of the liberty of Edmund, bishop of Salisbury, who has replied that he has taken Thomas and put him in prison, but that he cannot hand him over because he is sick.

20 May 20 Hen. VII [1505]. Inquisition at Fyssherton' Auger before John Erneley by Richard Popyngay, Robert Wulle, William Ploweman, Robert Hayward, Edward Milson, Thomas Silvestre, Henry Bole, John Rodman, William Alowe, Roger Colman, John Boleyn, and Robert Towereman.

No lands or chattels in Wilts. C 131/87 no. 27

58 Hugh Barley, 'clothemaker', of Pottehorn

13 May 20 Hen. VII [1505]. *Capias* returnable on the morrow of All Souls next [3 Nov.], sued out by John Kyme, citizen and mercer of London, to whom Hugh acknowledged 108*l.* on 20 Apr. 19 Hen. VII [1504] before Henry Colet, knight, then mayor of the Staple of Westminster, payable at Midsummer then next. Like writs to the sheriffs of Lond. and Mdx.

20 Oct. 21 Hen. VII [1505]. Inquisition at Bishops Cannynges before John Ernley by John Eyre, William Chancton, gentleman, Robert Wylkes, Robert Redman, John Cainnick, Humphrey Sterke, Richard Pollampton, Hugh Miller, William Terre, William Hurt, John Dolman, and Richard Fuller.

In possession of a fulling-mill in Levyngton Bysshop parish worth 60*s.* yearly, for 85 years by the grant of Margery Blake, relict of John Blake, at a yearly rent of 33*s.* 4*d.* C 131/87 no. 29

10 Nov. 21 Hen. VII [1505]. *Liberate* returnable in quin. of Hil. next [27 Jan.]; with *capias* against Hugh's body.

Endorsed. John Gawen, esquire, sheriff, has delivered the mill.

C 131/253 no. 2

59 William Changton, gentleman, of Shalbourn

3 Oct. 21 Hen. VII [1505]. *Capias* returnable on the morrow of the Purification next [3 Feb.], sued out by Thomas Bonham, gentleman, to whom William acknowledged 100*l.* on 7 July 18 Hen. VII [1503] before Henry Colet, knight, then mayor of the Staple of Westminster, payable at Eas. then next [7 Apr.]. Like writ to the sheriff of Mdx. C 131/89 no. 1

13 Jan. 21 Hen. VII [1506]. Inquisition at New Salisbury before John Gawen, esquire, by Robert Bowre, William Kyng, Thomas Tarrant, John Raulens, Thomas Swevyng, John Cove, John Whelour, John Hayward, John Barley, Thomas Penycot, Henry Crede, and John Ploughman.

Seised in his demesne as of fee of: the manors of Estwyke and Westcourte in Shalborne; in Shalborne, Estwyke, Westcourte, Harden, Westbedwyn, and Buttermere 16 messuages, 2 carucates and 8 virgates of land, 20 a. of meadow, 60 a. of wood and 60*s.* in rents; the advowson of the chapel of the manor of Westcourt in Shalborne. Total 12*l.* yearly.

12 Feb. 21 Hen. VII [1506]. *Liberate* returnable on the morrow of Ascension next [21 May]; with *capias* against William's body.
Endorsed. William has not been found. C 131/90 no. 2

Certification that the above lands were delivered on 1 Apr. 21 Hen. VII [1506].
C 131/89 no. 1

60 Richard Hany, 'wexchaundeler', of New Salisbury

20 Oct. 21 Hen. VII [1505]. *Capias* returnable in quin. of Hil. next [27 Jan.], sued out by Henry Seryche, 'fysshemonger', of New Salisbury, to whom Richard acknowledged 16*l.* on 28 Aug. 20 Hen. VII [1504] before John Gander, then mayor of the city and Staple of Winchester, payable at Christmas then next.
Endorsed. Richard has not been found. His lands have been appraised by the oath of William Hill, John Fen, Robert Doo, and James Nore.

12 Jan. 21 Hen. VII [1506]. Inquisition at New Salisbury before John Gawen, esquire, by William Eston, Henry Upton, John Aporte, Richard Bartilmewe the younger, John Cuff, John Grey, Thomas Sydgave, John Gylpurn, William Lynsey, William White, John Colplese, and William Thorneley.

Seised in his demesne as of fee of: 2 messuages, 11 tenements, and a garden in New Salisbury worth 4 marks yearly.
C 131/89 no. 7

61 Nicholas Chaffyn, mercer, of New Salisbury

5 Nov. 5 Hen. VIII [1513]. *Capias* returnable in oct. of Hil. next [20 Jan.], sued out by Mary Ymbar, relict and executrix, and John Aleyn and Richard Gerveys, executors, of Robert Ymbar, citizen and mercer of London, to

whom Nicholas acknowledged 158*l.* 4*s.* 9*d.* on 1 Sept. 4 Hen. VIII [1512] before William Broun, then mayor of the Staple of Westminster, payable on 12 Dec. then next. Like writs to the sheriffs of Hants, Som., and Dors.

Wed. after the Conception 5 Hen. VIII [14 Dec. 1513]. Inquisition at New Salisbury before William Compton, knight, bailiff of the liberty of Edmund, bishop of Salisbury, of his city of New Salisbury, by virtue of a warrant from John Danvers, knight, sheriff, dated 28 Nov. 5 Hen. VIII [1513] by Henry Upton, John Bartilmewe, John Reynolde, William Hoskyns, John Newman, Robert Arundell, Edward Vavasour, Philip Godfrey, Robert Assheton, Thomas Barker, William Harrold, and John Poynour.

In New Salisbury seised in his demesne as of free tenements in the right of his wife Agnes of: 3 messuages in Carternstrete and 3 cottages in Brounestrete worth 60*s.* yearly; a tenement in which Nicholas himself lives in Winchesterstrete in the south part, opposite a ditch of water, worth 26*s.* 8*d.* yearly.

Various goods listed on the attached schedule worth 8*l.*

'Invytory of the goodes and catalles of Nicholas Chafyn.

In the hall		
A counterbourde	4*s.*	
3 fourmes		16*d.*
A cubberd of joyn' worke	4*s.*	
3 shorte bankeres of verder	2*s.*	4*d.*
2 shorte carpittes of verder olde		12*d.*
6 olde cusshyns of corder		4*d.*
A laver of laten		12*d.*
20 yardes of olde hangynges stayned	3*s.*	4*d.*
In the parlour		
An olde counterbourde	3*s.*	
2 cheyers		12*d.*
5 olde cusshyns	2*s.*	
16 yerdes of olde hangynges	2*s.*	
In the buttery		
Half a garnysshe of pewter vasselles	6*s.*	8*d.*
2 basons of laten		8*d.*
3 basons of pewtour		12*d.*
2 olde chaffyngdisshys		6*d.*
6 small candelstikes		12*d.*
In the kechyn		
2 small pannys of brasse olde		16*d.*
2 small ketylles of brasse		10*d.*
Oon oder ketyll of brasse		10*d.*
2 bronde yrons		6*d.*
3 small pottes of brasse	2*s.*	4*d.*
A lytell broche of yron		6*d.*
An aundeyron		4*d.*
A stonon morter		6*d.*

In the chamber above		
A lytell counterbourde		16*d.*
3 fetherbeddes	20*s.*	
A matteresse of floxe		16*d.*
3 bolsters	3*s.*	
2 pillowys		20*d.*
6 payre of shetes	8*s.*	
A payre of blankettes		12*d.*
An olde quylte		8*d.*
4 coverlettes	4*s.*	
6 chestes	6*s.*	4*d.*
An olde tabull bourde		8*d.*
An olde fourme		4*d.*
A payre of olde trestelles		4*d.*
A olde banker		6*d.*
8 bedstedes	4*s.*	
2 trokull beddes		16*d.*
A coster with 3 curteyns	2*s.*	4*d.*
3 olde hangynges of stayned cloth conteynyng 60 yerdes	10*s.*	
2 olde small chestes		12*d.*
An olde cheyer		6*d.*
In the shope next the strete		
4 chestes olde	6*s.*	8*d.*
A dosen peynted forcers	3*s.*	
40 dosen ferthyng gyrdelles	3*s.*	4*d.*
8 dosen whipcorde		10*d.*
8 dosen ferthyng glassys		18*d.*
2 dosen synaper pauper		6*d.*
9 childern cappes		16*d.*
2 reme course pauper	2*s.*	
4 payre of balance olde	2*s.*	
A payre of grete balance of laten with a beme of yron	3*s.*	4*d.*
Small weights		6*d.*
A neste of small boxes		8*d.*
6 oder boxes		6*d.*
2 dosen ferthyng bedys		6*d.*
A dosen treyns		8*d.*
6 olde barelles		6*d.*
3 olde sope chestes		8*d.*
24 yerdes of narrow valance olden hangyng aboute the same shope		12*d.*
In a noder shope within the same shoppe		
A grete cheste	3*s.*	4*d.*
2 sope chestes		12*d.*
3 dosen olde crewsys		6*d.*
In the shoppe in the yerde		
2 olde bokeram chestes	3*s.*	4*d.*

A noder olde cheste	8*d*.
2 shorte tabull bourdes	12*d*.
A payre of olde trestelles	4*d*.
In the yerde	
A bokeram cheste	20*d*.
12 olde sope chestes	2*s*. 4*d*.
10 olde barelles	2*s*.'

C 131/100 no. 7

62 Thomas Marmyon, esquire, of Kyngesdon

16 Feb. 5 Hen. VIII [1514]. *Capias* returnable in quin. of Eas. next [30 Apr.], sued out by William Botrie, citizen and mercer of London, to whom Thomas acknowledged 100*l*. on 18 Mar. 4 Hen. VIII [1513] before William Broun the younger, then mayor of the Staple of Westminster, payable at All Saints then next [1 Nov.]. Like writs to the sheriffs of Lond., Mdx., Lincs., and Berks.
Endorsed. The lands were delivered to the king on 20 Mar. 5 Hen. VIII [1514]. Thomas has not been found.

18 Mar. 5 Hen. VIII [1514]. Inquisition at Wilton before John Danvers, knight, by William Mondye, Christopher Payne, Robert Eyre, Robert Newman, gentlemen, Robert South, John Gildon, Thomas Combe, John Goldyng, John Nobull, John Brynde, Thomas Manton, James Austen, Robert Burges, William Wolff, Philip Clerke, and John Sawyar.

Seised as of a free tenement in the right of his wife Anne for her life of the manor of Kevell and 10 messuages, 300 a. of land, 400 a. of pasture, a water-mill and 6*s*. in rents in Calston, Chesylden, Lyddington, Wanborowe, Walcott, Rodburne, and Heydon, worth 20 marks yearly.

C 131/100 no. 31

5 July 6 Hen. VIII [1514]. *Liberate* returnable in quin. of Mich. next [13 Oct.]; with *capias* against Thomas's body. Like writ to the sheriff of Berks. in respect of lands there worth 26*l*. yearly. C 131/260 no. 22

63 Thomas Broke, Lord Cobham

18 Mar. 5 Hen. VIII [1514]. *Capias* returnable in quin. of Trin. next [25 June], sued out by Nicholas Shelton, citizen and alderman of London, to whom Thomas acknowledged 200*l*. on 12 Feb. 4 Hen. VIII [1513] before William Broun the younger, then mayor of the Staple of Westminster, payable at Eas. then next [27 Mar.]. Like writs to the sheriffs of Oxon., Berks., Som., and Dors.
Endorsed. The lands were delivered to the king on 26 July 6 Hen. VIII [1514]. Thomas has not been found.

20 June 6 Hen. VIII [1514]. Inquisition at New Salisbury before John Danvers, knight, by William Cuff, John Jones, Richard Jamys, James Marten, Robert Eston, William Yong, William Grey, Robert Tymber,

Richard Cooke, Thomas Combell, Thomas Ledehall, Richard Crowchell, and Walter Bakar.

Seised in his demesne as of fee of the manor of Bynknoll and 9 messuages, 300 a. of land, 400 a. of pasture in Bynknoll, worth 20*l.* yearly. Thomas has not been found. C 131/100 no. 33

29 Aug. 6 Hen. VIII [1514]. *Liberate* returnable on the morrow of All Souls next [3 Nov.]; with *capias* against Thomas's body. Like writ to the sheriff of Oxon. in respect of a manor and lands there worth 40*l.* yearly.
Endorsed. The lands were delivered on 21 Sept. 6 Hen. VIII [1514].
C 131/260 no. 26

64 Richard Maynyard, 'taylor', of New Salisbury

18 May 12 Hen. VIII [1520]. *Capias* returnable in quin. of Mich. next [13 Oct.], sued out by William Bon', merchant of the Staple of Westminster, to whom Richard acknowledged 10*l.* on 13 Feb. 11 Hen. VIII [1520] before James Yarford, then mayor of the Staple of Westminster, payable on 23 Feb. then next.
Endorsed. Richard has not been found.

Edward Darell, knight, sheriff, has sent the writ to William Compton, knight, bailiff of the liberty of Edmund, bishop of Salisbury, of his city of New Salisbury, whose answer is annexed.

[*Undated*]. Inquisition at New Salisbury before William Compton, knight, bailiff of the liberty of Edmund, bishop of Salisbury, of his city of New Salisbury, by Thomas Marten, John Hobbis, Leonard Goldsmyth, Maurice More, John Alder, John Havey, Francis Cheverell, Stephen Millet, John Wall, Vincent Kyng, Thomas Sam, and Humphrey Smyth.

Seised in his demesne as of fee of ½ tenement in New Salisbury, St. Thomas the Martyr's parish, which is now occupied by Nicholas Dyker, worth 26*s.* 8*d.* yearly.
C 131/104 no. 20

65 Roger Frampton, gentleman, of Childefrome, Dorset

12 Nov. 18 Hen. VIII [1526]. *Capias* returnable in quin. of Martinmas next [25 Nov.], sued out by Thomas Keyle, citizen and mercer of London, to whom Roger acknowledged 30*l.* on 23 Nov. 16 Hen. VIII [1524] before James Yarford, knight, then mayor of the Staple of Westminster, payable at the Purification then next [2 Feb.]. Like writs to the sheriffs of Lond., Mdx., Som., and Dors.
Endorsed. Roger has not been found.

23 Nov. 18 Hen. VIII [1526]. Inquisition at Upton Lovell before John Bourghchier, knight, by Robert Bray, John Stevyns, John Croche, Thomas Prior, William Hille, William Prior, John Slye, Roger Hayward, John Lyde, John George, John Curtes, John Byffeasshe, and Richard Stephyns.

Seised in his demesne as of fee of a yearly rent of 12*l*. 13*s*. 4*d*. payable to Roger in fee from the manor of Uppton Lovell at St. Nicholas [6 Dec.], with power, in default, to re-enter and distrain for the rent and arrears. Thomas, duke of Norfolk, then tenant, had yielded the rent.

C 131/108 no. 20

4 Dec. 18 Hen. VIII [1526]. *Liberate* returnable in oct. of Hil. next [20 Jan. 1527]; with *capias* against Roger's body.
Endorsed. The sheriff has delivered the rent.

C 131/268 no. 15

66 William Dowlyng, husbandman, of Alkanynges

24 Oct. 20 Hen. VIII [1528]. *Capias* returnable on the morrow of Martinmas next [12 Nov.], sued out by William Button, gentleman, of London, to whom William acknowledged 100*l*. on 18 Nov. 19 Hen. VIII [1527] before Thomas Seymer, knight, then mayor of the Staple of Westminster, payable at St. Andrew then next [30 Nov.].
Endorsed. William has not been found.

6 Nov. 20 Hen. VIII [1528]. Inquisition at Alcainynges before Anthony Hungerford, knight, by Godfrey Smethewyke, gentleman, Thomas Surrey, William Thyrkyll, John Crooke, John Nycholles, John Dene, Thomas Ryng, William Miles, John Bartlet, John Hedde, John Acreman, Robert Karre, and Robert Hollwey.

Seised in his demesne as of fee of 3 messuages, 5½ virgates of land, 12 a. of meadow, and 40 a. of pasture in Alcainynges, and pasture for 100 ewes and 12 avers in the pastures of the manor of Alcainynges, worth 4*l*. 6s. 8*d*. yearly.

C 131/110 no. 15

67 Anthony Sayntmound, knight, of Wormynghurste, Sussex, and Francis Hastingis, gentleman, of Beynton, Yorkshire

8 Aug. 21 Hen. VIII [1529]. *Capias* returnable in a month from Mich. next [29 Oct.], sued out by John Broke, citizen and mercer of London, to whom Anthony and Francis acknowledged 1,000*l*. on 4 Dec. 20 Hen. VIII [1528] before Thomas Seymer, knight, then mayor of the Staple of Westminster, payable at Christmas then next. Like writs to the sheriffs of Surr. and Suss.
Endorsed. Anthony and Francis have not been found.

22 Sept. 21 Hen. VIII [1529]. Inquisition at Alyngton before John Erneley, esquire, by Godfrey Smethewyke, John Burdon, gentlemen, John Croke, Edmund Long, Thomas Krekysby, John Colet, John Benet, John Bartlet, Richard Phelpes, John Hyscoke, John Foode, and Rarnold Busshup.

Francis had no goods or lands in Wilts.

John Dudley, Henry Owen, John Bryggys, Roger Copley, knights, Owen West, Nicholas Strelley, Edward Lewkener, esquires, Thomas Shelley, clerk, Anthony Styleman, and Aldhelm Lambe were seised to the use of Anthony, his wife Anne, and their heirs of the manor of Alyngton and 12 messuages, 1,000 a. of land, 500 a. of pasture, 100 a. of meadow, and 40 a. of wood in Alyngton worth 26*l.* yearly. C 131/111 no. 7

4 Nov. 21 Hen. VIII [1529]. *Liberate* returnable in quin. of Martinmas next [25 Nov.]; with *capias* against the bodies of Anthony and Francis.
Endorsed. The lands were delivered on 8 Nov. 21 Hen. VIII [1529]. Anthony and Francis have not been found. C 239/1 no. 14

68 Cowdrey Strangwayse, esquire, of Brympton, Somerset

20 Mar. 21 Hen. VIII [1530]. *Capias* returnable in oct. of S.J.B. next [1 July], sued out by Richard Hardyng, 'yoman', to whom Cowdrey acknowledged 100*l.* on 26 Jan. 17 Hen. VIII [1526] before James Yarford, knight, then mayor of the Staple of Westminster, payable at Midsummer then next. Like writs to the sheriffs of Lond. and Salop.
Endorsed. Cowdrey has not been found.

10 June 22 Hen. VIII [1530]. Inquisition at Mylton Lylbon before John Horsey, esquire, by John Whyttard, Robert Cary, Henry Cary, William Browne, John Holydaye, Thomas Pyle, John Frankelyn, Walter Pollard, William Wyatt, John Brygger, Edward Pyle, and John Pydman.

Seised of the manor of Milton Lylbone and 12 messuages, 1,000 a. of land, 1,000 a. of pasture, 200 a. of meadow, 100 a. of wood, and 200 a. of gorse and heath in Milton Lylbone, Fyffed, Mylcot, and Haveryng, worth 19*l.* yearly. C 131/111 no. 14

69 William Rede, knight, of Borstall, Buckinghamshire, and Anthony Sayntmond *alias* Wroughton, son of Richard Beauchamp, knight, and Margaret Wroughton

5 May 22 Hen. VIII [1530]. *Capias* returnable in oct. of Mich. next [6 Oct.], sued out by John Fyssher, bishop of Rochester, and master Hugh Assheton, clerk, archdeacon of York, to whom William and Anthony acknowledged 1,000*l.* on 18 July 11 Hen. VIII [1519] before James Yarford, knight, then mayor of the Staple of Westminster, payable at Mich. then next. Like writs to the sheriffs of Devon, Hunts., Berks., Beds., Bucks., Lond., Mdx., Kent, Suss., and Herts.

21 May 22 Hen. VIII [1530]. Inquisition at Okyngham before John Horsey, esquire, by David Johnson, Ralph Mason, Ralph Mylward, John Myllward the elder, John Myllward the younger, William Assheby, Thomas Gyles, Oliver Bradford, Nicholas Lythyng, William Chayne, William Goswell, John Oswester, Thomas Taylour, John Goswell, and Thomas Wyllamson.

William had no lands or goods in Wilts.

Anthony Sayntmond, Thomas West, knight, and other co-feoffees were seised to the use of Anthony and his heirs of: the manor of Charylton and 12 messuages, 300 a. of land, 100 a. of meadow, 300 a. of pasture, and 40 a. of wood in Charylton worth 18*l.* yearly. John Dudley, Henry Owen, John Brigges, Roger Copley, knights, Owen West, Nicholas Strelley, Edward Lewkener, esquires, Thomas Shelley, clerk, Anthony Styleman, and Aldhelm Lambe were seised, after the day of the recognizance, to the use of Anthony, his wife Anne, and their heirs of: the manor of Alyngton and 12 messuages, 1,000 a. of land, 500 a. of pasture, 100 a. of meadow, and 40 a. of wood worth 26*l.* yearly. C 131/111 no. 18

30 May 22 Hen. VIII [1530]. *Liberate* returnable in quin. of S.J.B. next [8 July]; with *capias* against the bodies of William and Anthony. Like writ to the sheriff of Devon in respect of the manor of Ipelpen and various lands worth 50*l.* 6*s.* 8*d.* yearly.
Endorsed. The lands have been delivered. William and Anthony have not been found. C 239/1 no. 32

70 Anthony Sayntmond, knight, of Wormynghurst, Sussex, and Thomas Rowthall, gentleman, of Mulshoo, Buckinghamshire

12 July 23 Hen. VIII [1531]. *Capias* returnable in oct. of Mich. next [6 Oct.], sued out by James Danyell, citizen and merchant tailor of London, to whom Anthony and Thomas acknowledged 200*l.* on 13 June 20 Hen. VIII [1528] before Thomas Seymer, knight, then mayor of the Staple of Westminster, payable on 13 Dec. then next; as James has affirmed in person in Chancery that a previous writ of *capias* has been accidentally lost. Like writs to the sheriffs of Lond., Mdx., Surr., Suss., Bucks., and Northants.
Endorsed. Anthony and Thomas have not been found.

12 Sept. 23 Hen. VIII [1531]. Inquisition at Alyngton before [Thomas Yorke, esquire], by Godfrey Smythewiche, John Burden, Edmund Long, Edward Hoochyns, William Carter, William Burden, Robert Burden, John Bartlett, John Forde, Richard Phelps, John Hiscockes the elder, John Stanburgh, and John Beele.

Anthony was seised in his demesne as of fee of the manor of Alyngton and 9 messuages, 600 a. of land, 100 a. of pasture, 20 a. of meadow, 6 a. of marsh, and 14*s.* 11*d.* and 1 lb. of pepper in rents in Alyngton, worth 26*l.* yearly.

Thomas had no lands or goods in Wilts.

19 Oct. 23 Hen. VIII [1531]. *Liberate* returnable on the morrow of All Souls next [3 Nov.]; with *capias* against the bodies of Anthony and Thomas.
Endorsed. The lands have been delivered. C 131/113 no. 2

71 Charles Wrothesley *alias* Wyndesor, esquire, of London

15 Nov. 29 Hen. VIII [1537]. *Capias* returnable in quin. of Hil. next [27 Jan.], sued out by John Warneford, gentleman, to whom Charles acknowledged 300*l.* on 10 Feb. 27 Hen. VIII [1536] before John Baldewyn, knight, chief justice of the Common Pleas, payable on 14 Feb. next. Like writs to the sheriffs of Lond. and Mdx.
Endorsed. Charles has not been found.

12 Jan. 29 Hen. VIII [1538]. Inquisition at Ambresbury before John Brygges, knight, by Thomas Walrond, Thomas Stephyns, William Garard, Simon Yate, Thomas Mille, John Jones, Thomas Yate, Thomas Masklyn, Thomas Russheley, John Messenger, Thomas Matew, Leonard Mawes, and William Cockes.

Seised in his demesne as of fee of 6 messuages, 2 water-mills, 4 orchards, 6 tofts, 8 a. of pasture, 16 a. of land, and 40 a. of meadow in Crykelade, Chelworth, and Pyrton, worth 6*l.* 3*s.* 4*d.* yearly.

C 239/7 no. 22

72 Thomas Walwyn, gentleman, of Bishop's Lawington

2 July 30 Hen. VIII [1538]. *Capias* returnable in quin. of Mich. next [13 Oct.], sued out by Edmund Walwyn, gentleman, late of Northertydworth, to whom Thomas acknowledged 500*l.* on 15 Nov. 25 Hen. VIII [1533] before John Fitzjames, knight, chief justice of the King's Bench, payable at Christmas then next. Like writs to the sheriffs of Lond.
Endorsed. The sheriff has taken Thomas and put him in prison.

1 Sept. 30 Hen. VIII [1538]. Inquisition at Highworth before John Brygges, knight, by Thomas Stephyns, William Garrard, Thomas Mylle, James Chaterton, William Webbe, John Curteys, John Messenger, Thomas Dixxe, Richard Shurborne, William Baus, Walter Tayte, Robert Alyn, and John Davys.

No lands or goods in Wilts.

C 239/8 no. 8

73 Thomas Hele, merchant, of New Salisbury

4 Nov. 34 Hen. VIII [1542]. *Capias* returnable in oct. of Martinmas next [18 Nov.], sued out by Thomas Woodlock, citizen and 'haberdassher' of London, to whom Thomas acknowledged 500*l.* on 5 Mar. 32 Hen. VIII [1541] before Ralph Waren, mayor of the Staple of Westminster, and Roger Cholmeley, recorder of London, knights, payable at Lady Day then next.
Endorsed. Goods to the value of 142*l.* 11*s.* 4*d.* have been appraised by the oath of John Milbrydye, Nicholas Subden, William Acton, John Regent, Robert Randall, and John Mason. Thomas has not been found.

22 Nov. 34 Hen. VIII [1542]. 'An invytory takyn the xviith day of November the yere and rayne our soverayne lorde kyng Henri the viiith XXXIIII [1542] of all the goodes of Thomas Helys late of the cytie of New Sar', merchant, sessenyd and appraised by thes men whowse namys here after by resytyd: John Mylbrydy, mercer, Nycholas Subdean, taylor, Wyllm. Acton, brewer, Rychard Sawnders, barber, Robard Elyott, grosser; aldermannes. George Chaffyn, mercer, John Clape, mercer, William Coxby, capper, John Hawkyns, sergant.

9½ lb. of gynger at 2*s.* a lb.	19*s.*
7½ lb. of graynes at 16*d.* a lb.	10*s.*

3½ lb. of sawnderes at 2*s.* 2*d.* a lb.	7*s.*	0½*d.*
1 lb. of dattes		4*d.*
3 lb. of turnsole at 10*d.* a lb.	2*s.*	6*d.*
2 lb. of nuttmeges at 20*d.* a lb.	3*s.*	4*d.*
1 lb. of gynger	2*s.*	
2 lb. of clovys at 4*s.* 8*d.* a lb.	9*s.*	4*d.*
½ lb. of maces	2*s.*	8*d.*
Isenglas to the valeu of		2*d.*
2 lb. of brayde auruefele		12*d.*
3 lb. of turnesole cours	2*s.*	
½ lb. of pepper		10*d.*
A byll of sartayne wares to the valeue of	10*s.*	
20 lb. of ryce at 2*d.* a lb.	3*s.*	4*d.*
8 lb. of annys at 2*d.* a lb.		16*d.*
18 lb. of cowranc at 3*d.* a lb.	4*s.*	6*d.*
28 lb. of brassell at 1½*d.* a lb.	3*s.*	6*d.*
43 lb. of dype prynt sope at 3*d.* a lb.	15*s.*	9*d.*
3½ doss. of strawyn hattes at 6*d.* a doss.	2*s.*	3*d.*
2 doss. of Brygys threde brayde at 16*d.* a bat.	32*s.*	
37 lb. of Collyn threde in bottans at 8*d.* a lb.	24*s.*	7*d.*
3 lb. of Collyn threde at 8*d.* a lb.	2*s.*	8*d.*
2 lb. of otnall' threde at 10*d.* a lb.		20*d.*
¾ lb. of otnall' threde		7½*d.*
1 cwt. 24 lb. of Normandy hempe at 18*s.* a cwt.	26*s.*	8*d.*
5½ doss. of cadysse peces at 3*d.* a pec'	16*s.*	6*d.*
1½ doss. of cadys peces at 3*d.* a pec'	4*s.*	6*d.*
3 doss. 3 peces of saye at 3*d.* a pec'	9*s.*	9*d.*
2 doss. 4 saye peces at 4½*d.* a pec'	10*s.*	6*d.*
3 peces of checkes with golde at 16*d.* a pec'	4*s.*	
9 check peces with golde at 18*d.* a pec'	6*s.*	
4 peces hande brede saye at 8*d.* a pec'	2*s.*	8*d.*
¾ lb. of ope sylck 2 ownces at 6*d.* a nownc'	7*s.*	
½ lb. of otnall threde		4*d.*
1 lb. of Brygys threde		8*d.*
10½ doss. of 1*d.* ware gyrdelles of caddys rownde at 8*d.* a doss.	6*s.*	1*d.*
5 grosse of Brytysche lace at 3*d.* a grosse		15*d.*

Total 12*l.* 18*s.* 4*d.*

A grosse of rownde lace		12*d.*
1 lb. of cadys		9*d.*
5 doss. of scole wexcke bandes at 6*d.* a doss.	2*s.*	6*d.*
¼ lb. of blacke threde		3*d.*
1 doss. of *ob.* comys		3*d.*
10 cloutes of Flawnderes pynys at 2*d.* a clowte		20*d.*
3 m. of London pynys		15*d.*
9½ doss. of brode cardes at 14*d.* a doss.	11*s.*	1*d.*

5 boltys of Parrys threde at 12*d.* a bolt	5*s.*	
14 lb. of Venys sope	2*s.*	
2 lb. of lycorys		3*d.*
1½ doss. of chyldryn ware	9*s.*	
8 coyffys at 2*d.* a pec'		16*d.*
2 boxys of trasche		12*d.*
2 lb. of flexe		4*d.*
2 rondes of pacthrede		4*d.*
19 lb. of Collyn hempe at 3*d.* a lb.	4*s.*	9*d.*
8 yardes of rolde bockeram at 5*d.* a yarde	3*s.*	4*d.*
16 yardes of past bockeram at 4*d.* a yarde	5*s.*	4*d.*
1 pec' of fustean for lynyng	10*s.*	
4½ yardes of bevernax fustean at 5*d.* a yarde	2*s.*	1*d.*
26 yardes of Holmys fustean at 7*d.* a yarde	15*s.*	2*d.*
22 yardes of Geyne fustean at 5*d.* a yarde	9*s.*	2*d.*
5 yardes of blacke seye at 18*d.* a yarde	7*s.*	6*d.*
13½ yardes of blacke seye at 12*d.* a yarde	13*s.*	6*d.*
6½ yardes of brode rowsettes at 20*d.* a yarde	10*s.*	10*d.*
25 yardes of rowsettes at 12*d.* a yarde	25*s.*	
14 yardes of rowsettes at 16*d.* a yarde	18*s.*	8*d.*
½ a nell of wostede		20*d.*
½ a yarde of blacke velvett	5*s.*	
½ a yarde ½ a part of whyte velvet	6*s.*	
2½ yardes of strypytt sylcke at 4*d.* a yarde	10*s.*	
11 yardes of Brygis satyn at 18*d.* a yarde	16*s.*	6*d.*
5 yardes of Brygis satyn at 18*d.* a yarde	7*s.*	6*d.*
3 doss. of Salybery laces at 7*d.* a doss.	2*s.*	4*d.*
2 chylldryn shertes		14*d.*
¼ lb. of otnale threde		2*d.*
7 yardes of unwater chamlett at 16*d.* a yarde	9*s.*	4*d.*
2 yardes of waterde chamlett	4*s.*	
1¾ yardes waterd chamlett	3*s.*	
3¾ yardes of sengill sarsenett at 3*s.* 4*d.* a yarde	12*s.*	6*d.*
53 yardes of corse bult at 1*d.* a yard	4*s.*	5*d.*
6 yardes of bultez at 1*d.* a yard		6*d.*
Total 12*l.* 7*s.* 5*d.*		

14 yardes of fustean remnawntes at 5*d.* a yarde	5*s.*	10*d.*
1¼ yardes of black fustean apys		20*d.*
20½ yardes of dornex at 6*d.* a yarde	10*s.*	
4 yardes of chalkyd fustean at 7*d.* a yarde	2*s.*	4*d.*
7 yardes of dornex at 4*d.* a yarde	2*s.*	4*d.*
13 yardes of Northyn cottyn at 5*d.* a yarde	5*s.*	10*d.*
3¾ yardes of Northyn whyte at 5*d.* a yarde		19*d.*
4½ lb. of Castell sope at 3*d.* a lb.		14½*d.*
38 hattes throwmyd at 2*d.* a pec.	6*s.*	4*d.*
29 strawyn hattes at 1*s.* a doss.	2*s.*	1*d.*

7 lb. of Castell sope		21*d.*
1½ nell of holonde at 10*d.* a nell		15*d.*
12 ells ,, ,, ,, 8*d.* ,, ,,	7*s.*	4*d.*
4 ,, ,, ,, 8*d.* ,, ,,	2*s.*	8*d.*
12½ ,, ,, ,, 6½*d.* ,, ,,	6*s.*	9*d.*
6½ ,, ,, ,, 7*d.* ,, ,,	3*s.*	9*d.*
5 ,, ,, ,, 6*d.* ,, ,,	2*s.*	6*d.*
2 ,, ,,		16*d.*
2¾ ,, ,, ,, 6*d.* ,, ,,		16½*d.*
2 ,, ,, ,, 11*d.* ,, ,,		22*d.*
2 ,, ,,		16½*d.*
4½ yardes of fustean Holmys at 7*d.* a yarde	2*s.*	7*d.*
14¼ ells of Normandy canvas at 6½*d.* a nell	7*s.*	9*d.*
17 awndes of canvas of the trasyll at 6*d.* a nawnd'	8*s.*	9*d.*
38 awndes of the crosse at 5½*d.* a nawnd'	17*s.*	9*d.*
18 awndes of the halfe crosse at 5*d.* a nawnd'	7*s.*	6*d.*
7 awndes of the halfe crosse at 5*d.* a nawnd'	2*s.*	11*d.*
7 awndes of vytore at 4½*d.* a nawnd'	2*s.*	7½*d.*
7 ells of canvas at 4½*d.* a nell	2*s.*	7½*d.*
29½ ells of lambolde at 4*d.* a nell	9*s.*	10*d.*
18½ ells of vyttre at 4*d.* a nell	6*s.*	2*d.*
21½ ells of vyttre at 4*d.* a nell	7*s.*	2*d.*
4 ells of vettre at 4*d.* a nell		16*d.*
25 ells of sulteg' at 4*d.* a nell	8*s.*	4*d.*
32 ells of slayeter at 1½*d.* a nell		4*d.*
20 remys of browne paper at 7*d.* a reme	11*s.*	8*d.*
A whyte cover		12*d.*
21 olde fosseres at 1*d.* a pec'		21*d.*
3 dowbyll chestes	26*s.*	8*d.*
A slydynge cheste	3*s.*	4*d.*

Total 10*l.* 5*s.* 9*d.*

The valenc' abowte the shope	2*s.*	
Casse of boxis		10*d.*
½ lb. of suger candy		4*d.*
2 lb. of Parys threde	2*s.*	
3 maces		8*d.*
8 boxys		8*d.*
A wrytyng deske		6*d.*
A barell with trekyll	2*s.*	
A brassyn morter with a irone pystell	15*s.*	
30 lb. of brokyn sope	3*s.*	9*d.*
A lede with 40 gallens of woll oyle at 14*d.* a gallen	46*s.*	8*d.*
The lede with the troo	12*s.*	

In the ware howse

30 ells of sarpler at 1½*d.* a nell	3*s.*	9*d.*

2 ells of sarpler at 2½*d.* a nell			4*d.*
3 cordes to the valew of			16*d.*
3 suger chestes			12*d.*
A nolde frame			6*d.*
6 payre of Flawnders valenssis		2*s.*	
A beme of iron with a payre of bassyns		3*s.*	4*d.*
A pylle wayt			8*d.*
9 lb. of brassyn wayttes			18*d.*
4 sworde gyrdelles of cruoll'			8*d.*
5 oyle mesuris			10*d.*
A smale tunnell			1*d.*
2 bordes			4*d.*
In the butre			
1 cwt. of brocke sope		13*s.*	4*d.*
10 bages of olle wayng' 15½ cwt. at 12*s.* a cwt.	6*l.*	6*s.*	
A pype with 12 gallons of oylle at 14*d.* a gallon		14*s.*	
The pype with the bassyn that they draw the oyle with			12*d.*
A nanvell			12*d.*
4 hoghedes of yowlege valoryd at		30*s.*	
A beme of tymber		5*s.*	
2 olde carpyttes			12*d.*
A nyron beme with the scalys		6*s.*	8*d.*
4¾ cwt. of ledyn wayttes		19*s.*	
6 towme stonys with certayne plattes in them with armys		4*s.*	
2 suger chestes			8*d.*
The olde tymber in the butre			8*d.*
A styllytory		3*s.*	4*d.*
Total 16*l.* 8*s.* 5*d.*			
2 bokyngtubys			12*d.*
In the warehowse next the kychyn			
3 whyte chestes brokyn		3*s.*	
The slayter abowte the warehowse		5*s.*	
2 peces of a rede lest		2*s.*	
3 whyte coffers with other trasche to the valew of		5*s.*	
A beme of tymbar			16*d.*
In the halle			
2 cowterbordes		12*s.*	
3 formys		2*s.*	
1 rownde borde			20*d.*
9 yardes of olde dornexe at 8*d.* a yarde		6*s.*	
A doss. of cowsshyons of grys at 12*d.* a pec'		12*s.*	
6 smale cowsshyns			12*d.*
A cowbard with a descke		6*s.*	8*d.*
3 latyn bassyns and 2 yewrys		5*s.*	
A towrnde chayer			12*d.*
The hangynges of saye with the borderes		6s.	8*d.*

The bankeres of saye	2*s.*	
A cowbarde clothe		6*d.*
4 olde pyntes pottes		8*d.*
A byble	12*s.*	
4 clothys paynted with a nawngell		20*d.*
In the buttere in the hall		
3 charchers	3*s.*	
2 platteres, 3 potyngers, 1 sawser	3*s.*	
2 standynge candelstyckes with a bassyn	2*s.*	8*d.*
2 quarte pottes, 1 pynte potte, 3 candellstyckes	5*s.*	
A drynkyng cupe of tyne		4*d.*
A nolde cowbard		8*d.*
A nalmery		8*d.*
A powdrynge tube		4*d.*
A nolde tabyll clothe with 3 shelffe clothys		12*d.*
2 tabylclothys of canvas of 5 ells		12*d.*
3 olde tabyllclothys		16*d.*
A tabyllclothe of dyaper of 4 ells	3*s.*	4*d.*
A nolde tabyllclothe of dyaper of 4 ells		20*d.*
A nolde dyaper clothe for a rownde borde		4*d.*
A towell of bleyte clothe of 2½ ells		12*d.*
A doss. of napkyns	3*s.*	
½ a doss. of olde towelles		18*d.*
Total 5*l.* 18*s.*		

In the parler		
A cownterborde	10*s.*	
A carpytt of rede with armys of 5½ yardes at 8*d.* a yarde	3*s.*	8*d.*
A forme		8*d.*
A cowbarde	6*s.*	8*d.*
A cowbarde clothe		12*d.*
2 browyshys		4*d.*
A course towell		4*d.*
A bassyn of tyne		12*d.*
A pynt pott		2*d.*
2 chayer stolys		8*d.*
4 lb. of besscattes and carawayes	2*s.*	8*d.*
The hangynges of saye in the parler with the borderes	3*s.*	4*d.*
A payre of awnderes	3*s.*	4*d.*
2 bankeres of saye		12*d.*
2 trestylles with stokys in them		12*d.*
In the kychen		
5 kettelles	5*s.*	
6 brasse pottes	6*s.*	8*d.*
1 frynge pane		8*d.*
2 drypyngpanys		12*d.*

A chafforne 3*s.* 4*d.*
A chafyngdysche with a fotte 16*d.*
2 lattyn ladelles 8*d.*
A skymmar with a flesche hooke 6*d.*
3 candelstyckes 16*d.*
A stoppe of tyne 12*d.*
A 1*d.* pot, *ob.* pottes 2*d.*
A holywatter pott with a brokyn candelstycke 12*d.*
A gyrderne 6*d.*
3 pothengys, 2 coterelles 8*d.*
1 racke 6*d.*
A nolde chafforne 12*d.*
2 brochys 16*d.*
1 cwt. of lede waytes 4*s.*
A stew for suger 6*s.* 8*d.*
1 shett of canvas 12*d.*
1 choppyng knyfe 2*d.*
2 holberdes 12*d.*
2 pollexys 12*d.*
A pyle of iron 4*d.*

In the bulliyng howse

2 doss. platters 12*s.*
9 potyngers 4*s.* 6*d.*
9 sawsers 2s. 3*d.*
2 smale morteres with a pestyll of brasse 2*s.* 8*d.*
A doss. of tynny sponys 2*d.*
2 doss. of trencheres 2*d.*
A bowltyng wyche with 2 knedyng kyveres 2*s.*

Total 5*l.* 5*d.*

The chambar over the parler

A fether bede with 2 bolysters 26*s.* 8*d.*
2 pyllowys of fethers 2*s.*
A pyllowtye 4*d.*
A whovyn coverlede of dyaper 5*s.*
A payre of shettes to the bede 4*s.*
A framyd bedstede with the fotte stolys abowte 8*s.*
A tester of bockeram with the cowrtaynes of rede and yalowe 6*s.* 8*d.*
3 barrys of iron for the same bede 12*d.*
A smale cowterborde 3*s.* 4*d.*
A carpytt of rede 12*d.*
A chayer 6*d.*
A lore cover 8*d.*
A nolde carpyt of dornex 6*d.*
A bow and a quever 20*d.*
The hanynges in the chamber with the borderes 5*s.*

A fyer showle		6*d*.
A gowne furryd with conne	20*s*.	
A gowne of pucke lynyd with bockram	10*s*.	
The chamber over the shope		
A bedstede		20*d*.
3 fotte stolys for the bede		12*d*.
A tester grene saye with 2 curtaynes	4*s*.	
A whyte tester		8*d*.
15 lb. of course yaryn at 4*d*. a lb.	5*s*.	
9 yardes of dornexe at 8*d*. a yarde	6*s*.	
10 yardes of carpytt of whyte and rede with armys	6*s*.	8*d*.
2½ brode yardes of Northyn clothe	4*s*.	2*d*.
7 yardes of payntyd clothe		21*d*.
The hanynges in the chamber	6*s*.	8*d*.
A cowbarde	3*s*.	4*d*.
A presse to laye wherynge gere in		5*d*.
The chamber over the buttere		
A fetherbed with 2 bolysters and 1 pyllow	16*s*.	
A payre of shettes of canvas	2*s*.	
A cowverle of whyte weyved	3*s*.	4*d*.
2 olde testers	2*s*.	
2 bedstedes		12*d*.
The hanynges in the chamber		20*d*.
The chamber over the buttere		
A fetherbede with 2 bolysters	10*s*.	
A payre of canvas shettes	2*s*.	
A whyt wevyd cowverlede	3*s*.	4*d*.
A flocke bede and a fether bolyster	4*s*.	
2 coverledes	4*s*.	
A payre of olde shettes		16*d*.
2 stayned testers	2*s*.	8*d*.
The hangynges of the chamber	4*s*.	
2 bedstedes with a trowkyll bede		18*d*.
A presse	5*s*.	
Total 40*l*. 6*s*. 7*d*.		
2 sope chestes		8*d*.
A cape presse		6*d*.
3 canvas shettes	3*s*.	
The seller next the stabyll		
A tylte of canvas of 40 ells	6*s*.	8*d*.
2 maylyng ropys		16*d*.
3 hoggyshedes with smale remnantes of yowlege	6*s*.	8*d*.
2 bowsshelles of baye salte		12*d*.
2 lode of haye	10*s*.	
In a loffte		
6 score fote of borde	3*s*.	

7 score selynge bordes at $\frac{1}{2}$*d.* a pec'	5*s.*	10*d.*
28 bordes at 2*d.* a pec'	4*s.*	8*d.*
24 square pec' at 2*d.* a pec'	2*s.*	
A fyer pane		1*d.*
6 planckes	3*s.*	
12 bordes at 2$\frac{1}{2}$*d.* a pec'	2*s.*	6*d.*
8 lb. of fethers	2*s.*	
A nolde holberde		4*d.*
A beme with a payre scalys	6*s.*	8*d.*
2 waytes of lockes and linite	10*s.*	
A whyt chest		12*d.*
A planck, a borde with a pec' of tymbar		8*d.*
In the backe lofte		
A bedestede		8*d.*
In carvyd stoffe	10*s.*	
36 bordes at 2*d.* a pec.	6*s.*	
6 planckes at 6*d.* a pec.	3*s.*	
7 lore pypys	4*s.*	8*d.*
4 bares of irone for a bede		16*d.*
3 ode ballys to the valew of	40*s.*	
14 bowsshelles of ode sede at 2*s.* a bowsshell	32*s.*	8*d.*
In the chambar over the yatt		
1 fetherbede, 1 bolyster	26*s.*	8*d.*
A nolde fetherbede	10*s.*	
A pyllowe of fethers		16*d.*
1 blancatt of flannell		12*d.*
A cowverled of gyrys	26*s.*	8*d.*
A wyt tester	3*s.*	4*d.*
A bede of joyne worcke	40*s.*	
The hangynges of the chamber with the borders	10*s.*	
A cownterborde	5*s.*	
A presse with a back of a nawter	13*s.*	4*d.*
A nawter of ymagory payntyd with golde	5*s.*	
3 tabylles of alybaster	2*s.*	
A Saynt John the Baptist	2*s.*	
Total 15*l.* 19*s.* 10*d.*		

A valenc' for a nawter	5*s.*	
A cope of yalowe sylck	2*s.*	
A pawle of yalowe sylck	2*s.*	
A tabylclothe of Normandy canvas	5*s.*	
A tabyll clothe of dyaper	2*s.*	
3 pyllowe tyes	3*s.*	4*d.*
3 payre of shettes of Garnesy clothe	12*s.*	
A shete of holonde	2*s.*	8*d.*
A shete for a bedeys hede		12*d.*
A valenc' of whyt for a bede		8*d.*

A dyaper towell		12*d.*
A stole	2*s.*	
A nolde pyllowe of satyn	2*s.*	
4 whyt chestes	8*s.*	
Total 50*s.* 8*d.*		

In the taverne next to the howse

In the shope		
The hangynges in the shope	4*s.*	
A forme		8*d.*
In the hall		
A tabylborde		8*d.*
A carpytt		4*d.*
A forme		8*d.*
2 cheyers		8*d.*
A lytelborde		6*d.*
The hanynges in the hall	6*s.*	
In the parler		
A tabylborde with 2 trestylles	3*s.*	4*d.*
A forme		16*d.*
A chayer		4*d.*
The hanynges in the parler		20*d.*
In the seller		
2 hogyshedes of clarett wyne	46*s.*	8*d.*
A hogyshede ½ full of clarett wyne	10*s.*	
A hogyshede of yowlege	13*s.*	4*d.*
1 but secke ½ full	30*s.*	
A towbe with 3 legges		6*d.*
A lytyll gymlattes with a funnell		3*d.*
3 bede stedes		2*d.*
A lytelborde		4*d.*
Total 6*l.* 4*s.* 2*d.*		

Total 98*l.* 2*s.* 10*d.*

Item for a lesse made by Thomas Chaffyn senyor, mercer of Sar', for 41 yeres for 4*l.*, by the yere of the wyche 41 yeres remaynyth to cumme 37 yeres to cum, for the wyche 37 yeres ys extendyd in valew 20*s.*

Item for a lesse made by Nycholas Bowre, chantre prest of Our Lady Chirch, the which is the londes nowe of Syr Thomas Mackes, clercke, the which was Thomas Helys and now yt is to the yowys of Thomas Wodlock, which ys value by synne namyd 3*s.* 4*d.*'

22 Nov. 34 Hen. VIII [1542]. *Liberate* returnable in quin. of Martinmas next [25 Nov.] with *des in mandatis* to the bailiff of the bishop of Salisbury's liberty. 'These parcells ensuing praysed in Bemerton; item the woodd prysed 21*s.* 8*d.*; a fetherbede with a coverlette, a pyllow and a bolster, wyth hangyng

clothes of the same chamber, wyth a tabylborde and trestells and 2 formes, price 16*s*. 8*d*.; the implements of the hales, viz., 2 paynted clothes, a borde, 2 trestells and a forme, a carpett, price 6*s*. 6*d*.; item a flokbede, a covering and 2 stayned clothes, 2 bedstedes, price 6*s*. 8*d*.; 2 brasse pottes and a skilete, 2 platters, 2 sawsers, 1 canstyke, 3 cawderns, 1 olde fornes, 1 frying panne, 1 drypyng panne, 1 broche, 1 aundyern and a gredeyern, 1 tryvete, price 15*s*. 8*d*.; 1 tramele, 1 castyng nette, price 10*s*.; item the woodd being upon the seid ferme of Bemerton with 1 mylle to grynde the said woode and other implements in the seid wooddhouse, 40*l*.' Total 43*l*. 6*s*. 4*d*. Total of the goods within and without the bishop of Salisbury's liberty 142*l*. 11*s*. 4*d*.

C 239/11 no. 44

74 Richard Olyver, 'husbondman', of Wotton Basset, son and heir of Nicholas Olyver, 'husbondman', late of Lydeard Treigose

9 Nov. 34 Hen. VIII [1542]. *Capias* returnable in quin. of Hil. next [27 Jan.], sued out by Thomas Gore, gentleman, of Aldryngton, to whom Richard acknowledged 50*l*. on 16 Dec. 15 Hen. VIII [1523] before John Wilkyns, then mayor of the town and Staple of Bristol, and John Williams and John Shipman, constables of the Staple, payable at St. Clement then next [23 Nov.].
Endorsed. Richard has not been found.

18 Nov. 34 Hen. VIII [1542]. Inquisition at Great Sherstone before John Mervyn by Thomas Hayes, Nicholas Williams, Robert Hort, Thomas Hort, . . . [*MS. blind*] Saye, William Morwey, John Lane, William Northe, William Benet, William Farmer, Anthony Stychall, and John Broune.

Seised in his demesne as of fee of: 30 a. of land, 6 a. of meadow, 20 a. of pasture, and 4 a. of wood in Great Sherstone, worth 40*s*. yearly; a messuage and 30 a. of meadow in Swyndon, worth 35*s*. yearly; a cottage and a close of land in Wotton Basset, worth 15*s*. yearly. Total 4*l*. yearly.

C 131/114 no. 16

75 Thomas Changton *alias* Shangilton, gentleman, of Shalbourne

3 July [37] Hen. VIII [1545]. *Capias* returnable on the morrow of All Souls next [3 Nov.], sued out by Thomas Wenman, gentleman, and Nicholas Aschefell, of London, to whom Thomas acknowledged . . . [*MS. blind*] *l*. on 9 May 26 Hen. VIII [1534] before Robert Norwiche, knight, then chief justice of the Common Pleas, payable at Whitsun then next [1 June].

Mon. 21 July 37 Hen. VIII [1545]. Inquisition at Shalbourne before Anthony Hungerford, knight, by John Daunsey, John Horsell, John Jenewey, John Wylmott, John Bryan, John Perese, Thomas King, John Farmer, Richard Barton, William Bayley, John Soper, and John Flower.

In Shalbourne seised in his demesne as of fee of: a plot of land called 'Radman' and 'Horscroft' worth 13*s*. 4*d*. yearly; messuages held by Robert Bocher (17*s*.), John Bryan (24*s*.), and the rector of Shalbourne (10*s*.); a cottage held by John Wilmott (6*s.*); ½ a messuage held by Thomas Emmes; ½ a messuage held by Isabel Dawnsey, widow, (11*s.*); free rent of 2*s.* yearly from the lands of Thomas Cheverell; cottages held by Lettice Parker, widow, (5*s.*) and William Buckland (6*s.*); a pasture called 'Westhardinges' held by John Daunsey . . . ; cottages held by John Thrussher, Robert Potter, and Joan Ludloo (6*s.* 8*d.* each); a messuage held by Thomas Romcey (6*s.* 8*d.*).

C 131/116 no. 4

76 Walter Singleton, gentleman, of Shalborne, son and heir of Thomas Singleton, gentleman, of Shalborne, deceased, and Nicholas Thorne, gentleman, of Sonnyng, Berkshire

13 Feb. 37 Hen. VIII [1546]. *Capias*[1] returnable in 3 weeks from Eas. next [16 May], sued out by Katherine Dormer, widow, and John Dormer, executors of Michael Dormer, citizen and alderman of London, to whom Walter and Nicholas acknowledged 200*l.* on 31 Oct. 31 Hen. VIII [1539] before Edward Mountague, knight, then chief justice of the King's Bench, payable at Christmas then next. Like writs to the sheriffs of Oxon. and Berks. *Endorsed.* Walter and Nicholas have not been found.

20 Apr. 37 Hen. VIII [1546]. Inquisition at Collyngborn Kyngston before Charles Bulkeley, esquire, by Thomas Cordrey, William Sotwell, Godfrey Gunter, gentleman, John Andrewes, Thomas Brounton, Edward Mondey, John Wythorn, Thomas Noyes, Thomas Chylde, Robert Busshell, Robert Dower, and Henry Norres.

Walter was seised in his demesne as of fee of: a capital messuage, 40 a. of arable land, 10 a. of meadow, a pasture called the 'Tegg lease', and 6 a. of pasture called 'Benett Hardyng' held by Walter himself and worth 40*s.* yearly; messuages held by William Geoffrey (6*s.* 8*d.*), Robert Potter (8*s.*), John Thrussher,[2] Robert Cholles (6*s.*), Robert Douney (6*s.* 8*d.*), Robert Broun,[2] Thomas Romsey (6*s.* 8*d.*), William Bos . . . (6*s.* 8*d.*),[2] John Bawleyne,[2] John Harres (6*s.* 8*d.*), Elizabeth Daunce (6*s.* 8*d.*), Robert Brissher,[2] John Daunce (20*s.*), William Farmer (10*s.*), John Kyng,[2] and William Buckland (6*s.* 8*d.*); a plot or parcel of land and pasture held by the rector of Shalborn (13*s.* 4*d.*) and a plot called 'Radmans' held by Francis Chock (10*s.*). Various other outhouses and buildings and other parcels of land belonging to the manor of Shalborn Westcourt (20*s.*): 'a parlour and the lofte over the parlour and . . . ground called a barton as far forth as the pound with [?within] and a barn wyth a gardeyn dycched aboute a lytell safferon ground dycched aboute'; 2 parcels of meadow called . . . [*MS. blind*] held by Walter himself; a messuage held by Thomas Peers (10*s.*).

Nicholas had no lands or goods in Wilts. C 131/116 no. 6

. . . [*MS. torn*] 38 Hen. VIII [1546–7]. *Liberate* returnable in 3 weeks from Trin. next. C 239/11 no. 110

[1] Writ printed in full in Appendix, p. 127.
[2] MS. blind.

77 John Hyll, gentleman, of Kington, Radnorshire

17 Nov. [*recte* Sept.] 2 Edw. VI [1548]. *Capias* returnable in quin. of Mich. next [13 Oct.], sued out by Robert Grome, gentleman, and his wife Joan, executors of Thomas Brygges, citizen and 'clothworker' of London, to whom John acknowledged 10*l*. on 16 Dec. 34 Hen. VIII [1542] before Ralph Waren, knight, mayor of the Staple of Westminster, and Roger Cholmeley, knight, then recorder of London, payable on 20 July then next.

23 Oct. 2 Edw. VI [1548]. Inquisition at Wynterborne Erles before Silvester Davers, esquire, by John Smyth, John Pryver, Richard Eston, Robert Tynham, William Note, Robert Bynder, Thomas Cole, William Pruett, Thomas Durman, John Martyn, Richard Hynton, John Arker, and Thomas Long.

Seised of a messuage and a water-mill in Wynterborne, worth 3*l*. 6*s*. 8*d*. yearly. John has not been found.

24 Nov. 2 Edw. VI [1548]. *Liberate* returnable in quin. of Eas. next [5 May]; with *capias* against John's body.

Endorsed. The above were delivered on 3 May 3 Edw. VI [1549] by Ambrose Dauntesey, esquire, sheriff, to John Hooper, gentleman, attorney of Robert and Joan Grome, to hold to their use. John has not been found.

C 239/13 no. 22

78 Robert Leversage, esquire, of Frowmselwood, Somerset

1 Feb. 3 Edw. VI [1549]. *Capias* returnable in 1 month from Eas. next [19 May], sued out by William Button, executor of William Button, gentleman, of Alton, to whom Robert acknowledged 500 marks on 29 Mar. 24 Hen. VIII [1533] before Robert Norwiche, knight, then chief justice of the Common Pleas, payable at Eas. then next [13 Apr.]. Like writs to the sheriffs of Som. and Glos.

Endorsed. Robert has not been found.

24 May 3 Edw. VI [1549]. Inquisition at Marleboroughe before Ambrose Dauntesey, esquire, by Simon Baskerffeyld, John Benger, Godfrey Gunter, John Spencer, gentlemen, Robert Pyke, Thomas Crypps, Thomas Noyes, William Monday, Thomas Baylly, Andrew Brunysdon, John Hardyng, and William Se . . . [*MS. blind*].

On 20 Mar. 24 Hen. VIII [1533] and on the day of the recognizance, seised in his demesne as of fee of: the manor of Rudlowe in Boxe parish and 8 messuages, 100 a. of pasture, 50 a. of meadow, 300 a. of arable land, 20 a. of wood, and 40 a. of gorse and heath in Rudlowe and Boxe, worth 10*l*. yearly; 24 messuages, a fulling mill, 300 a. of pasture, 100 a. of meadow, 300 a. of arable land, 20 a. of wood, and 60 a. of gorse and heath in Wesbery under the 'Playne' and in Lye, Heywodd, Hawkerygg, and Sewall in Wesbury parish, worth 20*l*. yearly.

28 May 3 Edw. VI [1549]. *Liberate* returnable in quin. of Trin. **next [30**

June]; with *capias* against Robert's body. Like writ to the sheriff of Som. to deliver lands there worth 31*l*.
Endorsed. The above lands were delivered on 15 June 3 Edw. VI [1549]. Robert has not been found.

C 239/14 no. 1

79 John Smyth, 'clothier', of le Vise, and John Smyth, his eldest son

6 July 7 Edw. VI [1553]. *Capias* returnable on the morrow of All Souls next [3 Nov.], sued out by Anthony Calthorpe, citizen and mercer of London, to whom John and John acknowledged 100*l*. on 17 Apr. 5 Edw. VI [1551] before Edward Mountague, knight, then chief justice of the Common Pleas, payable at . . . [*MS. torn*].

C 239/18 no. 20

80 John Beckyngham, merchant, of New Salisbury

8 Dec. 1 Mary [1553]. *Capias* returnable in quin. of Hil. next [27 Jan.], sued out by John Abyn, 'clothier', of New Salisbury, to whom John acknowledged 200*l*. on 1 Mar. 37 Hen. VIII [1546], before Richard Lyster, knight, then chief justice of the King's Bench, payable at Midsummer then next.
Endorsed. John Erneley, sheriff, has sent the writ to the bailiff of the liberty of John, bishop of Salisbury, of his city of New Salisbury, whose answer is annexed.

19 Jan. 1 Mary [1554]. Inquisition at New Salisbury before Robert Jones, gentleman, bailiff of the liberty of John, bishop of Salisbury, of his city of New Salisbury, by virtue of a warrant from John Erneley, esquire, sheriff, by John Coryett, Robert Eyer, Richard Holt, Richard Canon, George Wilton, Edward Meryvale, William Jorden, John Morall, Thomas Bassett, William Coxe the elder, William Davy, John Pylgram, William Dyer, John Belynger, Thomas Westcott, and John Venard.

In New Salisbury seised in his demesne as of fee of: the site of the late college of St. Edmund, recently dissolved, with dovecote, orchard, garden, yard, curtilage, and ditch adjoining the site, worth 4*l*. yearly; a garden in Saynt Edmondes strete (5*s*.); herbage of the churchyard of the parish church of St. Edmund (6*s*. 8*d*.).

Taken in his demesne as of right of the advowsons of the rectories of the parish churches of St. Edmund and St. Martin, each worth 12*d*. yearly.

In possession of: a tenement called 'the Cell Corner' and 12 other tenements in Newe strete, Crane strete, Broun strete, Dragon strete, [and Wynchester strete] which John holds from Henry Woodall, esquire, for a term of years, worth 4*l*. 10*s*. yearly; 4 tenements and a garden in Castelstrete, Saynt Edmondes strete, and Grene Croft strete, which John holds from [Stephen] Cheke for a term of years, worth 36*s*. yearly.

The following goods: in the hall a table with a form (*scanno*) and 2 'trestelles' (*tripodibus*), worth 2*s*. 6*d*.; a 'bason' (*pelve*) . . . [*MS. torn*] 'laver' worth 2*s*. 4*d*.; a 'coberd' (*abace*) worth 12*d*. In the 'parler' (*cenaculo*) 2 tables with trestles worth 8*s*.; 2 'formys' worth 3*s*.; . . . 2 'joyned stoles' (*selatoriis*) worth 4*s*. 2*d*.; 6 'fotestoles' (*suppedaneis*) worth 18*d*.; 6 'chears' worth [2*s*.; 'iron crepers'] (*parva creparili ferri*) . . . a 'fyer pyke' (*furca ignar'*) worth 4*d*., a 'payer of tonges' (*forcipe*) worth 8*d*.; a 'tostyng iron' (*furcula ignaria*) worth 4*d*.; 8 'stayned clothes' (*peripetasmatis*) worth 10*s*.; 6 'grene cuysshyns' (*virid' pulvinar'*) worth 3*s*. In the kitchen 7 'broches' (*verubus*) worth 5*s*.; 2 'dreapyng pannes' (*sartaginibus*) worth 16*d*.; 2 'grydyerons' (*cratis*) worth 8*d*.; 2 iron supports (*sustentalis ferreis*); [10 'pannes' (*vasis ferreis*) worth] 26*s*. 8*d*.; 2 'fryeng pannes' (*fryxor'*) worth 12*d*.; a 'skymmer' (*despumator'*) worth 6*d*. . . . worth 12*d*. . . . 2 'chafers of bras' (*situlis eris*) worth 13*s*. 4*d*.; a 'fote of bras for a chafyngdyshe' (*pede eris*) worth 12*d*.; 4 'bras pottes' worth 20*s*.; an 'yeren potte' worth 12*d*.; a 'mortar and a pestell' (*mortar' et pistill'*) . . . worth 20*s*.; a 'pappan' (*batre*) worth 2*d*.; a 'lytell pott of bras' (*parva auxilla eris*) worth 4*d*.; a 'collender' (*colator'*) . . . worth 3*s*. 4*d*.; a 'ladyll' (*cocleare sulinar'*) worth 4*d*.; a 'pott hooke' (*cathena olaris*) worth 2*d*. . . . [a 'bedsted' and a 'flockbedd' (*lect' tomentat'*)] worth 8*s*.; 2 'cosers' (*capsulis*) worth 10*s*. In the middle chamber, a 'fether bedde' (*culcitra* . . .) and a 'coverlet' (*stragula*), worth 30*s*.; 2 'cosers' (*capsulis*) worth 6*s*.; [2 'paynted clothes'] (*peripetasmatis*) worth . . . ; ' . . . of tapstare' worth 5*s*.; a 'presse' (*abaca*) worth 40*s*.; a 'pillowe of fethers' (*pulvinar'*) worth 12*d*.; a 'bedstedd' (*fulchra*), a [canopy] 'with curtaynes' (*cagnobo cum velis*) worth 6*s*. 8*d*.; a 'fetherbedde' (*culcitra tomentata*), worth 40*s*.; a 'rusett [gown]' (*toga ian' coloris*) . . . [a 'coser' worth 3*s*. 4*d*.; 3 'stayned clothes' worth 3*s*.] . . . In 'the mill howse' (*domo molendinar'*), a thrave (*trava*) . . . a 'payer of scalis' worth 5*s*.; 'two hundred wayght and a halffe of leade' (*ducentis duodenis et dimidium plumbi*) worth 13*s*. 4*d*.; 3 vessells (*vascell'*) . . . 2 'lodes of heye' (. . . *carectat'*) worth 20*s*.; a 'lytle cart' worth 2*s*. . . . [In the storeroom (*promptu'*)] . . . 6 'candylstyckes of bras' worth 3*s*. 4*d*.; a 'pottell' pott of tyn' (*ciatho enii*) worth [16*d*.; a 'quarte pott of tynn' (*ciatho enii*) worth 8*d*.;] . . . 5 'platters', 5 'potyngers' (*pattinis*), 5 dishes (*scutellis*) . . . (*culcitra plumar'*), [a 'bolster'] (*cervicale*), [a 'helyng' (*operiment'*), a 'pyllowe' (*pulvinar'*)], a 'flockebedde'.

14 Feb. 1 Mary [1554]. *Liberate* returnable in . . . ; with *capias* against John's body.

Endorsed. John Erneley, esquire, sheriff, has sent the writ to the bailiff of the liberty who has replied that he delivered the above on 31 Mar. 1 Mary [1554].

C 239/19 no. 27

81 John Cryppes the elder, 'yoman', of Meyseyhampton, Gloucestershire

10 Oct. 2 & 3 Philip and Mary [1555]. *Capias* returnable on the morrow of All Souls next [3 Nov.], sued out by John Chamberlayne, 'yoman', of Sparsholt *alias* Sparshold, Berks., to whom John acknowledged 400*l*. on 15 Feb. 6 Edw. VI [1552] before Edward Mountagu, knight, then chief justice of the Common Pleas, payable at Lady Day then next. Like writ to the sheriff of Glos.

27 Oct. 2 & 3 Philip and Mary [1555]. John has not been found. The lands have been delivered to the king and queen.

26 Oct. 2 & 3 Philip and Mary [1555]. Inquisition at Crykelade before Robert Hungerforde, esquire, by Henry Cove, John Ferys, gentlemen, William Brynd, William Bryan, Thomas Kemble the elder, Thomas Burgys, John Brawn, John Telynge, Thomas Wake, Thomas Raseley, William Telyn, Robert Sherndon, Thomas Galfrey, Thomas Hynton, Thomas Telynge, and John Cull.

In Castyll Eaton seised in his demesne as of fee of: a meadow or close of pasture called 'Overborsed' of *c*. 15 a.; a meadow or close of pasture called 'Netherborsed' of *c*. 10 a. These lands were lately held by Richard Verney, knight, and, after the recognizance, by a charter dated 28 Jan. 1 & 2 Philip and Mary [1555], John granted the lands to Anthony Ayleworth, esquire, in fee and Anthony is now so seised in his demesne. The lands are worth 42*s*. yearly.

Seised in his demesne as of fee of: a tenement in Pwlton parish now held by Richard Miller, worth 3*s*. 4*d*. yearly; a tenement in Merston in Mesye Hampton *alias* Merston Meysie parish now held by Edith Snell, worth 14*s*. yearly; a tenement in Marston now held by Martin Bradforde, worth 20*s*. yearly. The tenements contain *c*. 30 a. of pasture, 110 a. of arable land, 20 a. of meadow, and 2 a. of wood, gorse, and briar.

7 Nov. 2 & 3 Philip and Mary [1555]. *Liberate* returnable in oct. of Martinmas next [18 Nov.]; with *capias* against John's body. Like writ to the sheriff of Glos.

C 239/21 no. 3

82 Lancelot Stokker, gentleman, of Malmesbury

25 June 4 & 5 Philip and Mary [1558]. *Capias* returnable in oct. of Mich. next [6 Oct.], sued out by Matthew Kynge, 'clothier', of Malmesbury, to whom Lancelot acknowledged 300*l*. on 24 Apr. 4 & 5 Philip and Mary [1558] before Robert Broke, knight, chief justice of the Common Pleas, payable at Eas. then next [10 Apr.]. Like writs to the sheriffs of Herts., Glos., and Lond.
Endorsed. Lancelot has not been found.

30 Sept. 5 & 6 Philip and Mary [1558]. Inquisition at Cowfold grange before Walter Hungerford, knight, by Richard Helyer, David Serney, Francis Meryett, Robert Aphoall, Henry Mydwynter, Robert Bruoer, Richard Olyver, William Coren, Edward Smythe, John Browne, William Woderoffe, Thomas Millard, and John Symkyns.

The following goods: 3 'broches' (*vera*) worth 3*s*. 4*d*.; 3 'mylkepanes' (*vasa*) and a 'tubbe' worth 14*d*.; a table with 2 'tresselles' (*instrumentis*) worth 6*d*.; a 'pewter pott' worth 16*d*.; 3 other pots called 'pichers' and a dish (*disco*) worth 6*d*.; a vessel (*vas*), 6 quart pots (*quadras*), and 2 barrels worth 2*s*. 8*d*; a net (*rete*) called a 'tocknett' worth 4*d*.; a 'sedeler' with cover (*copertur*') worth 4*d*.; a mirror with studded case (*speculum cum vagina sticat*') worth 2*d*.; a round table, a 'trendell', a measure of seed (*mensuram seminis*) called 'senvy seade' worth 14*d.*; a table, 2 trestles, and 2 chairs worth 5*s.*; 'chesevates' and a 'beame' worth 2*s.*; a 'bowcase' (*vaginam*) with a 'qwyver' worth 8*d.*; 2 'stiroppes' with their gear worth 8*d.*; various linen cloths (*panna linea*) called '[han]gynges' worth 5*s.*; a table with 3 trestles worth 16*d.*; a 'chorne', a 'morter', a dozen quart pots and 3 dishes worth 11*d.*; a 'syve', a piece of a table (*pecia mense*), a 'whiche', and a 'trendell' worth 3*s.* 8*d.*; 3 pairs of iron (*para ferrei*) called 'andyers' worth 5*s.*; an instrument called a 'fire pyke flyse' worth 6*d.*; a 'grydier' with 'clever, hatchen, and brondier' worth 16*d.*; a table with 3 stools (*stolis*) worth 4*s.*; a chair, a cloth (*pannum*) called 'a carpett clothe', and 3 [*blank*] called 'koyshens' worth 6*s.* 8*d.*; a 'chafyndishe', 2 'platters', and 2 'bottelles' worth 3*s.* 4*d.*; a 'brasse pott' with a 'cawdron' worth 6*s.* 8*d.*; a feather-bed (*lectum plumial'*) with a 'bolster' worth 26*s.* 8*d.*; a 'flockbedd', a 'mattres', 2 'coverlettes' (*copert'*), a 'bolster', 2 linen sheets (*lintea*) called 'blankettes', a linen sheet (*linthea*) called a 'shete' with hangings for the bed (*pendent' lecti*) worth 17*s.* 2*d.*; 4 'chestes' (*arcas*) worth 12*s.*; 8 boxes (*cassos*) worth 16*d.*; 8 'baskettes' (*bucell'*) worth 12*d.*; a dish with a 'bottell' worth 5*d.*; 2 wagon-loads (*plaustrat'*) of oats, barley, and hay worth 18*s.*; 2 wagon-loads of hay worth 7*s.* Total 7*l.* 2*s.* 8*d.*

C 239/23 no. 53

83 Thomas Stantor, esquire, of Great Hornyngsham

1 Aug. 5 & 6 Philip and Mary [1558]. *Capias* returnable in oct. of Mich. next [6 Oct.], sued out by John Thynne, knight, to whom Thomas acknowledged 400*l.* on 24 June 2 & 3 Philip and Mary [1556] before Robert Broke, knight, chief justice of the Common Pleas, payable at Mich. then next. Like writs to the sheriffs of Som. and Dors.
Endorsed. Thomas is dead.

12 Sept. 5 & 6 Philip and Mary [1558]. Inquisition at Horningsham before Walter Hungerford, knight . . . [*MS. blind*].

C 239/24 no. 1

84 Richard Lyster, esquire, of Pryours Husbourne, Hampshire

2 Dec. 3 Eliz. I [1560]. *Capias* returnable in quin. of Eas. next [28 Apr. 1561], sued out by John Stockman, gentleman, of Abbottes Anne, Hants, to whom Richard acknowledged 200*l.* on 25 June 2 & 3 Philip and Mary [1556] before William Portman, knight, then chief justice of the Queen's Bench, payable at St. James then next [25 July]. Like writs to the sheriffs of Hants and Herefs.
Endorsed. Richard has not been found.

14 Apr. 3 Eliz. I [1561]. Inquisition at Chipenham before James Stumpe, knight, by John Webbe, John Gale, John Vyves, Thomas Noble, John Ladd, Francis Gulwell, Robert Wastfyld, William Bone, Nicholas Amer, Robert Harrys, William Harrys, and Thomas Bowghton.

No lands or goods in Wilts. C 239/27 no. 8

85 John Care, of Kekkebear'

13 Jan. 5 Eliz. I [1563]. *Capias* returnable in 1 month from Eas. next [9 May], sued out by Martha Carewe, relict and administratrix of Ormond Carewe, knight, to whom, in the name of Ormond Carewe, gentleman, John acknowledged 500*l*. on 6 Jan. 23 Hen. VIII [1532] before John Blakaller, then mayor of the Staple of Exeter, and Richard Martyn and John Seller, then constables of the said Staple, payable at Whitsun then next [19 May]. Like writs to the sheriffs of Som., Devon, and Cornw.
Endorsed. John has not been found.

13 Apr. 5 Eliz. I [1563]. Inquisition at Stapleford before George Penruddoke, esquire, by Nicholas Snowe and William Balch, gentlemen, John Hayter, John Baseley, Charles Tuck . . . [*MS. blind*], John Gylbert, John Barley, Nicholas Down, gentleman, John Bygges, John Randoll, William Kendoll, William Brown, John . . . , Alexander Percye, and William Hulett.

After the day of the recognizance, 7 Apr. 32 Hen. VIII [1541], seised in his demesne as of fee of: $\frac{1}{3}$ of a messuage, 9 tofts, a garden, 400 a. of land, 6 a. of meadow, 300 a. of pasture, and 6 a. of wood in Partewood *alias* Parteworth, worth 43*s*. 4*d*. yearly. On 14 Apr. 32 Hen. VIII [1541] John alienated and bargained the said third to John Marvyn, of Pertwood, to hold in fee.

The above were delivered to the queen on 14 Apr. 5 Eliz. I [1563].

14 Feb. 7 Eliz. I [1565]. *Liberate* returnable in quin. of Eas. next [6 May]; with *capias* against John's body. C 239/29 no. 7

86 Humphrey Essex, gentleman, of Highworth

7 Feb. 6 Eliz. I [1564]. *Capias* returnable in quin. of Eas. next [16 Apr.], sued out by Thomas Essex, esquire, of Chilrey, Berks., to whom Humphrey acknowledged 600*l*. on 1 July 5 Eliz. I [1563] before Robert Catlyn, knight, chief justice of the Queen's Bench, payable at St. James then next [25 July].
Endorsed. Humphrey has not been found. The lands and goods were delivered on 13 Apr.

13 Apr. 6 Eliz. I [1564]. Inquisition at Maggatt Myll before John Erneley, esquire, by Giles Mylles, gentleman, Arthur Dereng, John Sadler, Arthur Beynton, Henry Sevegar, Arthur Clyde, William Saundere, John Spencer, John Cox, John Squyer, William Cuttler, William Burges, Lawrence Cuffe, Valentine Crappes, Thomas Wyse, and William Whyttway.

On the day of the receipt of the writ seised and possessed in his demesne as of fee of a messuage called 'Maggatt Myll' in Hyeworth parish, worth 4*l*. yearly.

The following goods: 18 cows worth 24*l*.; 8 oxen worth 12*l*.; 2 geldings (*spadon*') worth 4 marks; 2 horses worth 40*s*.; 6 mares and a bullock worth 18*s*.; 2 boars and a sow worth 15*s*.; 6 a. of wheat worth 46*s*. 8*d*. and 12 a. of barley worth 48*s*. C 239/30 no. 25

87 John Servyngton, esquire, of Falson

2 Aug. 6 Eliz. I [1564]. *Capias* returnable in quin. of Mich. next [13 Oct.], sued out by Edmund Mathewe, mercer, of New Salisbury, to whom John acknowledged 700*l.* on 7 Nov. 4 Eliz. I [1562] before Robert Catlyn, knight, chief justice of the Queen's Bench, payable at Christmas then next. Like writ to the sheriff of Dors.

14 Sept. 6 Eliz. I [1564]. Inquisition at New Salisbury before John Ernley, esquire, by William Morgerydye, gentleman, Thomas Belly, William Walker, Thomas Boston, John Thorpe, Robert Olyver, William Bedford, William Grafton, John Grey, Nicholas Huland, William Hyckes, Robert Bachet, James Perham, and Thomas Heath.

Seised in his demesne as of fee of: the manor of West Harnam and 10 messuages in West Harnam [and Fycherton Auger], in the several tenures of John Wekes, Joan Shuter, widow, Ralph Mory, John Soppe, James Clythman, John Hybbard, Joan Pryme, Richard Manyngton, Robert Nottyng, and John Younge, gentleman, worth 7*l.* 4*s.* yearly; 3 tenements in Damerham worth 4*l.* yearly. C 239/30 no. 99

88 Humphrey Redynge, 'tanner', of Wokingham, Berkshire

26 Aug. 6 Eliz. I [1564]. *Capias* returnable in quin. of Mich. next [13 Oct.], sued out by John Cater, citizen and vintner of London, to whom Humphrey acknowledged 160*l.* on 7 Mar. 4 Eliz. I [1562] before Thomas Offeley, knight, then mayor of the Staple of Westminster, and Ralph Cholmeley, esquire, then recorder of London, payable at Whitsun then next [17 May]. Like writ to the sheriff of Berks.
Endorsed. Humphrey has not been found.

10 Oct. 6 Eliz. I [1564]. Inquisition at Wokyngham before John Erneley, esquire, by William Planner the elder, William Hyde, Thomas Mattynglye, William Tyckener, Ralph Hygges, William Planner the younger, John Banyster, Thomas Crockefurd, William Well, Ralph Dorwell, Thomas Soper *alias* Gyles, and Thomas Mylward.

In Wokyngham parish seised in his demesne as of fee of: a barn called '[Bolt House] barne', 4 closes of arable land adjoining it of *c.* 12 a., and an orchard and curtilage, worth 55*s.* 3*d.* yearly; 2 messuages, 2 gardens, 5 closes of arable land and pasture of *c.* 12 a., now held by Richard Yonge, worth 39*s.* yearly.

27 Oct. 6 Eliz. I [1564]. *Liberate* returnable in oct. of Martinmas next [18 Nov.]; with *capias* against Humphrey's body. Like writ to the sheriff of Berks. in respect of lands there worth 6*l* 19*s.* 2*d* yearly.

C 239/30 no. 101

89 Richard Pexsall, esquire, of Bewrepaire, Hampshire

29 Oct. 7 Eliz. I [1565]. *Capias* returnable in quin. of Martinmas next [25 Nov.], sued out by Henry Redyngfyld and Thomas Cornewallis, knights, and

Brian Holland, esquire, executors of Richard Freston, esquire, of Mendham, Suff., and his wife Anne, to whom Richard acknowledged 300*l.* on 19 Feb. 35 Hen. VIII [1544] before Edward Mountagu, knight, then chief justice of the King's Bench, payable at Eas. then next [13 Apr.]. Like writ to the sheriff of Hants.
Endorsed. Richard has not been found. The lands were delivered to the queen on 21 Nov. 8 Eliz. I [1565].

21 Nov. 8 Eliz. I [1565]. Inquisition at Clacke before William Button, esquire, by Adam Orcharde, John Curteis, Thomas Pelyver, Thomas Gale, ... [*MS. blind*], John Orcharde, Ralph Jelycoxe, John Podington, John Browne, Thomas Reve, William Newnton, William Walter, and William Jacobbe.

Seised in his demesne as of fee of the manor of Clacke, worth 10*l.* yearly, and a wood next to Clacke called 'Woodloxhey', worth 200*l.*

C 239/31 no. 75

90 Henry Peckham, esquire, of London

7 Feb. 8 Eliz. I [1566]. *Extendi facias* returnable in quin. of Eas. next [28 Apr.], for John Ayleworth, esquire, to whom Henry acknowledged 3,000*l.* on 26 Oct. 5 Edw. VI [1551] before Edward Mountague, knight, then chief justice of the Common Pleas, payable at All Saints then next [1 Nov.]; as John had sued out a *capias* to which the sheriff has returned that Henry is dead and that the writ was delivered too late for execution. Like writs to the sheriffs of Beds., Glos., and Herts.
Endorsed. Henry is dead.

20 Apr. 8 Eliz. I [1566]. Inquisition at Pyrton before John Eyre, esquire, by Thomas Wyntersall, gentleman, Anthony Geringe, William Morse, John Lyminginge, Anthony Deynton, James Forde, Henry Sevegar, John Ryman the younger, Thomas Telinge, John Warman, Henry Richman, and Thomas Taylour.

After the day of the recognizance, 9 Apr. 1 Mary [1554], seised in his demesne as of fee of a close of pasture in Pyrton called 'Templeclose' and a meadow adjoining it, worth 40 marks yearly.

C 239/32 no. 18

91 Gabriel Pledell, gentleman, of Mouncketon in Chippenham parish

2 Jan. 9 Eliz. I [1567]. *Capias* returnable in quin. of Eas. next [13 Apr.], sued out by Robert Colman, citizen and skinner of London, to whom Gabriel acknowledged 200*l.* on 20 June 6 Eliz. I [1564] before Robert Catlyn, knight, chief justice of the Queen's Bench, payable at St. James then next [25 July]. Like writs to the sheriffs of Lond. and Mdx.
Endorsed. The sheriff has sent the writ to the bailiff of the liberty of Henry Sharington, esquire, of his hundred of Chippenham, who has returned no answer.

11 Apr. 9 Eliz. I [1567]. Inquisition at Chippenham before Nicholas Snell,

esquire, by Thomas Exham, John Beryman, Henry Hacker, Thomas Nashe, John Newman, Robert Wastfylde, Robert Scott, Thomas Stratton, David Jeffrey, Robert Prater, Richard Shepard, and William Brewer.

No lands or goods in Wilts. C 239/33 no. 12

92 John Lake and William Ellmes, each 'yoman', of Bishop's Cannynges

8 May 9 Eliz. I [1567]. *Capias* returnable in oct. of Trin. next [1 June], sued out by William Darrell, esquire, of Lytlecote, to whom John and William acknowledged 400 marks on 1 May 6 Eliz. I [1564] before Robert Catlyn, knight, chief justice of the Queen's Bench, payable on 5 May.

Endorsed. The sheriff has taken John and put him in prison. William has not been found.

3 June 9 Eliz. I [1567]. Inquisition at Devizes before Nicholas Snell, esquire, by John Flower, Edward Purye, Thomas Carpenter, John Whyte, John Hardinge, William Horte, John Dyck, Nicholas Stycklowe, William Lewdon, Christopher Dobbes, Robert Clowde, and William Steavens.

John and William have no lands in Wilts.

John has the following goods: 18 oxen worth 33*l.*, 5 horses called 'horse beastes' worth 6*l.* 13*s.* 4*d.*, 2 cows worth 3*l.*, 4 bullocks worth 4*l.*, 4 bullocks worth 3*l.*, 6 horses called 'horse beastes' worth 7*l.*, 35 pigs worth 5*l.*, and 9 pigs worth 53*s.* 4*d.*; 12 [qr.] of wheat worth 6*l.*, 138 a. of land sown with wheat, barley, and other types of grain in certain fields in Mounckton parish worth 56*l.*; 5 carts (*curros*) called 'cartes and waynes' worth 6*l.* 13*s.* 4*d.*, 6 yokes and 6 'stringes' worth 10*s.*, 30 cart-loads of wood worth 5*l.*, 4 qr. of wheat worth 40*s.*, 4½ a. of land in 'Cannynges Fylde' sown with wheat worth 45*s.* and 54 a. sown with barley worth 18*l.*, 6 cart-loads of wood and 2 cart-loads of timber worth 20*s.*, and 12 sheep in the care of John Truslowe worth 28*l.*

William has the following goods: 202 sheep worth 33*l.* 6*s.* 8*d.*, 65 lambs worth 6*l.* 13*s.* 4*d.*, 4 oxen worth 6*l.*, 3 cows worth 3*l.* 15*s.*, a horse called a 'nagge' worth 26*s.* 8*d.*, and 2 piglets worth 6*s.*; a 'rike' of corn with *c.* 8 qr. of wheat worth 4*l.*, 5 a. of land in 'Horton Fylde' sown with wheat worth 55*s.* and 13½ a. sown with barley worth 4*l.* 10*s.*, and 5 a. of land in 'Rundweys Fylde' sown with wheat worth 50*s.* and 7 a. sown with barley worth 50*s.* Total 256*l.* 17*s.* 8*d.*

8 Nov. 9 Eliz. I [1567]. *Liberate* returnable in quin. of Martinmas next [25 Nov.]; with *capias* against William's body.

Endorsed. The lands and goods have been delivered. William has not been found. C 239/33 no. 44

93 George Jones, gentleman, of Fyfeld parish

12 Nov. 10 Eliz. I [1568]. *Capias* returnable in quin. of Eas. next [24 Apr.], sued out by David Lewes, esquire, doctor of civil law, to whom George

acknowledged 500*l.* on 1 May 8 Eliz. I [1566] before Robert Catlyn, knight, chief justice of the Queen's Bench, payable at Whitsun then next [2 June]. Like writs to the sheriffs of Som. and Dors.
Endorsed. George has not been found.

1 Apr. 11 Eliz. I [1569]. Inquisition at Fyfyelde before George Ludlow, esquire, by Henry Good, John Ogborne, Thomas Barter, Thomas Knight, Thomas Lawes, John Cane, Robert Everlye, Peter Flatcher, Nicholas Rendall, Thomas Elmes, John Streate, and John Deane.

Possessed of the manor of Fyfield, worth 20*l.* yearly.

The following goods: 2 . . . [*MS. torn*], worth 40*s.*; 56 a. of land sown with wheat in the 'Westfeilde' in Fyfield parish, worth 37*l.* 6*s.* 8*d.*, and 6 a. sown with 'fetches' (*vesicis*), worth 4*l.*; 41 a. sown with barley in the 'Eastfielde' worth 27*l.* 6*s.* 8*d.* Total 70*l.* 13*s.* 4*d.*

C 239/34 no. 96

94 Thomas Goddard, gentleman, of Alborne

4 Dec. 11 Eliz. I [1568]. *Elegit* returnable on the morrow of the Purification next [26 Mar.], upon Thomas's nonappearance in Chancery to answer Henry Compton, esquire, of Compton Uyniates, Warws., to whom he acknowledged 200*l.* in Chancery on 3 Oct. 8 Eliz. I [1566], payable at Christmas then next; upon a *scire facias* to the sheriffs of London, who have returned that Thomas has not been found; as Thomas was given until oct. of Martinmas [18 Nov.] to make his answer, but failed to appear then in Chancery.

C 239/35 no. 12

95 Thomas Chatterton, gentleman, of Lydiatt

13 Feb. 11 Eliz. I [1569]. *Elegit* returnable in quin. of Eas. next [24 Apr.], sued out by William Reade, gentleman, of Bristol, to whom Thomas acknowledged 200*l.* in Chancery on 6 June 6 Eliz. I [1564], payable at Midsummer then next; upon a *scire facias* to the sheriffs of London, who have returned that Thomas has not been found.
Endorsed. The writ was received by George Ludlowe, sheriff, too late for execution.

11 May 11 Eliz. I [1569]. *Elegit* returnable in quin. of Mich. next [13 Oct.], upon Thomas's nonappearance in Chancery to answer William Reade.

C 239/35 no. 29

96 John Hamlyn, gentleman, of Surrendell

28 Apr. 12 Eliz. I [1570]. *Capias* returnable in quin. of Trin. next [4 June]; upon a *levari facias* to the sheriff of Mdx. for John Fawnte, clerk, vicar of Willesden, Mdx., who recovered 50*l.* against John; as the sheriff has returned that John held no lands or goods in his bailiwick from which the debt could be levied.
Endorsed. The sheriff has sent the writ to the bailiff of Chippenham hundred who has given no answer.

C 131/272 no. 37

97 William Horton, gentleman, of Iford

2 May 12 Eliz. I [1570]. *Extendi facias* returnable in oct. of Martinmas next [18 Nov.], for William Reade, gentleman, to whom William acknowledged 100*l.* in Chancery on 14 Feb. 11 Eliz. I [1569], payable on 17 Aug. then next; as William had sued out an *elegit* by default for 70*l.* of the debt to be levied from William's chattels and half of his lands in Wilts., following William's nonappearance in Chancery in 3 weeks from Eas. [1 May] after various writs of *scire facias* executed by the sheriffs of London, who also returned that William had no lands or goods there.

1 Sept. 12 Eliz. I [1570]. Inquisition at Stepleasheton before John Thynne, knight, by Anthony Styleman and John Lambe, gentlemen, Christopher Baylie, John Willys, Richard Allen, John Wylliams, Walter Wylkyns, Richard West, John Merywether, John Longe, William Lucas, and Henry Shaston.

Seised in his demesne as of fee of: 2 messuages, 3 tenements, 70 a. of land, 40 a. of meadow, and 100 a. of pasture in Chippenham parish, worth 16*l.* yearly; 12 messuages, 6 tenements, 22 a. of land, 8 a. of meadow, 6 a. of pasture in Trowbridge (10*l.*); a messuage and a tenement, 12 a. of land, 2 a. of meadow, and 14 a. of pasture in Iford in Westwoode parish (40*s.*); a tenement, 20 a. of land, 3 a. of pasture, and 3 a. of meadow in Byttessonne (16*s.*). Yearly value of the moiety 14*l.* 8*s.*

C 131/118 no. 12

98 Anthony Hungerforde, esquire, of Stocke

12 June 12 Eliz. I [1570]. *Capias* returnable in quin. of Mich. next [13 Oct.]; upon a *levari facias* to the sheriff of Mdx., for Humphrey White, citizen and merchant tailor of London, who recovered 100*l.* against Anthony in Chancery; as the sheriff has returned that Anthony held no lands or goods in his bailiwick from which the debt could be levied.

C 131/272 no. 41

99 William Sturton, knight, Lord Sturton, and Roger Sturton, esquire

24 Nov. 13 Eliz. I [1570]. *Capias* returnable in quin. of Trin. next [4 June], sued out by Thomas Charde, executor of William Charde, gentleman, of London, to whom William and Roger acknowledged 300*l.* on 26 June 32 Hen. VIII [1540] before John Baldwyn, knight, then chief justice of the Common Pleas, payable at Mich. then next. Like writs to the sheriffs of Dors. and Som.

Endorsed. William and Roger are dead.

12 Nov. 13 Eliz. I [1571]. *Extendi facias* returnable in quin. of Hil. next [27 Jan.] for those lands that have not descended by the law of heredity to any heir who is under age or passed into the queen's hands by attainder and for all goods and chattels.

17 Jan. 14 Eliz. I [1572]. Inquisition at Devises before Edward Baynton, esquire, by Edward Pyrry, Richard Harvest, William Sloper, Richard Wood-

roffe, John Duke, Robert Townesend, William Tayler, William Creche, William Good, Roger Segar, Thomas Page, and William Waddin'.

William was seised in his demesne as of fee of: the manor of Westbury worth 10*l.* yearly and 5 messuages and 400 a. of land, meadow, pasture, and wood in Westbury (6*l.* 3*s.* 4*d.*); the manor of Easton Greye (5*l.*); the manors or farms of Ablington, Alton, and Wellow in Fyhelden *alias* Fyelden parish and 2 capital messuages and 1,500 a. of land, meadow, pasture, and wood (20*l.*); 10 messuages in Potthorne and Cheverell (5*l.* 11*s.* 2*d.*); the manor of Westeashton and 10 messuages and 800 a. of land, meadow, and pasture in Westashton (10*l.* 10*s.* 8*d.*); the manor of Hilperton (4*l.* 13*s.* 4*d.*); 4 messuages in New Salisbury (6*l.*).

William and Roger had no other lands at the time of the recognizance and no goods at the times of their deaths.

15 Feb. 14 Eliz. I [1572]. *Liberate* returnable in quin. of Eas. next [20 Apr.]. Like writ to the sheriff of Som. for lands there worth 7*l.* yearly.
Endorsed. The lands were delivered on 12 Mar. 14 Eliz. I [1572].
C 239/37 no. 9

100 Henry Woodrofe, 'yoman', of Cawne, and John Michell, of Calston

19 Jan. 13 Eliz. I [1571]. *Elegit* returnable in 3 weeks from Eas. next [6 May] upon Henry and John's nonappearance in Chancery to answer John Warde, citizen and grocer of London, to whom they acknowledged 80*l.* in Chancery on 28 Feb. 11 Eliz. I [1569] payable at Eas. then next [10 Apr.]; as John had sued out a *scire facias* to the sheriffs of London, William Dane and Henry Becher, who returned that Henry and John had no lands or goods in London and had not been found; when Henry and John failed to appear in Chancery they were given until quin. of Eas. [9 Apr.] on which date they still failed to appear.

Because of the above writ the sheriff has delivered to John Warde the following goods of John Michell, appraised by William Taylor, William Browne, William Colman, Valentine Norton, Richard Hyscoxes, John Danyell, Thomas Gyles, John Bere, Thomas Gawyn, and Walter Segar: a 'barly reke' (*pira hordii*) with *c.* 40 cart-loads, worth 10*l.*; 2 'rekes of haye' (*piras feni*), 1 in the 'Sandes' and the other in Chowberowghe, worth 5*l.*; an 'yerne bound weyne' (*plaustrum ferrat'*) and all the gear belonging to a cart, worth 13*s.* 8*d.*; a 'dragge' (*rethe*) worth 8*s.* 8*d.*; a pair of 'ethes' worth 2*s.*; a 'solewe' worth 2*s.*; a 'joyned bedsted' (*lecticam*), a 'flockbed', a 'bolster' (*cervicale*), a 'coverlet' (*cooperturium*), a pair of 'blankettes' (*lancathecarum*), worth 17*s.* 4*d.*; a cupboard (*abacum*) with covering (*velamini*) and a chair, worth 6*s.* 4*d.*; 127 lb. of 'pewter' (*stanni*) worth 52*s.*; a 'joyned bedsted' worth 30*s.*; a 'flockbed', a bolster, a pair of blankets, and a coverlet, worth 20*s.*; a 'truckle bed' (*lecticam*), a 'flockbed', a pair of blankets, a coverlet, and a bolster, worth 25*s.*; 6 brass pots and a 'skellet' weighing 77 lb., worth 16*s.*; a furnace (*fornacem*), a cooking-pot (*cacabum*), 2 'brasse pannes' (*vasa enea*), a 'drip-pynge panne' and a 'chavendyshe' (*patena carbonifera*) weighing 53 lb., worth 19*s.* 4*d.*; a 'fetherbed' (*lectum plumalem*), a bolster, a pair of blankets, and a coverlet, worth 30*s.*; a horse (*equum*) worth 50*s.*; 5 'cosshynges' (*pulvinaria*) and a cupboard (*abacum*) worth 6*s.* 8*d.*; a 'fryinge panne' and 2 'dripping pannes' worth 2*s.*; 5 'broches' weighing 59 lb. worth 8*s.*; 3 candelsticks worth 4*s.*; a cupboard and 3 'hanginges' worth 6*d.*; a black gelding (*spadonem*) worth 31*s.* 8*d.*

The sheriff has delivered the following goods belonging to Henry Woodroff: a 'reke of wheate' (*piram frumenti*) worth 3*l.* 6*s.* 8*d.*

As the above are not sufficient to pay the debt, the sheriff has delivered the following lands belonging to John Michell: a 'tuckyng mylle' (*molendin' fullonicum*) and a close called 'Meryettes' now held by William Mathewe with *c.* 2 a. of pasture in Cawston, worth 10*l.* yearly; a messuage, a garden, a curtilage, 6 a. of arable land, and 2 a. of meadow in Cawne now in the occupation of Valentine Norton (40*s.*); a messuage and a close of 2 a. of pasture and 2 a. of meadow in Cawne now held by John Wayne (10*s.*); a messuage and a close with *c.* 3 a. of pasture in Cawne now held by Godfrey Percy *alias* Daye (20*s.*); a messuage and a close with *c.* 3 a. of pasture in Cawne parish now held by Richard Ilsley (26*s.* 8*d.*); a messuage and a close with *c.* 1 a. of pasture in Cawston parish now held by William Mathewe (20*s.*); a messuage and a garden in Cawston parish now held by Thomas Bassett (13*s.* 4*d.*); a messuage and a close with *c.* 3 r. of pasture in Cawne parish now held by Richard Buckland (13*s.* 4*d.*); a messuage and a close with *c.* ½ a. of pasture in Kennyt parish now held by John Cue (7*s.* 4*d.*); a messuage and a close with *c.* ½ a. of pasture in Cleve Annsey parish now held by Roger Harper (6*s.* 8*d.*); a messuage and a close with *c.* 3 r. of pasture in Cawne parish now held by Richard Burton (13*s.* 4*d.*). Half the above lands have been delivered to John Warde.

Henry Woodroff has no lands in Wilts. C 239/37 no. 18

101 William Latiwere, gentleman, of Brynckeworth

22 May 13 Eliz. I [1571]. *Capias* returnable in quin. of Trin. next [24 June], sued out by Edmund Stokes, 'yoman', of Langley Berrell, to whom William acknowledged 500*l.* on 26 May 5 Eliz. I [1563] before Robert Catlyn, knight, chief justice of the Queen's Bench, payable at Midsummer then next.

12 June 13 Eliz. I [1571]. Inquisition at Brynkworth before William Button, esquire, by John Smyth *alias* Davys the elder, John Pynnell, Thomas Beale, John Wynkworth, John Sherer, John Smyth *alias* Davis the younger, William Frye, William Beale the elder, Thomas Baylye, John Myll, James Scull, John Mathewe, William Busshell, and John Henley.

In Brynckeworth seised solely in his demesne as of fee on the day of the recognizance and on 1 June 13 Eliz. I [1571] of: a tenement called 'Trapps'; closes of meadow or pasture called 'Home Lease', 'Paddocke', 'Russhe Grove Hill', 'Russhe Grove Meade', the 'Breach', 'Litle Lakes', 'Rounsthyll Close', and 'Wyndmyll Fyeld', worth 18*l.* yearly.

C 239/37 no. 67

102 William Stourton, knight, Lord Stourton[1]

29 Feb. 14 Eliz. I [1572]. *Capias* returnable in quin. of Eas. next [20 Apr.], sued out by William Burde, esquire, executor of Thomas Longe, 'clothmaker', of Trowbrige, to whom William acknowledged 2,000*l.* on 22 Sept. 36 Hen. VIII [1544] before Ralph Waren, then mayor of the Staple of Westminster, and Roger Cholmeley, then recorder of London, knights, payable at Christmas then next. Like writs to the sheriffs of Som., Dors., and Mdx.
Endorsed. William is dead.

C 239/38 no. 38

103 Edward Morgan, esquire, of Whitchurche, and Thomas Stafford, esquire, of Bromham

19 June 14 Eliz. I [1572]. *Capias* returnable in quin. of Mich. next [13 Oct.], sued out by James Altham, esquire, of Latton, Essex, to whom Edward acknowledged 200*l.* on 20 May 13 Eliz. I [1571] before Robert Catlyn, knight, chief justice of the Queen's Bench, payable at Whitsun then next [3 June]. Like writs to the sheriffs of Lond. and Berks.
Endorsed. The lands were delivered to the queen on 6 Oct. 14 Eliz. I [1572]. Edward and Thomas have not been found.

30 Sept. 14 Eliz. I [1572]. Inquisition at Wylton before Edward Baynton, esquire, by Humphrey Bydlecombe, Henry Saunders, William Hayter, Christopher Mackes, Edward Hayward, Hugh Kynge, Thomas Clark, John Kynge, William Whytmershe, John Bampton, John Lyghte, and Roger Eastman.

Edward was seised in his demesne as of a free tenement of Rowde rectory and various lands in Rowde, Stanley, and Chipenham, worth 6*l.* 10*s.* yearly.

Thomas was seised in his demesne as of a free tenement in the right of his wife Isabel of: the manors of Tollard Baynton (8*l.*), Falston (20*l.*), and Lavington Fox and Lavington Baynton (20*l.*); the manor, farm, and sheep pasture of Temple Ruckley, commonly called Temple Downe (11*l.*).

C 239/38 no. 68

104 Anthony White, citizen and 'haberdassher' of London

8 Aug. 14 Eliz. I [1572]. *Capias* returnable in oct. of Mich. next [6 Oct.], sued out by John Conyers, mercer of London, to whom Anthony acknowledged 320*l.* on 15 Nov. 13 Eliz. I [1571] before Robert Catelyn, knight, chief justice of the Queen's Bench, payable at Christmas then next. Like writ to the sheriffs of Lond.
Endorsed. The sheriff has taken Anthony and put him in Fyssherton Auger prison. The lands have been delivered to the queen.

17 Sept. 14 Eliz. I [1572]. Inquisition at Wylton before Edward Baynton, esquire, by Humphrey Bydlecombe, Henry Saunders, William Hayter, Christopher Mackes, Edward Hayward, Hugh Kynge, Thomas Clark, John

[1] See 131 for further action on this case.

Kynge, William Whytmershe, John Bampton, John Lyghte, and Roger Estman.

At the time of the receipt of the writ seised in his demesne as of a free tenement with his wife Mary of ½ Falston manor worth 10*l.* yearly.

C 239/38 no. 81

105 Anthony Whyte, citizen and 'haberdassher' of London

27 Aug. 14 Eliz. I [1572]. *Capias* returnable in oct. of Mich. next [6 Oct.], sued out by Thomas Browne, citizen and merchant tailor of London, to whom Anthony acknowledged 240*l.* on 9 July 13 Eliz. I [1571] before Thomas Offley, knight, mayor of the Staple of Westminster, and William Fletewood, esquire, recorder of London, payable at St. James then next [25 July].
Endorsed. Anthony has not been found.

17 Sept. 14 Eliz. I [1572]. Inquisition at Wilton before Edward Baynton, esquire, by Humphrey Bydlecombe, Henry Saunders, William Hayter, Christopher Mackes, Edward Hayward, Hugh Kynge, Thomas Clark, John Kynge, William Whytemershe, John Bampton, John Lyght, and Roger Eastman.

Seised in his demesne as of a free tenement with his wife Mary of ½ the manor of Falston *alias* Fallersden worth 10*l.* yearly.

. . . [*MS. torn*] Oct. 14 Eliz. I [1572]. *Liberate* returnable in . . . , with *capias* against Anthony's body.

C 239/38 no. 82

106 Henry Beckingham, fishmonger, of New Salisbury, and Thomas Beckingham, merchant, of Norwic'

4 May 15 Eliz. I [1573]. *Capias* returnable in oct. of Mich. next [6 Oct.], sued out by Henry Wallys and Thomas Trunbull, citizens and fishmongers of London, to whom Henry and Thomas acknowledged 200*l.* on 1 Feb. 9 Eliz. I [1567] before Robert Catelyn, knight, chief justice of the Queen's Bench, payable at Eas. then next [30 Mar.].
Endorsed. Henry and Thomas have not been found.

6 July 15 Eliz. I [1573]. Inquisition at New Salisbury before John Seintjohn, esquire, by Thomas Crowche, gentleman, John Randall, William Feltham, Henry Warde, Edward Strugnell, Thomas Hayward, William Dyer, William Scamell, Thomas Dollynge, John Bacon, John Pile, Gilbert Best, and Gregory Cooke.

In New Salisbury Henry was seised in his demesne as of fee of: a capital messuage called the 'Colledge' now held by John Barkley, knight, worth 5*l.* yearly; a messuage called the 'Hermitage' now held by Henry himself worth 40*s.* yearly; a messuage with various gardens adjoining held by Richard Yonge worth 3*l.* yearly.

Thomas had no lands or goods in Wilts. C 239/39 no. 59

107 William Chatterton, esquire, of Brodefelde, and Henry Chatterton, gentleman, of Yowyn

16 Oct. 15 Eliz. I [1573]. *Capias* returnable in oct. of Hil. next [20 Jan.], sued out by James Altham, esquire, of London, to whom William and Henry acknowledged 600*l.* on 8 Dec. 10 Eliz. I [1567] before Robert Catelyn, knight, chief justice of the Queen's Bench, payable at Christmas then next. Like writ to the sheriff of Mdx.
Endorsed. The sheriff has issued a warrant to the constable of the town and liberty of Wooksey, parcel of the duchy of Lancaster, who replied that William and Henry have not been found.

Wed. 15 Jan. 16 Eliz. I [1574]. Inquisition at Wooksey before Thomas Ellys, constable and minister of the queen's liberty of Wooksey, parcel of the duchy of Lancaster, by a warrant from Walter Hungerford, knight, sheriff, by James Unnyng, William Coulston, William Baker, Walter Kyte, Richard Mager, William Browne, John Hayes, William Peers, John Palmer, John George, William Myllard, and Thomas Packer.

The following goods: a 'mowe' (*tasse*) of wheat and barley worth 12*l.*; 8 pigs worth 16*s.* 8*d.*; a parcel of hay, straw, and oats worth 20*s.*; 8 geese worth 4*s.*; 6 'ganny burdes' worth 2*s.*; 12 measures of wheat worth 24*s.*; a mill called 'a querne' worth 2*s.*; 2 brass pots worth 6*s.* 8*d.*; 2 brass vessels called 'pannes' worth 5*s.*; a pair of hooks (*hamor'*) called 'eyryns' worth 5*s.*; 2 pans (*patenis*) and 3 dishes (*paropsidis*) worth 2*s.*; 1½ cwt. of wood (*roborum*) worth 5*s.*; a wagon worth 2*s.*; a brass vessel called 'a cawdron' worth 12*d.*

3 Mar. 16 Eliz. I [1574]. *Capias* returnable in quin. of Eas. next [25 Apr.], as it is understood that William and Henry had other goods and also lands within the area of the sheriff's jurisdiction.
Endorsed. William and Henry have not been found. C 239/39 no. 109

11 Mar. 16 Eliz. I [1574]. Inquisition at Wotton Basset before Walter Hungerford, knight, by Nicholas Webbe, Richard Bathe, Thomas Parker, Thomas Jacobb, Robert Trynder, William Edwardes, John Hedland, Thomas Francklyn, Richard Heskyns, John Maslyn, Thomas Arman, and Thomas Bathe.

Henry had the following goods: 2 bedsteads (*thoralibus*) called 'standing bedstedes' and 2 other bedsteads of which 1 is called 'a . . . [*MS. torn*] bedsted' worth 23*s.* 4*d.*; 5 'fetherbeddes' worth 5*l.* 6*s.* 8*d.*; a pair of linen sheets (*lodicis lintor'*) called 'canvas sheetes' worth 5*s.*; 4 'coverlettes' (*coopertur'*) worth 10*s.*; 7 woollen sheets (*lodicis lane*) called 'blankettes' worth 15*s.*; 6 broaches (*verua*) worth 10*s.*; a cask of food (*doleolum cibi*) called 'a tubb of sowse' worth 16*d.*; a peck of butter worth 2*s.* 8*d.*; a 'flocke bedd' and a bolster worth 6*s.* 8*d.*; 8 pans (*paten'*) and a 'sawcer' (*patibul'*) worth 9*s.*; 4 brass vessels of which 1 is called 'a furnes' and 3 are called 'cawdrons' worth 24*s.*; a piece of iron called 'a dripping panne' worth 12*d.*; 2 pieces of iron called 'andyerns' worth 2*s.*; 2 pieces of iron called 'cobyrons' worth 4*s.*; a piece of iron called a 'fyer pyke' worth 16*d.*; 3 tables called 'table bordes' with forms (*scannis*) worth 10*s.*; 10 boxes (*cassis*) worth 2*s.*; 2 books of which one is called 'a bible' and the other 'Chawcer' worth 8*s.*; a crossbow (*balist'*), a piece of iron called 'a rack' and 2 arrows worth 16*s.*; 2 pigs worth 8*s.*; a vessel called 'a washefatt' worth 12*d.*; 2 parcels of hay worth 5*s.*; 3 vessels called 'chesefates' and 2 spoons (*coclear'*) worth 12*d.*; 2 vessels called 'a crocke' and 'a posnet' worth 3*s.* 4*d.*; a pair of painted boards (*pict' tabulor'*) worth . . . [*MS. torn*] *s.*; a piece of cloth (*panni*) called 'a curten' worth 12*d.*; 6 pillows (*sulsitr'*) called 'fether bolsters' and 3 called 'fether pillos' worth 35*s.*; 5 'flower pottes' worth 2*s.*; a 'water pott' worth 12*d.*; a chest (*cista*) called 'a coser' worth 2*s.*; a halter (*capistro*), a table, and a piece of iron called 'a curteyne rodd' worth 18*d.*; an altar (*ara*), 2 pieces of iron called 'a marking iron' and 'a chisell', and a scythe (*fasse*) worth 16*d.*; 2 jugs (*obbis*) called 'tynnen bottelles' worth 12*d.*; 3 lbs. of butter worth 22*d.*; a piece of iron called 'a frying pann' worth 12*d.*; 2 pieces of iron called 'a pestell' and 'a gredyren' worth 18*d.*; a brass pan (*paten'*) called 'a bason' worth 8*d.*; a gallon vessel (*legena*) of 'otemeale' worth 6*d.*; 3 casks (*doleolis*) of the drink called 'bere' worth 13*s.* 4*d.*; 2 pots of 'grese' (*pinguidinis*) worth 2*s.* 8*d.*; 7 pieces of cloth called 'say curtens' and 'a tester' worth 26*s.* 8*d.*; 6 vessels called 'a boulting whiche', 2 'vurkyns, a churne, a chesepresse, and a barrell' worth 3*s.* 6*d.*; a cupboard (*abbaca*) called 'a chayrt cubberd' worth 2*s.*; 2 pieces of iron called 'iron cheynes' worth 12*d.*; 2 . . . [1] worth 14*d.*; an axe (*secur'*) called 'a hatchyett' worth 8*d.*; 'paynted clothes' worth 3*s.* 4*d.*; 3 geese worth 2*s.*; a 'hawking glove' (*chereteca*) worth 6*d.*

C 239/40 no. 39

108 Thomas Chatterton, esquire, of Lydearde

26 Feb. [16] Eliz. I [1574]. *Capias* returnable in quin. of Eas. next [25 Apr.], sued out by James Altham, esquire, of Latton, Essex, to whom Thomas acknowledged 1,000*l.* on 29 Nov. 9 Eliz. I [1566] before Robert Catelyn, knight, chief justice of the Queen's Bench, payable at Christmas then next. *Endorsed.* Thomas has not been found.

8 Mar. 16 Eliz. I [1574]. Inquisition at Marlebrough before Walter Hungerford, knight, by William Kyng, Thomas Venny, Edward Gardner, John Stumpe, William Skory, John Grygge, William Croke, Walter Elmes, Thomas Parker, Robert Lasye, Henry Lawe, Thomas Lancaster, Robert Eaton, John Brusshe, and Robert Mylles.

Seised in his demesne as of fee of: the manor of Lyddeard Myllysent and messuages, mills, cottages, outhouses, barns, stables, dovecotes, gardens, orchards, lands, meadows, pastures, leasows, and feedings in Lyddeard Myllysent now or lately held by Thomas or his assigns; the chantry of Ramesbury and the house with orchard adjoining called the 'chauntry howse'; the tenement in Ramesbury lately of a yearly rent of 3*s.* 4*d.*; the tenement, 4 a. of several pasture, 2 a. of meadow called 'Stanmeade', and 24 a. of arable land in Pyrton held by John Rymon or his assigns; the tenement in Pyrton,

[1] MS. reads *cam' clabris cutis.*

3 a. of several pasture, ½ a. in 'Stanmeade', 8 a. of meadow yearly divided between 4 people by tasses, and 18 a. of land held by John Jakes or his assigns; the tenement, 7 a. of several pasture, 6 a. in 'Stanmeade', and 20 a. of arable land held by Robert Plover or his assigns; the tenement, 3 closes of 3 a., 2 a. in 'Stansmeade', and 22 a. of land held by Thomas Wallyngton or his assigns; the tenement, 2 a. of several pasture, 3 a. in 'Stansmeade', and 10 a. of arable land held by William Pryddy or his assigns; the tenement, 2 a. of several pasture, 1½ a. in 'Stanmeade', 1 a. of arable land held by Thomas Phyllips or his assigns; the tenement, 3 a. of pasture, 1 a. of arable land held by John Messenger or his assigns; the tenement, 8 a. of several pasture, 2 a. in 'Stanemeade', 2 a. of arable land held by Edmund Oteley or his assigns; the tenement, 8 a. of several pasture, 2 a. of meadow called 'Stanmeade', 2 a. of arable land held by Joan Workeman, widow, or her assigns; a cottage held by Thomas Mair. Total 50*l.* yearly.

On 12 Mar. 16 Eliz. I [1574] all lands were delivered to the queen, except the capital messuage or manor-house of Lyddeard Myllysent. The sheriff approached this house with the intention of delivering it to the queen. Mary Chaderton, wife of Thomas, George Kettelby and Henry Kettelby, gentlemen, Peter Care, 'yoman', John Turke, 'yoman', John Saunders, 'husbondman', and John Bolley, 'tayler', all of Lyddeard Myllysent, together with other wrongdoers and disturbers of the queen's peace arrayed in hostile manner with force and arms, namely with firearms (*tormentis*), crossbows (*balistis*), stones, swords, shields (*clippeis*), daggers, sticks (*bacilis*), bill-hooks (*falcastis*), and other arms, assembled at the manor house and shut its doors against the sheriff. George Kettelby, holding two firearms and a crossbow with arrow ready to shoot, shouted loudly at the sheriff, "Yf thow come here to take any possessyon thow shalt be the first that shall dye for yt". Then George and Peter Care discharged their firearms at the sheriff and the people in his party who came to his aid before they were 12 paces from the house and they threw great stones out of the windows at the party. Thus the sheriff was unable to take the house on that occasion, but on 2 Apr. 16 Eliz. I [1574] he was able to deliver it to the queen.

C 239/40 no. 37

109 [*Name missing*]

8 Apr. . . . [*MS. torn*] Eliz. I . . . Inquisition at Calne before Walter Hungerford, knight, by Thomas Reed . . . Richard Edwardes, John Coates, Philip Jones, Giles Hellier, Thomas Oliffe, and George Olyver.

In New Salisbury seised in his demesne as of fee of: [a tenement] held by John Hellier for a yearly rent of . . .; a tenement held by Robert Hawker for a yearly rent of . . . ; [a tenement] held by . . . Sweataple for a yearly rent of 20*s.*; a tenement in Brounestrete held by James Lealand for a yearly rent of 4*l.*; . . . yearly rent of 4*l.*; a tenement in Dragonstrete held by Edmund Hongerford for a yearly rent of 40*s.*; 3 tenements . . . in the several tenures of Anthony Pore, Henry Luke, and John Barker for yearly rents of 20*s.*; a tenement called the 'Gryffyn' . . . [held by] Katherine Stevens and Henry

Stocker for a yearly rent of 40*s.*; a tenement called 'Gilderland' held by Thomas Andrewes for a yearly rent of . . . ; a tenement held by Thomas Andrewes for a yearly rent of 20*s.*; 2 tenements and 2 gardens with a barn belonging to the tenement held by Roger Luxmore for a yearly rent of 33*s.* 4*d.* Total value of the rents . . . *l.* 16*s.* 8*d.*

The rents have been delivered to Robert Smythe.

C 131/123 no. 17

110 John Jones, 'clothyer', of Kevell

17 May 17 Eliz. I [1575]. *Capias* returnable in quin. of Trin. next [12 June], sued out by William Reade, gentleman, to whom John acknowledged 300*l.* on 11 Feb. 10 Eliz. I [1568] before James Dyer, knight, chief justice of the Common Pleas, payable at Eas. then next [18 Apr.].
Endorsed. John has not been found.

26 May 17 Eliz. I [1575]. Inquisition at Devizes before John Danvers, knight, by Thomas Longe, Nicholas Hulbarte, John Longe, John Markes, Robert Prior, Thomas Carpenter, John Rooke, William Goodenowghe, Thomas Somner, Robert Somner, Thomas Wylkyns, and Robert Harrys.

In Kevell seised in his demesne as of fee of: a tenement, 3 a. of meadow, 4 a. of pasture, 26 a. of arable land, pasture for an ox [in] 'Oxen Lease' and for 3 animals in the 'Northwoode', lately held by John Jones and now by Roger Blagden or his assigns; 16 a. of meadow called 'Baches Meades' lately held by John or his assigns, worth 40*s.* yearly. C 239/41 no. 40

111 William Latnar, 'yoman', of Brinckeworth

23 June 17 Eliz. I [1575]. *Capias* returnable in oct. of Mich. next [6 Oct.], sued out by Thomas Estcourte, gentleman, of Shypton Moyne, Glos., to whom William acknowledged 200 marks on 13 June 14 Eliz. I [1572] before James Dyer, knight, chief justice of the Common Pleas, payable at Midsummer then next.
Endorsed. William has not been found.

7 Oct. 17 Eliz. I [1575]. Inquisition at Marlebroughe before John Danvers, knight, by Geoffrey Provender, gentleman, William Webbe, of Lyddeard, gentleman, William Blake, Thomas Baylye, of Uphaven, Robert Mondaye, William Lavington, of Newnton, Godfrey Goodman, John Harrys, Richard Baylye, John Crooke *alias* Whood, William Edwardes, and Ambrose Hawkyns.

In Brynckworth seised in his demesne as of fee of: a messuage called 'Trappers', in which William was living at the time of the recognizance, and 2 closes of pasture or meadow of *c.* 10 a. called 'Home Lezes', worth 5*l.* yearly; closes of pasture or meadow called 'Redinges' of *c.* 6 a., the 'Breache' of *c.* 10 a., 'Russhe Grove' of *c.* 10 a., 'Russhe Grove Meade' of *c.* 5 a., worth 13*l.* yearly. On 29 Mar. 4 & 5 Philip and Mary [1558] William by an indenture granted the said closes to Brian Lec, to have and hold for himself his executors or assigns from Mich. for 61 years, with reversion to William in fee. Thus at the time of the recognizance William was seised in his demesne as of fee of the reversion, worth ¼*d.* yearly.

C 239/41 no. 50

112 Thomas Page, 'yoman', of Calston

21 Nov. 18 Eliz. I [1575]. *Capias* returnable in oct. of the Purification next [9 Feb.], sued out by Thomas Wynterbrowne, 'baker', and Richard Adams, fishmonger, citizens of London, to whom Thomas acknowledged 200*l.* on 17 June 10 Eliz. I [1568] before Robert Catelyn, knight, then chief justice of the Queen's Bench, payable at St. Bartholomew then next [24 Aug.].
Endorsed. The lands were delivered to the queen on 20 Jan. 18 Eliz. I [1575]. Thomas has not been found.

31 Dec. 18 Eliz. I [1575]. Inquisition at Marleborough before Robert Longe, esquire, by Thomas Yonge, gentleman, William Lyddeard the younger, John Bukley *alias* Yate, Robert Browne, John Turrant, Robert Playster, Edward Langbridge, John Collyns, Thomas Peers, Henry Coke, Thomas Dawley, and John Peche, gentleman.

On the day of the inquisition seised in his demesne as of fee of a capital messuage, 144 a. of land, 6 a. of meadow, 30 a. of pasture, and 3 a. of wood in Calston Wily, now held by Thomas himself, and of a messuage, 8 a. of land, and 2 a. of pasture held by John Ferret and William Edmay, worth 4*l.* yearly.

C 239/42 no. 2

113 Thomas Hudsun, gentleman, of East Grafton

7 Dec. 19 Eliz. I [1576]. *Capias* returnable in oct. of Hil. next [20 Jan.], sued out by Richard Hickman and Richard Hayward, citizens and 'clothworkers' of London, to whom Thomas acknowledged 200*l.* on 26 Nov. 19 Eliz. I [1576] before Christopher Wray, knight, chief justice of the Queen's Bench, payable on 30 Nov. Like writ to the sheriffs of Lond.
Endorsed. Thomas has not been found.

17 Dec. 19 Eliz. I [1576]. Inquisition at Est Grafton before Thomas Wroughton, knight, by John Noyse, Edward Brinsdon, Humphrey Griffin, Thomas Somersett, John Pyper, Robert Romsey, William Bennett, Stephen Markes, John Shadwell, George Swyper, William Whitchurch, Thomas Hurlebatt, Robert Pyper, and Nicholas Porter *alias* Sapper.

On the day of the inquisition in possession of: 7 cows worth 13*l.*; 2 bullocks worth 4*l.*; 3 bullocks and a bull worth 7*l.*; 4 bullocks worth 4*l.* 6*s.* 8*d.*; 4 calves worth 46*s.* 8*d.*; 8 oxen worth 20*l.*; 4 horses and 'a blind gelding' (*spadone*) worth 13*l.*.; 2 'litle nagges' (*equillis*) worth 5*l.* 3*s.* 4*d.*; 4 sows worth 33*s.* 4*d.*; a 'stak or rike of ottes' (*meta avenarum*) with *c.* 10 qr. of oats, worth 3*l.* 6*s.* 8*d.*; 'stakes or rikes of wheat' (*metis tritici*) with *c.* 26 qr. of wheat, worth 26*l.*; 'a stake or rike of rey' (*meta siliginar'*) with *c.* 5 qr. of rye, worth 3*l.* 6*s.* 8*d.*; 'a stake or rike of beanes' (*meta fabarum*) with *c.* 2 qr. of beans, worth 26*s.* 8*d.*; 'stakes or rikes of barly' with *c.* 20 qr. of barley, worth 13*l.* 6*s.* 8*d.*; 'a stake or rike of fetches' with *c.* 3 qr., worth 40*s.*; 'a stake or rike of pese' (*meta pisa-*

rum) with *c*. 2 qr. of peas, worth 26*s*. 8*d*.; 'a stake or rike of barly' (*meta ordii*) with *c*. 5 qr. of barley, worth 3*l*. 6*s*. 8*d*.; 'a stake of hay' (*meta feni*) worth 53*s*. 4*d*.; a plough not fitted with iron tires (*caruca sine ferreo ligata*) worth 12*s*.; 2 ploughs fitted with iron tires (*caruca ferreo ligata*), worth 53*s*. 8*d*.; a 'vanne' worth 10*s*.; 48 a. sown with wheat in the fields of Grafton worth 26*l*. 13*s*. 4*d*.; 9 a. sown with rye and wheat in the close called 'the Parke' worth 6*l*.

28 June 19 Eliz. I [1577]. *Liberate* returnable in quin. of Mich. next [13 Oct.]; with *capias* against Thomas's body.
Endorsed. The goods have been delivered. Thomas has not been found.

C 239/43 no. 8

114 William Kelwaye, knight, of Rockeborne, Hampshire

6 June 20 Eliz. I [1578]. *Capias* returnable in 3 weeks from Trin. next [15 June], sued out by Thomas Essex, esquire, of Chilrey, Berks., and John Vaughan and his wife, Anne Knevett, to whom William acknowledged 1,000*l*. on 28 [May] 7 Eliz. I [1565] before Robert Catlyn, then chief justice of the Queen's Bench, payable at Whitsun then next. Like writ to the sheriff of Hants.

C 239/44 no. 63

115 James Morres, of Little Farryngton

. . . [*MS. torn*]. *Capias* returnable in . . . , sued out by John Mores, gentleman, [of Eastlache, Glos.], son and heir of James, to whom James acknowledged 1,000*l*. on 27 Oct. 10 Eliz. I [1568] before James Dyer, knight, chief justice of the Common Pleas, payable at [St. Andrew then next] [30 Nov.]. Like writs to the sheriffs of Berks., Oxon., and Glos.

15 Nov. 20 Eliz. I [1578]. *Liberate* returnable in oct. of Hil. next [20 June]; as the sheriff has returned that on 12 Nov. last James was seised of . . . pasture called 'Steit' in Hanington parish and in his wife's right of a tenement in Devises, worth 13*l*. 6*s*. 8*d*. yearly. Like writs to the sheriff of Glos. in respect of lands at Eastlache Turvile worth . . . yearly and of Oxon. for lands there worth 8*l*. yearly.

C 239/44 no. 94

116 Edward Essex, esquire, of Mildenhale

10 July 21 Eliz. I [1579]. *Capias* returnable in oct. of Mich. next [6 Oct.], sued out by Hugh Stuckley, gentleman, of London, to whom Edward acknowledged 1,000 marks on 9 May 3 Eliz. I [1561] before Robert Catlyn, knight, then chief justice of the Queen's Bench, payable at Midsummer then next.
Endorsed. Edward has not been found.

6 Aug. 21 Eliz. I [1579]. Inquisition at Chippenham before Henry Knyvett,

knight, by the oath of John Reade and Isaac Tailor, gentlemen, John Scott, Thomas Smarte, John Curteis, of Boxe, John Wastfeilde, Henry Kedwyn, William Brewer, Robert Force, Robert Harris, William Maltman, Robert Symons, and Richard Wastfeild.

Seised in his demesne as of fee of: the manor of Eston Pers in Kynton, held by John Snell, esquire, Isaac Taylor, gentleman, John Light, Nicholas Light, and Thomas Light, worth 18*l.* yearly; 2 messuages held by John Snell or his assigns in Yatton Kennel, worth 56*s.* 8*d.* yearly.

C 131/126 no. 6

117 John Mychell, gentleman, of Cawlston

4 Dec. 22 Eliz. I [1579]. *Elegit* returnable in oct. of Hil. next [20 Jan.], upon the nonappearance in Chancery of William Mougareyge, Katherine Michell, widow, and John Michell, gentleman, to answer Stephen Duckett, gentleman, of London, to whom John acknowledged 50*l.* in Chancery on 14 Feb. 15 Eliz. I [1573], payable at Eas. then next [22 Mar.]; as Stephen had sued out a *scire facias* to Edward Osborne and Wolstan Dixey, sheriffs of Mdx., who returned that John was dead, and had then sued out a *scire facias* for the appearance in Chancery of John's tenants, to which Robert Longe, esquire, sheriff, returned that through Richard Thorne, Laurence Woodman, John Baker, and Richard Hacker he had served the writ on William, Katherine, and John, who were tenants of a messuage, 3 mills, 200 a. of land, 30 a. of meadow, and 42 a. of pasture in Cawlston, which were the lands of John at the time of the recognizance.

12 Jan. 22 Eliz. I [1580]. Inquisition at Calne before Nicholas Seyntjohn, esquire, by Thomas Michell, gentleman, William Breache, George Ailmer, Richard Chandler, Henry Wilcockes, William Tayler, John Danyell, Robert Scott the elder, John Somers, John Rogers, William Good, and Roger Parrvus.

Seised in his demesne as of fee of a messuage, 3 mills, 200 a. of land, 30 a. of meadow, 42 a. of pasture in Calston and Calne, worth 63*l.* 6*s.* 8*d.* yearly.

The moiety was delivered to Stephen on 12 Jan. 22 Eliz. I [1580].

C 239/46 no. 11

118 John Jones, clothier, of Kevell

15 Feb. 22 Eliz. I [1580]. *Capias* returnable in quin. of Eas. next [17 Apr.], sued out by William Reade, gentleman, to whom John acknowledged 300*l.* on 11 Feb. 10 Eliz. I [1568] before James Dyer, knight, chief justice of the Common Pleas, payable at Eas. then next [18 Apr.].

23 Mar. 22 Eliz. I [1580]. Inquisition at Bradforde before Nicholas Seyntjohn, esquire, by John Baylye, Edmund Baylye, John Drewse, Anthony Drewse, Henry Rogers, John Paynter, William Hendy, Richard Chapman, Edward Rogers, William Gybbens, Thomas Crooke, Luke Stevens, and John Sonnycke.

Seised in his demesne as of fee of a messuage and 25 a. of land, meadow, and pasture called 'Stevens' in Kevell, now held by Roger Blagden, worth 40*s*. yearly. C 131/126 no. 11

119 Egion Wilson, gentleman, of Henton

14 Feb. 22 Eliz. I [1580]. *Extendi facias* returnable in quin. of Eas. next [17 Apr.] for Henry Calverley, citizen and mercer of London, to whom Egion acknowledged 100*l*. on 11 Jan. 9 Eliz. I [1567] before James Dyer, knight, then chief justice of the Common Pleas, payable at Midsummer then next; as Henry had sued out a *capias* to which the sheriff has returned that Egion is dead.

Endorsed. The lands have been delivered to the queen.

11 Apr. 22 Eliz. I [1580]. Inquisition at Calne before Nicholas Seyntjohn, esquire, by Roger Seagar *alias* Parsons, John Danyell, Walter Seagar *alias* Parsons, Robert Scotte the elder, John Scotte, Charles Tyler, Robert Coleman, William Goddard, Thomas Bryan, William Breach, John Somers, and John Beare.

No goods in Wilts.

In Little Henton in Stepleashton parish: a capital messuage, garden, and orchard with dovecote and 76 a. of land, meadow, and pasture held by Dorothy Wilson, widow, worth 53*s*. 8*d*. yearly; a garden and 22 a. of land, meadow, and pasture held by the same (10*s*.).

The following moieties in Stepleashton: a tenement, garden, orchard, and dovecote and 68 a. of land, meadow, and pasture held by John Ballard (53*s*. 4*d*.); a tenement and garden and 18 a. of land, meadow, and pasture held by William Longe (33*s*. 4*d*.); a close and 24 a. of land, meadow, and pasture held by William White (20*s*.); a close and 13 a. of land, meadow, and pasture held by William Palmer (7*s*.); a tenement and 12 a. of land, meadow, and pasture held by Robert Whyte (13*s*. 4*d*.).

The following moieties in Chrystenmalford: a tenement, garden, and 47 a. of land, meadow, and pasture held by John Danvers, knight, (12*s*.); a tenement and garden and 8 a. of land, meadow, and pasture held by Robert Hamerbrydge (8*s*.); a tenement, garden, and orchard and 8 a. of land, meadow, and pasture held by — [*blank*] Evered (8*s*.); a tenement, garden, and orchard and 4 a. of land, meadow, and pasture held by — [*blank*] Barnes (6*s*.); a tenement, garden, and orchard and 5 a. of land, meadow, and pasture held by William Compton (7*s*.); a tenement, garden, and 'backsyde' and 11 a. of land, meadow, and pasture held by John Polle (10*s*.); a 'shope' and a small close belonging of *c*. 15 ft. held by Adam Reade (4*d*.); a tenement and 'backsyde', 20 a. of land, meadow, and pasture held by Nicholas Plumer (24*s*.); a tenement, garden, and 'backsyde' and 8 a. of land, meadow, and pasture held by Thomas Saunders (10*s*.).

. . . [*MS. torn*] 22 Eliz. I [1579–80]. *Liberate* returnable in 3 weeks from Eas. next [24 Apr.]. C 131/126 nos. 13-14

120 John Mydelcott, 'yoman', of Bysshopstrow

17 June 22 Eliz. I [1580]. *Liberate* returnable in oct. of Mich. next [6 Oct.]; with *capias* against John's body; upon a *capias* sued out by John Toppes, citizen and merchant tailor of London, to whom John acknowledged 1,000 marks on 9 May 20 Eliz. I [1578] before Christopher Wraye, knight, chief justice of the Queen's Bench, payable at Whitsun then next [18 May]; as the sheriff has returned that on 13 Apr. last John was in possession of: Boram rectory for a term of years, worth 20*l.*; 'a griest myll' and 'a fullynge myll' in Bisshopps Trowe for 4 years from Lady Day last, worth 20*l.*; 10 a. of pasture called 'Mancombe' in Warmester for a term of years, worth 6*l.* 13*s.* 4*d.*; 10 cows worth 15*l.*; 6 cows worth 7*l.*; and that on the day of the recognizance he was seised in his demesne as of fee of: the manor of Bishopes Trowe and lands belonging thereto, worth 40*s.* yearly, beyond 20*l.* to be paid for 2 years to John Temes and 50*l.* to be paid yearly to John Temes and his heirs at the end of 2 years; a piece of pasture called 'Mote Hill' in Warmester, 5 a. of meadow in 'Pitt Meade' in the south of the piece called 'Mootehill' in Warmyster (5*l.* 6*s.* 8*d.*); a piece of pasture called 'Westpilles marshe' in Warmister held by Clement Bathe (26*s.* 8*d.*); 7 a. of meadow in 'Pitt Meade' in Warmister (40*s.*); a messuage with various lands in Sutton held by Stephen Henton (43*s.* 4*d.*); a messuage and a close belonging in Warmyster held by Richard Bullocke (20*s.*); 2 a. of pasture in severalty next to 'Smalbrookes mill', 5 a. of meadow in 'Spurtmeade' in Warmester held by John Chamberlyn (40*s.*). *Endorsed.* The lands were delivered on 5 July 22 Eliz. I [1580].

C 239/46 no. 94

121 Edward Darrell, knight, of Litlecote

20 May 23 Eliz. I [1581]. *Extendi facias*[1] returnable in quin. of Trin. next [4 June], for Hugh Stukely, esquire, administrator of William Essex, knight, of Chepynglamborn, Berks., to whom Edward acknowledged 80*l.* on 9 Sept. 38 Hen. VIII [1546] before Ralph Waren, knight, then mayor of the Staple of Westminster, and Ralph Broke, esquire, then recorder of London, payable at All Saints then next [1 Nov.]; as Hugh had sued out a *capias* with like writ to the sheriff of Berks., to which the sheriff has returned that Edward is dead.

23 May 23 Eliz. I [1581]. Inquisition at Calne before Michael Earneley, esquire, by Robert Francklyn, gentleman, Roger Seegar *alias* Parsons, Roger . . . [*MS. blind*], Edward Woodroffe, Thomas Gawen, Henry Eye, John Weare *alias* Broune, Thomas Bryan, . . . , John Daniell, William Goddarde, Robert Coleman, Edward Aymes, and John Carpenter.

Seised in his demesne as of fee of: the manors of Lytlecote, Bewley, and Winterborne Mounton; the manors of Fytleton, Combe, Compton, and Hackleston; 20 messuages, 10 gardens, 30 cottages, 10 tofts, 2,200 a. of land, 220 a. of meadow, 1,200 a. of pasture, 410 a. of wood, 11*l.* in rents in Litlecote, Bewley, Knyghton by Ramsbery, Ramsbery . . . Fytelton, Combe by Fytleton, Compton, Hackleston, and Winterborne Mounton, worth 115*l.* 13*s.* 8*d.* yearly.

C 131/127 no. 1

[1] Writ printed in full in Appendix, pp. 127-8.

122 William Chaderton

30 June 24 Eliz. I [1582]. Inquisition at Marlebrough before William Bruncker, esquire, by Richard Colman, John Stumpe, William Franckelyn, Thomas Wynde, William Wynde, Humphrey Stawnton, Laurence Woolridge, John Buckeley *alias* Yate, Stephen Pears, Richard Chapman *alias* Hiscockes, Robert Kyngsman, and John Dysmer.

On 13 May 21 Eliz. I [1579], seised in his demesne as of fee of: the manor or capital messuage of Lyddyard Myllysent and messuages, cottages, outhouses, barns, stables, gardens, orchards, lands, meadows, feeding, pasture, and a mill in Lydyard Millysent, Shawe, and Braydon, once held by Thomas Chaderton, gentleman, and which on 13 May 21 Eliz. I [1579] were held by William Chaderton or his assigns, and other messuages, lands, meadows, feeding, and pasture in common in Pyrton held by Michael Rymon, Robert Jakes, Robert Plover, William Pryddy, Thomas Phillippes *alias* Maior, Christopher Cleeter, Edmund Oteley, William Hellys, and Thomas Wallyngton or their several assigns, worth 50*l.* yearly.

Seised as of a free tenement for life of: ⅔ of the manor or capital messuage of Bradfyeld and ⅔ of a capital messuage, 100 a. of land, 40 a. of meadow, 100 a. of pasture, 15 a. of wood, *c.* 5 a. of gorse and briar in Bradfeild held by Joan Workeman, widow, or her assigns, worth 20*l.* yearly.

C 131/127 no. 10

123 John Yonge, of Durneford, and Edward Yonge, his son and heir apparent

22 Nov. 25 Eliz. I [1582]. *Capias* returnable in quin. of Hil. next [27 Jan.], sued out by Edward Horton, of Westwood, to whom John and Edward acknowledged 400*l.* on 13 May 22 Eliz. I [1580] before James Dyer, knight, chief justice of the Common Pleas, payable at Midsummer then next. Like writ to the sheriff of Berks.

Endorsed. John and Edward have not been found.

5 Dec. 25 Eliz. I [1582]. Inquisition at Fisherton Auger before William Brouncker by William Graye, Thomas Wresley, John Porter, Richard Wresley, Henry Saunders, Robert Collier, Anthony Kellawaye, John Downton, George Richardes, John Saffe, Walter Graye, and Anthony Forde.

John is seised in his demesne as of fee of: a messuage in Mayden Bradley now held by Peter Bristowe worth 8*l.* yearly; a messuage in Westharham held by John Yonge himself (20*l.*); 2 tenements in Fisherton Auger held by Thomas Hoskins and John Bastard (3*l.* 3*s.* 4*d.*); a tenement in Barford held by William Blacker, gentleman (5*l.*). Total 36*l.* 3*s.* 4*d.* yearly. No other goods or tenements except the capital messuage called Durneford and 6 tenements in Eastharham and various goods previously taken and passed into the queen's hands by virtue of another writ.

Edward has no lands or goods in Wilts.

C 131/128 no. 6

124 John Mody, of Foxley

22 Nov. 25 Eliz. I [1582]. *Capias* returnable in oct. of the Purification next

[9 Feb.], sued out by John Lovell, 'tanner', of Marleborough, to whom John acknowledged 100*l.* on 28 Oct. 22 Eliz. I [1580] before Christopher Wray, knight, chief justice of the Queen's Bench, payable at Christmas then next. *Endorsed.* John has not been found.

10 Jan. 25 Eliz. I [1583]. Inquisition at Calne before Walter Hungerford, esquire, by Anthony Goddard and John Head, gentlemen, Robert Colman, John Wastefeld the elder, Edward Butler, William Hale, Anthony Groome, Robert Scotte the elder, John Norborne, Thomas Milles *alias* Saunders, Richard Arnold, and John Hedland.

Seised in fee of the manor of Foxley and various lands, meadows, feeding, and pasture in Foxley worth 50*l.* yearly.

C 131/128 no. 8

125 Henry Hooper, gentleman, of Lyncolnes Inne, Middlesex

30 Oct. 25 Eliz. I [1583]. *Liberate* returnable in . . . [*MS. torn*] of Mich. next; with *capias* against Henry's body; upon a *capias* sued out by Edward Mathewe, gentleman, of Bulforde, to whom Henry acknowledged 1,000*l.* on 9 Feb. 21 Eliz. I [1579] before Christopher Wraye, knight, chief justice of the Queen's Bench, payable at Eas. then next [19 Apr.]; as the sheriff has returned that Henry has not been found and that on 5 Oct. 25 Eliz. I [1583] he had no goods in Wilts. and was seised in his demesne as of fee of: a capital messuage in New Salisbury in the west part of Castle Streete held by Christopher Ellyott or his assigns, and 2 gardens belonging to the messuage, worth 5*l.* yearly; 2 gardens next to the said garden held by John Odell or his assigns (20*s.*); a messuage and garden in Katheryne Streete called 'the Whyte Hart' held by Richard Vaughan or his assigns (40*s.*); a messuage and garden in Tanners street held by — [*blank*] Aston or his assigns (20*s.*); a messuage, garden, and close of land belonging and . . . [*MS. blind*] garden lying near the messuage in Fysherton Auger in the west part of a street there held by Anne Felt . . . assigns, (46*s.* 8*d.*); a toft with 2 a. of arable land and depasturing for 2 animals in Little . . . in Fysherton Auger held by John Penycott or his assigns (16*d.*). Total 11*l.* 12*s.*

C 239/49 no. 109

126 John Sturges, gentleman, of Wolverton *alias* Wolffington, Somerset

14 Nov. 25 Eliz. I [1583]. *Capias* returnable in quin. of Hil. next [27 Jan.], sued out by Roger Newborough, esquire, of Berkeley, Som., to whom John acknowledged 1,000*l.* on 30 Nov. 17 Eliz. I [1574] before Christopher Wray, knight, chief justice of the Queen's Bench, payable at Christmas then next. Like writ to the sheriff of Som.
Endorsed. John has not been found.

19 Dec. 26 Eliz. I [1583]. Inquisition at Warmyster before Jasper Moore, esquire, by Richard Mounpesson, esquire, William Middlecote, Philip Morgan, William Bower, and William Townsend, gentlemen, Robert Morren,

John Bowland, John Elderton, John Whatley, of Wesberye, Clement Bathe, John Yearberye, and William Bowcher.

Seised in his demesne as of fee of 17 messuages, a fulling-mill called 'Langnams Myll', 20 a. of land, 50 a. of meadow, 60 a. of pasture, 70 a. of wood, and 50 a. of gorse and briar in Langnam and Northbradley, worth 33*s*. 4*d*. yearly. C 131/128 no. 7

14 Feb. 26 Eliz. I [1584]. *Liberate* returnable in quin. of Eas. next [3 May]; with *capias* against John's body. Like writ to the sheriff of Som. in respect of lands there worth 26*l*. 13*s*. 4*d*. yearly.

The lands were delivered on 18 Feb. 26 Eliz. I [1584]. John has not been found. C 239/50 no. 38

127 Edward Essex, esquire, of Great Lamborne, Berkshire

17 Feb. 26 Eliz. I [1584]. *Capias* returnable in quin. of Eas. next [3 May], sued out by Hugh Stucley, gentleman, of London, to whom Edward acknowledged 500 marks on 24 Apr. 4 Eliz. I [1562] before Robert Catlyn, knight, then chief justice of the Queen's Bench, payable at Whitsun then next [17 May].

Endorsed. Edward has not been found.

31 Apr. 26 Eliz. I [1584]. Inquisition at Devizes before Jasper Moore, esquire, by Edmund Stokes, gentleman, William Edwardes, William Purnell, Richard Bayly, Matthew Benger, Paul Sammon, Richard Grene, Thomas Scott, Thomas Butcher, Anthony Hautt, Richard Ruddell, and William Roland.

Seised in his demesne as of fee of: the manor of Eston Pers in Kynton, held by John Snell, esquire, Isaac Taylor, gentleman, John Lyghte, Nicholas Lyghte, and Thomas Lyghte, worth 16*l*. yearly; 2 messuages held by John Snell or his assigns in Yatton Kennell, worth 56*s*. 8*d*. yearly. C 131/129 no. 3

128 William, Lord Mountjoye, Charles Blounte, esquire, and John Willoughbye, gentleman

17 Feb. 27 Eliz. I [1585]. *Capias* returnable in 3 weeks from Eas. next [2 May], sued out by Richard Arnold, citizen and grocer of London, to whom William, Charles, and John acknowledged 400*l*. on 2 Aug. 25 Eliz. I [1583], payable at Mich. then next.

5 . . . [*MS. torn*] 27 Eliz. I [1584–5]. Inquisition at Westburye before John Snell, esquire, by . . . William Trenchar, esquire, Walter Bashe, and Thomas Bennett, gentlemen, Thomas . . . Boocher, James Callard, William Rawlins, and William Bowyer.

On 18 May . . . Eliz. I William was seised in his demesne as of fee tail of:

½ of the manor of Brooke and Over[coorte] worth 75*l.* 6*s.* 8*d.* yearly . . . yearly value in rents and farms 3*l.* . . . of a capital messuage in Imber worth . . . yearly.

Charles and John have no lands or goods in Wilts.

C 131/129 no. 19

129 Thomas Chaderton, esquire, of Lydyard Millicent

25 Jan. 27 Eliz. I [1585]. *Elegit* returnable in quin. of Eas. next [25 Apr.] upon Thomas's nonappearance in Chancery to answer William Nele, esquire, of London, to whom Thomas acknowledged 120*l.* in Chancery on 9 Dec. 9 Eliz. I [1566], payable at Christmas then next; as William had sued out a *scire facias* to the sheriffs of Mdx., William Masham and John Spencer, who have returned that Thomas had no lands or goods in Mdx. and has not been found.

2 Mar. 27 Eliz. I [1586]. Inquisition at Crycklade before John Snell, esquire, by Richard Patsall, William Webbe, Henry Barnard, and William Garrett, gentlemen, William Rushlowe, of Chelworth, Richard Church the elder, Robert Looker, Richard Bathe the elder, Hugh Trynder, John Burge, Robert Hobbes, and William Symons.

In Lydyard Millisent seised in his demesne as of fee of: a capital messuage, a garden, an orchard, a 'backsyde', and a pasture called 'the Grove' next to the said messuage, worth 50*s.* yearly; a piece of land called the 'Brech' and a ruined wind-mill (40*s.*); a piece of land called the 'More' and 'Byrry fyldes' and the 'Stonefylde' (10*l.*); a pasture called 'Berry Marsh' (4*l.*); a field called 'Shylfynch' (40*s.*); 2 meadows called 'Borden brigge meade' and 'Lewe meade' (40*s.*); a meadow in Shawe in Lydyard Millisent parish (6*l.*); a wood within the common land of Braden in Lydyard Millisent parish (40*s.*).

Half of the above lands were delivered on 2 Mar. 27 Eliz. I [1586].

C 239/51 no. 15

130 William Poole, gentleman, son of Henry Poole, esquire, of Dicheninge, Sussex

4 Nov. 27 Eliz. I [1585]. *Capias* returnable in quin. of Martinmas next [25 Nov.], sued out by Margaret Poole, relict and administratrix of Henry Poole, to whom William acknowledged 1,000*l.* on 1 Dec. 22 Eliz. I [1579] before James Dyer, knight, then chief justice of the Common Pleas, payable at Christmas then next.

Endorsed. William has not been found.

13 Nov. 27 Eliz. I [1585]. Inquisition at Malmesburye before John Snell, esquire, by John Jaques, William Mabsoun, Henry Grayle, Richard Olyver, Richard Smarte, Nicholas Con . . . [*MS. blind*], all of Malmesburye, John Grymer, of Westpott, John Yowe and John Coole, both of Somerforde, William Broune, Giles Robertes, William Pytman, and Thomas Myles.

Seised in his demesne as of a free tenement for life of ½ of a farm and demesne lands called 'Somerford Mawdittes' and ½ of a water-mill called 'Kingesmede Mylne' in Somerford, worth 45*l.* yearly.

27 Nov. 28 Eliz. I [1586]. *Liberate* returnable in oct. of Hil. next [20 Jan.]; with *capias* against William's body.
Endorsed. The lands were delivered on 3 Dec. William has not been found. The writ was delivered by John Snell, former sheriff, to John Danvers, knight, sheriff. C 131/129 no. 9

131 William Stourton, knight, Lord Stourton[1]

8 June 28 Eliz. I [1586]. *Capias* returnable in 3 weeks from Trin. next [19 June], sued out by William Burde, esquire, executor of Thomas Longe, 'clothmaker', of Trowbridge, to whom William acknowledged 2,000*l.* on 22 Sept. 36 Hen. VIII [1544] before Ralph Waren, then mayor of the Staple of Westminster, and Roger Cholmley, then recorder of London, knights, payable at Christmas then next. Like writs to the sheriffs of Som., Dors., and Mdx.
Endorsed. William is dead.

The lands were delivered to Robert Chambers, gentleman, assignee of William Burde, on 25 Mar. 29 Eliz. I [1587]. C 239/52 no. 72

27 Oct. 28 Eliz. I [1586]. *Extendi facias* returnable in oct. of Martinmas next [18 Nov.].

31 Jan. 29 Eliz. I [1587]. *Liberate* returnable in quin. of Eas. next [30 Apr.]; as John Danvers, sheriff, has returned that William was seised in his demesne as of fee of: the manors of Danges Langford (40*s.*), Dennys Langford (40*s.*), and Westburye (10*l.*) and lands in New Salisbury (40*s.*) and Mayden Bradley (20*s.*); the manor of Yarnefeld and other lands in Yarnefeld (20*s.*); other lands by New Salisbury called 'Douse Courte' (10*s.*), and lands in Hildeverell called 'Southwigmores' and 'Estwigmores' and other lands in Hildeverell parish (3*s.* 4*d.*). Total 18*l.* 13*s.* 4*d.* The above were delivered to the queen on 17 Nov. last. Like writ to the sheriff of Som. in respect of manors and lands there worth 24*l.*, of Dors. for manors and lands worth 18*l.* 14*s.*, and of Mdx. for a messuage and lands there worth 4*l.* yearly.
C 239/38 no. 38

132 William, Lord Mountjoy

3 Dec. 29 Eliz. I [1586]. *Elegit* by default returnable in oct. of Hil. next [20 Jan.], sued out by Edward Skipwith, gentleman, of Westminster, to whom William acknowledged 100*l.* in Chancery on 1 Aug. 24 Eliz. I [1582]; upon a *scire facias* executed by Robert Howse and William Elkyn, sheriffs of Mdx.
Endorsed. The writ was received by the sheriff too late for execution.
C 239/53 no. 16

[1] See 102 for an earlier *capias*.

133 Thomas Crowche, 'yoman', of Fysherton Auger

7 June 29 Eliz. I [1587]. Inquisition at Fisherton Auger before Edmund Ludlowe by Alexander Liwater, gentleman, John Basterd, Edward Stringall, Robert Ward, George Michel, . . . [*MS. blind*] Randall, John Warde, Henry Stringall, John Marshall, Thomas . . . , Roger Cooke, Richard Ellis, and Robert . . .

Seised in his demesne as of fee of a messuage, a garden, an orchard, and a meadow of *c.* ½ a. belonging to the messuage and situated in Fyssherton Auger, lately held by Thomas himself and worth 3*s.* yearly.

8 July 29 Eliz. I [1587]. *Liberate* returnable in quin. of Mich. next [13 Oct.]; upon a *capias* sued out by Nicholas Mussell, gentleman, of Steple Langford, to whom Thomas acknowledged 200*l.* on 6 June 2 Eliz. I [1560] before Edmund Anderson, knight, chief justice of the Common Pleas, payable at Midsummer then next; as the sheriff has returned that Thomas died last Mar.

C 239/53 no. 109

134 [*Name missing*]

[*MS. torn*] [Inquisition at] . . . on . . . 29 Eliz. I [1586–7] before Edmund Ludlowe, esquire, by . . . Willis, gentleman, Robert Blackborraue, Walter West, Thomas Bartlett, William Temple, Richard Dewe, John Stanlocke, Roger Blackdeane, John Elderton, and William Carre.

In Lavington Baynton seised in his demesne as of fee of a messuage, 15 a. of meadow, 3 a. of pasture, 18 a. of land, a messuage . . . worth 36*s.* yearly; 5 a. of meadow, 3 a. of pasture, 21 a. of arable land and . . . (30*s.*); a messuage, 6 a. of meadow, 1 a. of pasture, 48 a. . . . now held by William Hiscockes (13*s.* 4*d.*); a messuage, 3 a. . . . held by Robert Andrewes (13*s.* 4*d.*); 3 . . . held by John Smithe (13*s.* 4*d.*); . . . [feeding] for 60 sheep and 6 animals held by Thomas Purches (13*s.* 4*d.*), Agnes Clarcke (13*s.* . . .), and Elizabeth Hille (10*s.*); . . . held by John Hurrell (13*s.* 4*d.*); a messuage, 28 a. . . . held by Agnes Clarcke *alias* Peirce (10*s.*); a messuage, 1 a. of meadow, 7 a. of land . . . Hille (6*s.* 8*d.*); a messuage, 4 a. of land, and pasture in common for 3 animals . . . 7 a. of arable land and pasture in common for 3 animals, held by Robert Sainisburye; . . . pasture in common for 3 animals, held by Henry Shettell . . . now held by John Dauntsey, esquire, (20*s.*); a cottage . . . ; a cottage held by Philip Browse (12*d.*); a water-mill and cottage held by Joan Cheyne, widow, (13*s.* 4*d.*); a cottage . . . held by Nicholas Reynolde (12*d.*); a cottage . . . held by Edith Howper (12*d.*); a messuage, a cottage, 1 a. of meadow, 1 a. of pasture . . . held by Laurence Stanlicke (21*s.*).

In Lavington Rector a messuage, a cottage, 6 a. . . . held by Thomas Godfreye (25*s.*); a messuage, 3½ a. of meadow held by Christian Newlon (13*s.* 4*d.*); 3 a. . . . and 12 animals, held by Christian Fitts (26*s.* 8*d.*); . . . 60 sheep and 6 animals, held by John Whoode (13*s.* 4*d.*); pasture in common for 60 sheep and 9 animals, and a cottage held by John Hampton; . . . 20 a. of arable land and pasture in common for 60 sheep and 6 animals held by . . . Maryard; . . . of meadow, 1 a. of pasture, 20 a. of arable land, and pasture in common for 60 sheep and 6 animals . . . ; . . . messuage, 1 a.

of meadow, ½ a. of pasture, 12 a. of land, and pasture in common for 3 animals . . . ; . . . cottages, 24 a. of land held by John Sainisburye . . . ; . . . called 'Ham Asheveylle' held by John Sainysburye; . . . a. of arable land and pasture in common for 2 animals held by . . . ; . . . held by William Rogers; . . . (4*s.*); a messuage and 2 a. of arable land . . . messuages, 4 a. of arable land . . . held by Nicholas Dunier . . . held by John Hame . . . (12*d.*); a cottage . . . held by Nicholas . . . ; . . . held by John Darrell . . . ; . . . held by Henry Hille . . . for 3 years to come from an estate lately dissolved . . . also the farm of Imber and lands belonging to it.

C 239/53 no. 223

135 William, Lord Mountjoye, and Charles Blount, of London

4 Dec. 30 Eliz. I [1587]. *Capias* returnable in oct. of the Purification next [10 Feb.], sued out by Randal Wolley, citizen and merchant tailor of London, to whom William and Charles acknowledged 200*l.* on 21 Nov. 27 Eliz. I [1584] before Edmund Anderson, knight, then chief justice of the Common Pleas, payable at Christmas then next. Like writs to the sheriffs of Dors., Devon, and Cornw.
Endorsed. William and Charles have not been found.

14 Feb. 30 Eliz. I [1588]. *Liberate* returnable in quin. of Eas. next [21 Apr.]; with *capias* against the bodies of William and Charles; as the sheriff has returned as follows. William was seised in his demesne as of fee of: ½ of the manors of Brooke and Overcourte, worth 87*l.* 12*s.* 8*d.* yearly; tenements in Paxcrofte, Henton, and Marston worth 3*l.* 5*s.* 11*d.* yearly; a capital messuage in Imber worth 33*s.* 4*d.* yearly; total 92*l.* 11*s.* 11*d.* Charles had no lands or goods in Wilts. The above were delivered to the queen on 24 Jan. last. Like writ to the sheriff of Dors. in respect of the manors of Lytton, Wydehooke, and Hadscombe, and ½ of the manor of Mangerton and ⅔ of the messuages and 'mynes' worth 58*l.* yearly.
Endorsed. The lands were delivered on 3 Mar. William and Charles have not been found.

C 239/54 no. 51

136 William Blount, Lord Mountjoy

21 May 30 Eliz. I [1588]. *Liberate* returnable in oct. of Trin. next [9 June]; with *capias* against William's body; upon a *capias* sued out by Thomas Dowse, gentleman, of Collingborne, to whom William acknowledged 500*l.* on 21 May 26 Eliz. I [1584] before Edmund Anderson, knight, chief justice of the Common Pleas, payable at Whitsun then next [7 June], with like writs to the sheriffs of Mdx., Lond., Devon, Surr., and Cornw.; as the sheriff has returned that William has not been found and that he was seised in his demesne as of fee tail of: ½ of the manors of Brooke and Overcote, worth in rents and farms 75*l.* 6*s.* 8*d.*; ½ of certain lands in Paxcroft and Henton, worth in rents and farms 33*s.* 4*d.*, worth 80*l.* 5*s.* 10*d.* yearly. Like writ to the sheriff of Dors. in respect of lands there worth 13*l.* 12*s.* 4*d.* yearly.
Endorsed. William has not been found.

C 239/54 no. 84 b

137 Simon Yate, son and heir of Thomas Yate, gentleman, late of Highworth, deceased

22 May 30 Eliz. I [1588]. *Scire facias, sicut alias* to the sheriffs of Mdx.[1] for Simon's appearance in Chancery in oct. of Trin. [9 June], to answer Margaret Proves, relict and administratrix of William Proves, 'yoman', of Eastegrenewiche, Kent, who died intestate on 29 Apr. 30 Eliz. I [1588], to whom Simon acknowledged 500*l.* in Chancery on 26 May 10 Eliz. I [1568], payable at Whitsun then next [6 June]; upon a *scire facias* for Simon's appearance in Chancery on the day after the Ascension [17 May]. Margaret is to have judgment by default, as Simon has failed to appear and Thomas Skynner and John Catcher, sheriffs of Mdx., have returned that he held no goods in Mdx. and has not been found. C 43/10 no. 171

20 Mar. 31 Eliz. I [1589]. Inquisition at Pirton before Walter Hungerford, knight, by Francis Kemble, Robert Blake *alias* Jaques, William Hellier, Edmund Oteley, Robert Plover, Thomas Wallington, Christopher Cliter, John Packer, Thomas Major, Michael Ryman, Leonard Pridye, and Arthur Iles.

Seised in his demesne as of fee of 4 messuages, 2 cottages, 2 barns, 80 a. of land, 30 a. of meadow, and 40 a. of pasture in the parish and fields of Highworth, Easthroppe, Westroppe, and Hampton Turvyll, worth 16*l.* yearly. Moiety delivered to John Bridges, gentleman, attorney of Margaret Proves. C 131/133 no. 12

138 Henry Baynton, esquire, of Edington

9 May 31 Eliz. I [1589]. *Scire facias* to the sheriffs of Mdx.[2] for Henry's appearance in Chancery on the morrow of Trin. [26 May] to answer Henry Cavendishe, esquire, of Tutburie, Staffs., and William Cavendishe, gentleman, of Grayes Inne, Mdx., to whom Henry acknowledged 400 marks in Chancery on 13 July 16 Eliz. I [1574], payable at Mich. then next; upon a *scire facias* dated 26 Mar. 31 Eliz. I [1589] for Henry's appearance in Chancery in one month from Eas. next [27 Apr.]. William and Henry are to have judgment by default, as Henry has failed to appear and Hugh Offley and Richard Saltonstall, sheriffs of Mdx., have returned that Henry held no goods in Mdx. and has not been found. C 43/10 no. 221

27 Sept. 31 Eliz. I [1589]. Inquisition at Trowbridge before Walter Hungerford, knight, by Walter Bushe and Anthony Webbe, gentlemen, Anthony Pickringe, Robert George, William Wilkins, William Widden, Richard Axford, Edward Rogers, Edmund Baylie, Henry Tylton, John Selfe, Thomas Pinchin, and Henry Bowell.

Seised in his demesne as of fee tail of the manor of Lavington, worth 30*l.* yearly, and the manor of Temple Rockley, worth 13*l.* 14*s.* 8*d.* yearly. In

[1] No writ to the sheriff of Wilts. has been found. See *Introduction*, p. 6.
[2] No writ to the sheriff of Wilts. has been found. See *Introduction*, p. 6.

possession of a yearly rent of 10*l.* from a messuage and various acres of land, meadow, and pasture held by John Hampton, gentleman. The moiety of these manors with the moiety of a messuage, 219 a. of land, 76 a. of meadow, and 178 a. of pasture in Lavington held by Jasper Moore, esquire, and his wife, Katherine, worth 3*l.* 2*s.* 8*d.* yearly, and the moiety of the yearly rent have been delivered.

C 131/133 no. 7

139 Andrew Rogers

28 May 31 Eliz. I [1589]. Inquisition at Urchefont before Walter Hungerford, knight, by John Flower, gentleman, William Edwardes, Thomas Dawndie, John Bewlie, William Purnell, John Sheareall, William Myntie, Thomas Lyne, John Phelpes, Robert Bewlie, John Benett, William Springe, John Saintsburye, Edward Giddings, and William Whood.

On the day of the recognizance, 4 July 27 Eliz. I [1585], seised in his demesne as of a free tenement for life in Urchfont of: a messuage or farm with 2 gardens, an orchard, 2 barns, a stable, a 'malthowse' (*domo bracear*'), a cowshed and a dovecote belonging to it; a pasture called 'Neither' of *c.* 12 a. and a pasture called 'Over Breach' of *c.* 20 a.; 20 a. of meadow called 'Filt Meade' and 4 a. called 'Harmerst Meade' and 50 a. of arable land in the common fields; a hill called 'sheepe downe', a piece of land called 'a yowe slayghte', 18 a. of meadow called 'Homismeade', 6 a. called 'Newe meade', 7 a. called 'Longe Lie', 2 a. called the 'Moore', 4 a. called 'White Crofte', and 60 a. of wood. All the above are held by George Mortimer by Andrew's grant for a yearly rent of 160*l.* payable to Andrew or his assigns.

C 131/133 no. 10

140 John Michell

2 June 31 Eliz. I [1589]. Inquisition at Calne *alias* Cawlne before Walter Hungerford, knight, by Roger Chevers, gentleman, Ralph Sloper, John Somers, Richard Warne, William Harris, Thomas Page, Richard Hutchins, John Philippes, Walter Browne, John Pountney, Henry Rogers, John Scott the younger, and Walter Stapleford.

Seised in his demesne as of fee of: a barn, a cowshed, and another outhouse, with close, garden, and orchard belonging, in Cawlston; 160 a. of arable land and a 'shepe pasture' in 'le Downe' in Cawlston fields; an outhouse with pasture and meadows called 'Knightes Mashe' in Stoke parish; a meadow called 'Dircuttes Meade' in Blaklande parish; 2 pastures called 'Ashones Meade', 2 meadows called 'Scutes Meade' and 'Marshs Close', and a tenement in Quemerforde with pastures and meadows, occupied by Richard Warne; a tenement occupied by Godfrey Pirrys; a pasture in Stockley called 'Chinniokes' occupied by John Freatos; tenements occupied by Isabel Mathew, widow, Thomas Bassett, Richard Bockland, Margery Youngs, and Godfrey Greneway. Total 46*l.* 13*s.* 4*d.*

The above were delivered to the queen so that they might be passed to Robert Wolters.

C 131/133 no. 9

141 William Goddard, gentleman, of Cherhill

13 Aug. 31 Eliz. I [1589]. *Capias* returnable in oct. of Mich. next [6 Oct.], sued out by Anselm Symes, 'yoman', of Clatford, to whom William acknowledged 200*l.* on 27 Nov. 31 Eliz. I [1588] before Edmund Anderson, knight, chief justice of the Common Pleas, payable at Christmas then next. *Endorsed.* William has not been found.

2 Sept. 31 Eliz. I [1589]. Inquisition at Cherill before Walter Hungerforde, knight, by Robert Nicholas, gentleman, Henry Crippes, Simon Sloper, William Good, John Reave, William Taylour, William Stratton, Richard [W]arren, William Harrys, John Somers, Henry Rogers, John Scott, William Dangerffyld, John Bradfeild, and John Felpes.

On the day of the recognizance and after, seised in his demesne as of fee simple of a messuage now or late called 'Walter House' and a virgate of land called 'a yarde lande' in Cherrell belonging, occupied by William or his assigns, worth 6*l.* 13*s.* 4*d.* yearly.

On the day of the inquisition, in possession of: 1 qr. of 'wheate', 1 qr. of 'barlye', 1 qr. of 'pease' worth 25*s.*; 2 cart-loads of 'haye' worth 10*s.* Total 35*s.*

13 Oct. 31 Eliz. I [1589]. *Liberate* returnable in oct. of Hil. next [20 Jan.]; with *capias* against William's body.
Endorsed. The above were delivered on 1 Dec. 32 Eliz. I [1589]. William has not been found.

The writ thus endorsed was delivered to Henry Willugby, esquire, sheriff, by Walter Hungerford, knight, on his departure from office.

C 239/55 no. 125

142 Henry Ferrers, gentleman, of Middle Temple, London

9 July 32 Eliz. I [1590]. *Elegit* returnable in quin. of Mich. next [13 Oct.] upon Henry's nonappearance in Chancery to answer Thomas Copley, gentleman, executor of Nicholas Lewkenor, gentleman, of Tunbridge, Kent, to whom Henry acknowledged 80*l.* in Chancery on 27 Mar. 14 Eliz. I [1572] payable at Whitsun then next [25 May]; as Thomas had sued out a *scire facias* to the sheriffs of Mdx., Thomas Skynner and John Catcher, who have returned that Henry had no lands or goods in Mdx. and has not been found.

21 Sept. 32 Eliz. I [1590]. Inquisition at Whiteparishe before Henry Willughby, esquire, by Roger Elkyns, John Hurste, Peter Wylkyns, Nicholas Sauram, William Morris, John Pressey, John Marchman, Robert Saye, John Hussey, and John Thorne.

Seised in his demesne as of fee tail of the following reversions: a water-mill, 100 a. of land, 30 a. of meadow, and 30 a. of pasture in Fysherton held by Eleanor Powell, widow, or her assigns, for a term of years for a yearly rent of 17*l.* 19*s.* 10*d.* payable in equal parts at Mich. and Lady Day; a messuage, 30 a. of land, 30 a. of meadow, and 20 a. of pasture held by Walter Belli on the same terms for a yearly rent of 5*l.* 15*s.* 4*d.*; a messuage, garden, and orchard held by Robert Parker for a yearly rent of 20*s.*; a messuage and 20 a. of land held by Richard Sponder on the same terms for a yearly rent of 20*s.*; $\frac{1}{4}$ of a messuage in New Salisbury known as the 'signe of the three swannes' held by Henry Bulle on the same terms for a yearly rent of 26*s.* 8*d.* Yearly rents from messuages in Fysherton held by the following: — [*blank*] Cooke or his assigns (16*d.*), John Hooper or his assigns (2*s.*), Walter Bonham, esquire, (9*s.* 1*d.*), Robert Warde (3*s.*), — [*blank*] Younge or his assigns (5*s.*), Arthur Langley (8*d.*), Agnes Hoskyns (12*d.*), and — [*blank*] Gauntlett (8*d.*).

Total value of the moiety 14*l.* 3*s.* 3*d.* yearly. The rents have been delivered.

C 239/56 no. 94 a

143 Hugh Ryley, gentleman, of Upton Lovell

19 Oct. 33 Eliz. I [1591]. *Capias* returnable in oct. of Martinmas next [18 Nov.], sued out by Thomas Oldefelde, gentleman, administrator of William Chambers the elder, to whom Thomas acknowledged 400*l.* on 23 Nov. 20 Eliz. I [1577] before James Dyer, knight, then chief justice of the Common Pleas, payable at Christmas then next.

Endorsed. Hugh has not been found.

11 Nov. 33 Eliz. I [1591]. Inquisition at Upton Lovell before [John Warneford, esquire,] by Thomas Flower, John Barnabye, gentleman, Oliver Moulton, John Chamberlayne, Hugh Huelett, Christopher Combes, John Tillye, Thomas Smithfield, Richard Moodie, Robert Steevens, William Hayward, William Steevens, and John Marshe.

In Upton Lovell seised in his demesne as of fee of: a capital messuage or farm and 800 a. of land, 8 a. of meadow, 3 a. of pasture, and pasture in common for 160 sheep, held by Hugh and his assigns, worth 3*l.* 6*s.* 8*d.* yearly; a messuage called a 'copie holde' and 30 a. of arable land, 2 a. of meadow, 1 a. of pasture, and pasture in common for 80 sheep, held by Andrew Tunstalle; a messuage called a 'copie holde' and 30 a. of arable land, 1 a. of pasture, 1 a. of meadow, and pasture in common for 80 sheep, held by Robert Cartere (13*s.* 4*d.*); a tenement called a 'copie holde' and 30 a. of arable land, 2 a. of meadow, and pasture in common for 80 sheep, held by William George and Edith Everett, widow, (13*s.* 4*d.*); a cottage, 1 a. of arable land, and pasture in common for 1 animal, held by Joan Hockins, widow, (2*s.*).

Possessed of 'sixteene akers of wheate nowe growinge at Upton', worth 8*l.* yearly.

C 131/135 no. 7

144 John Webbe, of Slaughtenforde

26 Oct. 33 Eliz. I [1591]. *Liberate* returnable in quin. of Martinmas next [18 Nov.]; with *capias* against John's body; upon a *capias* sued out by Elizabeth Staples, relict and executrix of Alexander Staples, gentleman, of Yate, Glos., to whom John acknowledged 400 marks on 19 May 29 Eliz. I [1587] before Christopher Wraye, knight, chief justice of the Queen's Bench, payable at Midsummer then next; as the sheriff has returned that John has not been found and that he was in possession for 4 years from 31 Aug. last of that part of the farm of Slaughtenford held by John Keynes, worth 40*l.* yearly, and that the above has been delivered to the queen.

C 239/57 no. 156 a

145 William Thorley, gentleman, of New Salisbury

9 Nov. 33 Eliz. I [1591]. *Liberate* returnable in quin. of Hil. next [27 Jan.] for Anthony Dyston, fishmonger, of Marleborough, to whom William acknowledged 300*l.* on 28 Jan. 21 Eliz. I [1579] before Christopher Wraye, knight, chief justice of the Queen's Bench, payable at Eas. then next [19 Apr.]; with *capias* against William's body; as Anthony had sued out a *capias*, with like writ to the sheriff of Berks., to which Walter Hungerforde, knight, former sheriff, has returned that William has not been found and that he was seised in his demesne as of fee of a tenement in Soley in Chilton Folyatt parish and 200 a. or more of arable land, meadow, pasture, and wood belonging, worth 24*l.* yearly, lately held by Edward Merivall the younger, now deceased, and that the lands were delivered to the queen on 23 Sept. 31 Eliz. I [1589].

C 239/57 no. 168

146 Henry Ferrers, esquire, of Baddesley Clynton, Warwickshire

11 Aug. 34 Eliz. I [1592]. *Elegit* returnable in oct. of Martinmas next [18 Jan.] upon Henry's appearance in Chancery and inability to deny the suit of Richard Henton and his wife, Elizabeth, administrators of John Beconsawe, gentleman, of Stoke, Hants, to whom he acknowledged 200*l.* in Chancery on 28 May 30 Eliz. I [1588]; as Richard and Elizabeth had sued out a *scire facias* to the sheriffs of Mdx., who have returned that Henry had no lands or goods in Mdx. and has not been found.

2 Nov. 34 Eliz. I [1592]. Inquisition at Fysherton before William Eyre, knight, by William Hewlett, gentleman, Robert Jones, John Richardes, John Waters, Thomas Burrowe, Thomas Myles, Edward Whittock, John Morrys, Richard Tompson, Richard Boldye, Richard Este, John Clare, John Haerford, and Anthony Hooper.

Seised in his demesne as of fee tail of the following reversions: a water-mill, 100 a. of land, 30 a. of meadow, and 30 a. of pasture in Fysherton held by Eleanor Powell, widow, or her assigns, for a term of years at a yearly rent of 17*l.* 19*s.* 10*d.* payable in equal parts at Mich. and Lady Day; a messuage, 30 a. of land, 30 a. of meadow, and 20 a. of pasture held by Walter Belli on the same terms for a yearly rent of 5*l.* 15*s.* 4*d.*; a messuage, garden, and orchard held by Lewis Harrys on the same terms for a yearly rent of 20*s.*; a messuage and 20 a. of land held by Richard Sponder on the same terms for a yearly rent of 20*s.*; ¼ of a messuage in New Salisbury known as the 'signe of the three swannes' held by Henry Bull on the same terms for a yearly rent of 26*s.* 8*d.* Yearly rents from messuages in Fysherton held by the following: — [*blank*] Cooke or his assigns (16*d.*), John Hooper or his assigns (2*s.*), Walter Bonham, esquire, (9*s.* 1*d.*), Robert Warde (3*s.*), — [*blank*] Younge or his assigns (5*s.*), Arthur Langley (8*d.*), Agnes Hoskyns (12*d.*), and — [*blank*] Gauntlett (8*d.*). Total of the moiety of the rents 14*l.* 3*s.* 4*d.*

Henry Willughbye, esquire, late sheriff, has delivered the moiety to Richard Henton as the assignee of Thomas Copley, executor of Nicholas Lewkner, because of an earlier writ of *elegit*. The half of the moiety of the rents, tenements, and reversions that is payable on Lady Day is worth 7*l.* 0*s.* 19*d.* and has been delivered to Richard Henton and his wife Elizabeth.

C 239/58 no. 137 a

147 Ambrose Button, gentleman, of Grayes Inne, Middlesex

26 Nov. 37 Eliz. I [1594]. *Capias* returnable in quin. of Hil. next [27 Jan.], sued out by Christopher Lidcott, then esquire, now knight, of Basselton, Berks., to whom Ambrose acknowledged 2,000*l.* on 26 Nov. 33 Eliz. I [1590] before Christopher Wray, knight, then chief justice of the Queen's Bench, payable at Christmas then next. Like writs to the sheriffs of Som. and Hants. *Endorsed.* Ambrose has not been found.

[*MS. torn*] 20 Jan. [37 Eliz. I] [1595]. Inquisition at Marleborough before [Edward Hungerforde, esquire,] by Thomas Fysher, John Fysher, and John Dorrington, gentlemen, Thomas . . . , . . . Cuffe, Richard Wilmotte, and Godfrey Wiett.

[Seised] of: the manors of Tockenham [(18*l.*), Lyneham and Preston (31]*l.* 6*s.* 8*d.*); pasture and meadows called 'Thickthorne' and tithe of hay in the said close, with herbage in Lyneham [(86*s.* 8*d.*); a meadow in Lyneham called 'Milham' of 7 a.] (8*s.*); a pasture in Littlecott called 'Brodeleaze' and another called 'Littlecott Marshe'; a meadow lying between [the said pastures, except for the crops and hay on 7 a. of meadow and herbage once a year in the west part] in Hilmerton (8*l.*); the crops in the meadow in Segre held by Adam Tucke or his assigns (10*s.*); [the manor of Roodashton and closes of meadow and pasture called 'Croswell Doune'] (5*l.*); the manors of Little Sutton (5*l.* 1*s.* 8*d.*), [Comerwell (8*l.*] 12*s.*), Burbage (3*l.* 7*s.* 4*d.*), [Northwraxall (8*l.*)], Compton Comerwell (6*l.*).

The following rents and reversions: 4 messuages, 4 gardens, 4 [orchards and 30 a. of land, 3 a. of meadow, and 3 a. of pasture in Calne,] 7 a. of meadow and 3 a. of meadow called 'Wemhille' in Calne fields, and a coppice in Studly (20*s.*); [a pasture and meadow called 'Tesworthe' *alias* 'Tessell' and other closes called 'Broadcraste' in Stocke and Stockley;] a messuage in Stoke and Stokley held by John Kinge for life (13*s.* 4*d.*); a messuage, garden, and orchard in Venny Sutton (6*s.* 8*d.*); a capital messuage and farm, garden, and orchard in Middleton [held by Richard Dewye for life (5*l.* 6*s.* 8*d.*)]; a cottage in Warmynster held by Henry Phillips for life (4*s.*); a messuage, garden, and orchard in Norton Bavent held by Henry Burman for life (5*s.*); a messuage, garden, and orchard in Westkington held by Richard Haywarden (20*s.*); [a messuage, garden and orchard, and close of pasture] of 3 a. and closes called 'Inockes' of 2 a., 'Hedlondes' of 4 a., 'Southleaze' of 5 a., 'Warleaze' of 6 a., 'Henley Shrewde', 'Newlande' of 6 a., 'Yellyn Crofte' of 3 a., 'Hurle Leaze' of 4 a., ['Chalkeleaze' of 7 a., and 'Coteby' of 3 a., a coppice called] 'Oxleaze', a coppice at 'Henley Shrewdes Grove', and 16 a. of arable land in Boxe (9*s.*); a tenement called 'Cussehayes', in English a 'routes tenement', a close called 'Ashebrooke' of . . . a. of arable land, and 3 a. of meadow in Boxe fields (3*s.* 8*d.*); the farm or capital messuage of Backhampton held by

. . . for life; [a messuage, garden, and orchard] held by John Reeves for life (6*l*. 0*s*. 6*d*.); ½ of a tenement in Stanmer held by [Thomas Hutchyns for life at a yearly rent of 26*s*. 8*d*.; 3] tenements, 3 gardens, and 3 orchards, 700 a. of pasture and 6 a. of wood in Shawe, and 30 a. of arable land in Shawe (22*s*.); a tenement in Lurgarshall held by . . . (17*s*.); tenements in Marleboroughe held by Richard Herste (40*s*.), Richard Clementes, clothier, (11*s*.), and Thomas Hobbes (12*s*.); a [tenement in Devises held by Henry Foxe or his assigns; ½ of a] . . . held by Thomas Baylie in le Devises (60*s*.); a tenement in Foulston held by — [*blank*] Bodenham, gentleman, [(20*s*.); a tenement in Maddington held by William Woodroofe] (11*s*. 8*d*.); a tenement in Bratton and Edington now or lately held by Widow Rawlins (20*s*.); a messuage, cottage, garden, and orchard in Ore *alias* Owre held by John Geale for life (8*s*. 3*d*.); a messuage, garden, orchard, [and 3 virgates of land in Mill . . .] held by Richard Greene for the life of his wife Joan (15*s*.); the manor and farm of Wodborgughe and 8 virgates of land; 30 a. of meadow and pasture in Maungford held by [John Mawdytt for life (3*l*.)] . . . ; a tenement and ½ virgate of land in Bottwell and Bechingstooke held by Andrew Smithe for life (13*s*. [4*d*.); a tenement, water-mill, garden,] orchard, and meadow called 'Millmeade' near Gooseham, a meadow by Patney called 'Millmeade', and 12 a. of arable land in Marden held by — [*blank*] Smithe, widow, for life (26*s*. 8*d*.). Total 129*l*. 14*s*. 9*d*.

12 May 37 Eliz. I [1595]. *Liberate* returnable in oct. of Trin. next [29 June]; with *capias* against Ambrose's body. Like writ to the sheriff of Hants in respect of manors and lands there worth 6*l*. 10*s*. 5*d*. yearly.

C 239/61 no. 6

148 Thomas Webbe, of Kevill, and Henry Webbe, of Great Sherston, gentlemen

22 May 37 Eliz. I [1595]. *Capias* returnable in quin. of Trin. next [29 June], sued out by John Fawne, gentleman, of London, to whom Thomas and Henry acknowledged 100*l*. on 4 Nov. 36 Eliz. I [1594] before Edmund Anderson, knight, chief justice of the Common Pleas, payable at St. Andrew then next [30 Nov.]. Like writ to the sheriff of Mdx.
Endorsed. Thomas and Henry have not been found.

2 June 37 Eliz. I [1595]. Inquisition at Sherston before Edward Hungerforde, esquire, by John Seborne *alias* Plumer, John Blake, Nicholas Poole, Richard Hobbes, William Horte, James Jefferyes, William Ponter, John Bussell, Thomas Fylder, Thomas Turke, Richard Boxe, Henry Cannape, Nicholas Wylson, and Edward Sergeant.

Henry is seised in the right of his wife Elizabeth for her life of a capital messuage called 'Ivyes' in Sherston and all lands, meadows, feedings, pastures, and other profits belonging to it, worth 13*l*. 6*s*. 8*d*. yearly.

On the day of the receipt of the writ, Henry possessed the following goods: 'twoe oxen' worth 5*l*.; 'a heiffer' worth 30*s*.; a horse worth 30*s*.

Total 8*l*.

3 June 37 Eliz. I [1595]. Inquisition at Kevell before Edward Hungerforde, esquire, by Roger Blackeday, Edward Hiscoxe, Robert Jorden, Nicholas Hancocke, Stephen Caundell, Walter Lucas, Christopher Jones, John Bellyn, John Jones, John Lucas, Thomas Tayler, and Richard Dalmer.

Thomas had no lands or goods in Wilts.

C 239/61 no. 51

149 Thomas Goddarde, gentleman, of Upham

24 July 37 Eliz. I [1595]. *Capias* returnable in quin. of Mich. next [13 Oct.], sued out by Anne Bewforest, administratrix of Luke Bewforest, to whom Thomas acknowledged 2,000*l.* on 12 Nov. 4 Eliz. I [1562] before James Dyer, knight, then chief justice of the Common Pleas, payable at Christmas then next.

The sheriff certifies that Thomas has not been found.

11 Oct. 37 Eliz. I [1595]. Inquisition at Marleborowe before Edward Hungerforde, esquire, by William Adye, Thomas Collyns, Thomas Bacon, Thomas Brende, Thomas Humfries, Robert Evans, Henry . . . [*MS. blind*], John Monday, John Bright, John Foster *alias* Knyght, Humphrey Sympson, John Clarke, and Thomas Fowler.

Seised in his demesne as of fee of: the manor of Swyndon and all messuages, lands, meadows, feedings, pasture, woods, underwood, rents, and all other profits and easements belonging, worth 66*l.* 13*s.* 4*d.* yearly; a messuage and divers lands, feedings, and pasture called 'Westcott Leasnes' in Wroughton parish, now held by Thomas himself (126*l.* 13*s.* 4*d.*); a 'ferme' called 'Court Pounde' and all messuages [*etc., as above*] belonging in Cheselden parish (26*l.* 13*s.* 4*d.*); 3 messuages, a cottage, and divers meadows in the common fields of Wanborowe and all lands [*etc.*] belonging, held severally by Richard Reason, Thomas Morecock, John Wilkins, and William Lewys (26*l.* 13*s.* 4*d.*); a messuage in Ogborne St. George and all lands [*etc.*] belonging (40*l.*); ½ of a farm in Blackland in Calne parish and divers messuages belonging and all lands [*etc.*] belonging (26*l.* 13*s.* 4*d.*); ½ of a farm called 'Beckington Ferme' in Abrey parish and all lands [*etc.*] belonging (20*l.*).

On the day of the receipt of the writ, in possession for a term of several years of: a tenement in Upham in Alborne parish now held by William Gearuthe and a tenement and 2 virgates called 'twoe yearde landes' in Snappe in Alborne parish (10*l.*); ⅔ of a 'ferme' in Alborne and all lands [*etc., as above*] belonging (13*l.* 6*s.* 8*d.*); a meadow in Alborne (5*l.*).

The following goods: 130 'kyne and steares' worth 230*l.*; 10 'calves' worth 3*l.* 6*s.* 8*d.*

Total value of the lands 361*l.* 13*s.* 4*d.* yearly and of the goods 233*l.* 6*s.* 8*d.*

C 239/61 no. 85

150 Richard Fyssher, 'yoman', of Everley

22 Oct. 37 Eliz. I [1595]. *Capias* returnable in quin. of Martinmas next [25 Nov.], sued out by Francis Bartlett, 'yoman', of London, to whom

Richard acknowledged 120*l.* on 21 May 33 Eliz. I [1591] before Edmund Anderson, knight, chief justice of the Common Pleas, payable at St. James then next [25 July]. Like writ to the sheriff of Dors.

The sheriff certifies that Richard has not been found.

12 Nov. 37 Eliz. I [1595]. Inquisition at Everley before Edward Hungerforde, esquire, by George Reynoldes and John Andrewes, gentlemen, Henry Heycrofte, John Cheyney, John Mackerell, Richard Kyneton the elder, Richard Kyneton the younger, Jasper Preter, John Kinge, John Collins, Robert Collens, Richard Kent, Richard Eddington, and William Kyneton.

On the day of the receipt of the writ, in possession for a term of years of a messuage in Everley and 63 a. and 3 yds. of arable land, 1½ a. of meadow and pasture, and pasture in common for 120 sheep belonging to the messuage, worth 20*l.* yearly, held by John Cheyney the younger by the grant of Richard for 5 years at a yearly rent of 21*l.* 11*s.*

The following goods: 'wheat, barley, and other grayne of divers sortes lyeing and being in the barnes and rykes' at Everley, worth 40*l.*; 'fyre woodd and tymber' at Everley, worth 80*s.*; 'twoe hogges' (*porcis*), worth 10*s.*; 'implements of howshold stuffe' (*vescellis*) in the messuage, worth 5*l.*

The above were delivered to the queen on 12 Nov. 37 Eliz. I [1595].

C 239/61 no. 103

151 John Hampden, knight, of Great Hampden *alias* Hampden on the Hill, Buckinghamshire

7 May 38 Eliz. I [1596]. *Capias* returnable on the morrow of Ascension next [20 May], sued out by Richard Mountney, administrator of Henry Ferrers, knight, of Baddysley Clynton, Warws., to whom John acknowledged 500*l.* on 2 July 16 Hen. VIII [1524] before James Yarford, knight, then mayor and constable of the Staple of Westminster, payable at St. James then next [25 July]. Richard is administrator through Constance, relict of Henry, Thomas Willoughbye, knight, Thomas Marrowe, and Thomas Atteholte, esquire, his executors.

Endorsed. John is dead.

C 239/62 no. 37

152 Thomas Webbe, gentleman, of Keevil

13 Aug. 38 Eliz. I [1596]. *Capias* returnable in 1 month from Mich. next [29 Oct.], sued out by James Langton, gentleman, and his wife Margery, as Thomas acknowledged 600*l.* to Margery, as Margery Hobbes, widow, of Bristol, on 21 Nov. 38 Eliz. I [1595] before John Popham, knight, chief justice of the Queen's Bench, payable at Christmas then next. Like writs to the sheriffs of Bristol and Hants.

Endorsed. Thomas has not been found.

15 Sept. 38 Eliz. I [1596]. Inquisition at Stepleashton before Henry Sadleir,

esquire, by Roger Blagden, George White, Andrew Vennell, John Shepperd, William Silverthorne, Richard Neete, Richard Hancock, Thomas Whatley, John Lorde, John Margerom, Thomas Langfeil[d], and John Hardinge.

After the recognizance seised in his demesne as of fee in Stepleashton and Eddington of the following moieties: closes of pasture called 'Brodecroftes', of *c.* 20 a., 'Lessam Leaze', of *c.* 20 a., 'West Adnell', of *c.* 30 a., and a meadow called 'Stert Meadowe', of *c.* 20 a., worth 16*l.* yearly.

16 June 39 Eliz. I [1597]. *Liberate* returnable in oct. of Mich. next [6 Oct.]; with *capias* against Thomas's body.

C 239/62 no. 74

153 Samuel Browne, 'clothier', of Calne

25 Oct. 38 Eliz. I [1596]. *Capias* returnable in quin. of Hil. next [27 Jan.], sued out by Thomas Browne, 'yoman', of Wynterburne Bassett, to whom Samuel acknowledged 100*l.* on 8 Feb. 37 Eliz. I [1595] before John Popham, knight, chief justice of the Queen's Bench, payable at Lady Day then next.

21 Jan. 39 Eliz. I [1597]. Inquisition at Calne before John Dauntesey, esquire, by Stephen Orrell, Robert Scott the elder, Robert Scott the younger, John Scott, Richard Warne, John Hiscockes, Henry Segar *alias* Parsons, William Lewes, Richard Burgys, John Hannam, Isaac Welsted, Thomas Jenkyns, John Phelpes, William Good, and Thomas Good.

Seised in his demesne as of fee of: a messuage in Calne held by Samuel himself, worth 50*s.* yearly; a messuage in Calne held by William Bedford or his assigns for 7 years by a grant of Samuel made before the recognizance, worth 20*s.* yearly during the term and 50*s.* 8*d.* yearly thereafter; a close of pasture in Stockley called 'Goseacre' (20*s.*); 1 a. of arable land in the common fields of Calston (2*s.* 6*d.*), and 1 a. of arable land in the common fields of Cherhill (2*s.* 6*d.*) held by Thomas Browne or his assigns; a close of meadow called 'Moreacre' in Stockley held by Robert Segar *alias* Parsons for 8 years by a grant of Samuel made before the recognizance, worth 6*s.* yearly and 16*s.* yearly after the term; a close of pasture called 'Wellandes Penn' in Calne, of *c.* 3 a. (90*s.*); 15 a. and $\frac{1}{2}$ virgate of arable land in the common fields of Calne held by Samuel or his assigns; pasture in common for 100 sheep in the common fields of Calne (59*s.* 7*d.*); 2$\frac{1}{2}$ a. and 1 virgate of meadow in the common fields of Calne held by Samuel or his assigns (13*s.* 6*d.*).

C 239/62 no. 86

10 Feb. 39 Eliz. I [1597]. *Liberate* returnable in 1 month from Eas. next [25 Mar.]; with *capias* against Samuel's body.
Endorsed. The lands were delivered on 11 Mar. 39 Eliz. I [1597]. Samuel has not been found.

C 239/63 no. 30

154 James Lovell, gentleman, of Bulforde

2 Dec. 40 Eliz. I [1597]. *Capias* returnable in quin. of Hil. next [27 Jan.], sued out by Richard Knighte, son and heir of Robert Knighte, gentleman, of Skeeres, Hants, to whom James acknowledged 1,000*l.* on 10 July 33 Eliz. I [1591] before Edmund Anderson, knight, chief justice of the Common Pleas, payable at St. James then next [25 July]. Like writ to the sheriff of Hants. *Endorsed.* James has not been found.

19 Jan. 40 Eliz. I [1598]. Inquisition at New Salisbury before James Marvin, knight, by John Daye, Christopher Marshman, William Hewes, Hugh Noyes, Walter Chubbe, Richard Chappell, Richard Bidlecombe, John Bampton, Henry Whitmershe, William Stamforde, William Stubbin, Humphrey Ditton, and Edward Page.

On 23 Jan. 33 Eliz. I [1591], seised in his demesne as of fee of Bulford rectory, worth 70*l.* yearly. On 20 Nov. 36 Eliz. I [1593], seised in his demesne as of fee of a capital messuage or farm and 2 water-mills in Bulford lately held by James Lovell and John Mathewe, worth 100*l.* yearly.

C 239/64 no. 14

155 William Waryn, gentleman, of Fifehyde Waryns

11 May 40 Eliz. I [1598]. *Capias* returnable on the morrow of Ascension next [26 May], sued out by William Jones the younger, gentleman, of Woodlandes in Myldenhall parish, to whom William acknowledged 300*l.* on 26 May 37 Eliz. I [1595] before Edmund Anderson, knight, chief justice of the Common Pleas, payable at St. James then next [25 July].
Endorsed. William has not been found.

17 May 40 Eliz. I [1598]. Inquisition at Marleborough before James Marvin, knight, by John Hiscoxe, Thomas Hall, and Thomas Tichiner, gentlemen, Stephen Peirce, John Constable, Adam Plat, Thomas Appleford, Nicholas Kimber, Robert Cooke, John Goddard, John Dismore, John Pope, John Waldron, and Vincent Eyres.

On the day of the inquisition seised in his demesne as of fee of the manor of Fifehyde Warryns worth 20*l.* yearly.

27 May 40 Eliz. I [1598]. *Liberate* returnable in quin. of Trin. next [25 June]; with *capias* against William's body.

C 239/64 no. 70

156 John Maskeleyn, 'inholder', of Marlebroughe

3 July 40 Eliz. I [1598]. *Capias* returnable in oct. of Mich. next [6 Oct.], sued out by Richard Hearst, 'yoman', of Marlebroughe, to whom John acknowledged 200 marks on 23 Oct. 33 Eliz. I [1591] before Christopher Wray, knight, chief justice of the Queen's Bench, payable at Christmas then next. *Endorsed.* John has not been found.

31 July 40 Eliz. I [1598]. Inquisition at Marlebroughe before James Mervin, knight, by John Spenser, John Streat, William Jones the elder, William

Gryffin, John Dismer, Thomas Hitchcock, Richard Willmott, John Plastede, William Blissatt, Thomas Plastede, Thomas Phelpes, and Thomas Sloper.

Seised in his demesne as of fee of a messuage and 2 gardens in Marlebroughe, being a common inn called the 'Beare', worth 3*l*. 6*s*. 8*d*. yearly.

In possession of the goods in the attached schedule, namely:—

1 'joyned bedsteede' (*junct' fulcrum*) and 1 'truckle bedsteede'	10*s*.	
1 featherbed (*lect' plumatic'*) and 1 feather bolster (*cervical' plumatic'*)	40*s*.	
1 'flockbed' (*lect' flocc'*)	4*s*.	
1 'tapestry coverlett' (*stragula*)	20*s*.	
1 'lyste coverlett'	3*s*.	4*d*.
2 'blankettes' (*lodicis*)	4*s*.	
1 table and 4 'formes' (*scanna juncta*)	5*s*.	
1 chair and 2 'lyverie tables'	3*s*.	4*d*.
1 'dornex carpett' (*tapet'*)	3*s*.	4*d*.
3 'curteynes' (*vela*) and 3 'curteyne rodds' (*virgat'*)	5*s*.	
1 feather bolster (*cervical' plumatic'*)	3*s*.	4*d*.
14 rods (*virgat'*) of 'dornex hanginges'	10*s*.	
1 'joyned bedsteed' and 1 'truckle bedsteed'	8*s*.	
1 featherbed	30*s*.	
1 'tapestry coverlett'	13*s*.	4*d*.
1 'flockbed'	3*s*.	4*d*.
1 'lyst coverlett'	2*s*.	6*d*.
2 'blankettes'	3*s*.	4*d*.
1 table and 1 'joyned forme'	5*s*.	
1 chair and 1 'livery table'	3*s*.	
3 'curteynes' and 3 'rods'	5*s*.	
2 feather bolsters	6*s*.	8*d*.
1 'joyned bedsteed' and 1 'truckle bedsteed'	8*s*.	
1 feather bolster	13*s*.	4*d*.
1 flock bed	2*s*.	6*d*.
1 'tapestry coverlett'	10*s*.	
1 'lyste coverlett'	2*s*.	
2 'blankettes'	3*s*.	4*d*.
1 table and 1 form	2*s*.	6*d*.
3 'curteynes' and 3 'rods'	3*s*.	4*d*.
2 feather bolsters	5*s*.	
1 'lyverie table'		12*d*.
1 chair, 2 'carpettes' (*tapetes*), and 1 'cusshion' (*pulvin'*)	5*s*.	
1 'joyned bedsteed' and 1 'truckel bedsteed'	8*s*.	
1 feather bed	13*s*.	4*d*.
1 flock bed	3*s*.	4*d*.
1 'dornex coverlett' and 1 blanket	6*s*.	8*d*.
1 table and 1 form	3*s*.	4*d*.
2 feather bolsters	3*s*.	4*d*.

3 'curteynes' and 3 'rods' and 1 chair	5*s.*	
2 'joyned bedsteeds'	10*s.*	
2 feather beds	20*s.*	
2 'coverlettes'	20*s.*	
2 'blankettes'	2*s.*	
1 table and 2 forms	5*s.*	
1 feather bed, 1 'truckle bedsted', 1 'coverlett', and 1 blanket	6*s.*	8*d.*
2 'wyndow curteynes'		6*d.*
3 feather bolsters and 1 flock bolster	5*s.*	
1 'joyned bedsteed' and 1 'truckle bedsteed'	7*s.*	
2 feather beds	20*s.*	
1 'coverlett'	5*s.*	
1 'list coverlett' and 1 'blankett'	2*s.*	
1 table and 1 form	2*s.*	
1 carpet and 3 cushions		12*d.*
3 'curteynes' and 3 'rods'	3*s.*	4*d.*
2 feather bolsters	4*s.*	
1 'bedsteed' and 1 feather bed	13*s.*	4*d.*
1 coverlet and 1 'blankett'	5*s.*	
1 table and 1 form	2*s.*	6*d.*
1 feather bolster	2*s.*	
2 'joyned bedsteeds'	6*s.*	8*d.*
2 feather beds	13*s.*	4*d.*
2 'coverlettes'	6*s.*	8*d.*
2 'blankettes'	3*s.*	
1 table, 1 form, and 2 'stooles' (*sedil'*)	2*s.*	6*d.*
1 'feild bedsted' (*fulchrum*) and 1 'close side bedsteede'	6*s.*	8*d.*
1 feather bed and 1 bolster	10*s.*	
1 flock bed	2*s.*	
2 'list coverlettes'	3*s.*	4*d.*
2 'blankettes'	2*s.*	
1 table and 1 'forme'	2*s.*	6*d.*
1 'mattres' (*culcitra*)	2*s.*	
1 chair, 1 carpet, 2 cushions, 1 'quilt' (*centon'*), and 1 'paire of billowes' (*folle*)	2*s.*	
3 'curteynes' and 3 'rods'	5*s.*	
1 'bedsteed' and 1 feather bed	20*s.*	
1 'lyste coverlett' and 1 'blankett'	5*s.*	
1 'table and frame' (*mensa et framea*)		12*d.*
2 feather bolsters and 1 'rugg' (*gausape*)	10*s.*	
3 'curteynes' and 3 'rods'	2*s.*	6*d.*
1 'bedsteed' and 1 feather bed	13*s.*	4*d.*
3 'lyst coverlettes' and 1 'blankett'	6*s.*	8*d.*
1 chest (*cista*) and 1 'trounk' (*truncella*)	2*s.*	6*d.*
1 'truckle bedsteed' and 1 flock bed	5*s.*	
1 'cubbard' (*abac'*)	2*s.*	6*d.*

1 feather bolster and 1 flock bolster		3*s*.	4*d*.
1 Bible (*biblia*), 1 'standishe' (*atramentar*'), 1 'lookinge glasse' (*vitrum*)		2*s*.	6*d*.
1 'bedsteed' and 1 feather bed		8*s*.	
1 'coverlett'		2*s*.	
1 'cubbard'			18*d*.
1 'close stoole' (*excrementor*') and 1 'screene'		2*s*.	
1 long table and 2 square tables (*mense quadrat*') with their frames and 1 'forme' (*long' scann*')		10*s*.	
1 table with frame and form		5*s*.	
12 'pewter platters' (*vasa*)		13*s*.	4*d*.
16 'pewter pottingers'		6*s*.	8*d*.
18 'sawsers' or 'frut dishes'		3*s*.	4*d*.
6 candlesticks 'of pewter' (*scanni*)		3*s*.	
10 'chamber pottes' (*matule*)		5*s*.	
3 'brasse pottes'		20*s*.	
4 'kettelles' (*cacab' ahenei*)		13*s*.	4*d*.
2 'brasse skillettes' (*situle*)			12*d*.
6 'broches' (*verua*)		6*s*.	
2 'dripping pans' (*vasa*)		3*s*.	4*d*.
2 'gredirons' (*cratis*)			12*d*.
2 'potthookes' (*ollares cathene*) and 3 'potthangers' (*ollares uncini*)		3*s*.	
1 'fryeng pan' (*frixorium*)			12*d*.
6 pairs of 'holland sheetes' (*lodic' lineorum*)	3*l*.		
12 pairs of 'canvas sheetes'	4*l*.		
6 pairs of 'holland pillowbers' (*pulvinar*')		20*s*.	
12 'pillowes' (*pulvin*')		26*s*.	8*d*.
1 'presse' (*abac*') and 1 chest (*cista*)		5*s*.	
12 'table clothes' (*mappe*)		40*s*.	
5 doz. 'table napkins' (*mantil*')		30*s*.	
2 doz. 'towelles' (*mantel*')		40*s*.	
8 'stable rackes' (*presep*') and 8 'mangers'		20*s*.	
4 'tubs' (*vasa lignea*), 3 'cowles', and 3 'kevers'		20*s*.	
3 'silver bolles' (*pocula argentea*), 1 silver salver (*salvum argenteum*), 6 silver 'spoones' (*cochlear*'), and 1 silver salver 'guilded' (*deaurat*')	10*l*.		
1 'bason and ewre' (*lotor*')		2*s*.	6*d*.

14 Oct. 40 Eliz. I [1598]. *Liberate* returnable in oct. of Martinmas next [18 Oct.]; with *capias* against John's body.
Endorsed. The goods have been delivered. John has not been found.

C 239/64 no. 116

157 Archadius Knight, gentleman, of Peters Ampney, Gloucestershire

27 Oct. 40 Eliz. I [1598]. *Capias* returnable on the morrow of Martinmas next [12 Nov.], sued out by John Fowell, gentleman, of Middle Temple,

London, and William Carnsew, gentleman, of the university of Oxford, to whom Archadius acknowledged 2,000*l.* on 14 Feb. 32 Eliz. I [1590] before Edmund Anderson, knight, chief justice of the Common Pleas, payable at Lady Day then next. Like writ to the sheriff of Glos.
Endorsed. Archadius has not been found.

9 Nov. 40 Eliz. I [1598]. Inquisition at Cricklade before James Marvin, knight, by Daniel Champnoll, Robert Kemble, Daniel Browne, Robert Watris, Edward Dunne, Richard Mathewe, Jenivere Tainter, Thomas Howse, Richard Newman, Jenivere Champnoll, Richard Symondes, John Pepwall, and John Walton.
Seised in his demesne as of fee of a messuage and 24 a. of pasture in Chelworthe *alias* Celworth in Cricklade, worth 20*s.* yearly.

16 Nov. 40 Eliz. I [1598]. *Liberate* returnable in quin. of Martinmas next [25 Nov.]; with *capias* against Archadius's body. Like writ to the sheriff of Glos. in respect of manors, messuages, and lands there worth 40*l.* yearly.

23 Nov. 41 Eliz. I [1598]. The sheriff certifies that on 21 Nov. 41 Eliz. I [1598] he delivered the above lands to Thomas Busshopp to the use and in the name of John and William.

C 239/64 no. 155

158 John Calley, gentleman, of Hilmerton

4 Nov. 40 Eliz. I [1598]. *Capias* returnable in oct. of Martinmas next [18 Oct.], sued out by Godfrey Bathe, gentleman, of Cirencestr', Glos., to whom John acknowledged 200*l.* on 8 May 32 Eliz. I [1590] before Christopher Wray, knight, chief justice of the Queen's Bench, payable at Whitsun then next [7 June].
Endorsed. John is dead.

12 Nov. 40 Eliz. I [1598]. Inquisition at Hilmarton before James Marvin, knight, by Robert Kinges, Thomas Brewer, William Eastonton, Ralph Hollowaye, Edward Stoute, Robert Jefferes, John Hopkins, William Arnolde, Edward Kene, William Paine, William Thomas, and Thomas Rutchins.
Long after the recognizance he possessed the goods listed in the attached schedule, worth 166*l.* 1*s.* 4*d.*

'A scedule of the severall goodes and chattells of John Calley of Hilmarton in the countie aforesaied taken and seased by James Marvin, knight, high shiryf of the saied countie, the xiith daye of November in the fortieth yere of the raigne of our soveraigne ladie Elizabeth by the grace of God queene of England, Fraunce, and Ireland, defender of the faieth, etc.

6 oxen and 2 black steeres	26*l.*	13*s.*	4*d.*
11 kyne and 1 bull	28*l.*		
9 heyfers and 1 steere	16*l.*	13*s.*	4*d.*

2 mares and 1 geldinge	7*l.*		
1 bason and 1 ewer, 1 pewter pott, 1 save, and 1 flaskett		16*s.*	8*d.*
2 chargers, 4 chamber pottes, 3 paire of pewter candlestickes, 1 doz. of platters, 13 fruite dishes, 2 platters, 3 basons, 8 sawcers, 6 potingers, 1 doz. of plates, 1 doz. of spoones, and 3 saltes	3*l.*	6*s.*	8*d.*
4 silver spoons		20*s.*	
1 fetherbed and 1 bedsteede, 1 bolster, 2 blankettes, 2 pilloes, 1 greene rugge, 1 paire of pilloes, 5 curtaines and curtaine roddes, 1 coverlett of tapistrie	9*l.*		
2 chaires		13*s.*	4*d.*
1 cheste		20*s.*	
1 feilde bedsteed with a canopie, 1 fetherbed, 2 fether bolsters, 1 paire of blankettes, and 1 coverlett	4*l.*		
1 square table and 1 cubbard		5*s.*	
2 cubbard clothes and 2 curtaines and curtaine roddes		10*s.*	
1 holberde		10*s.*	
2 stooles, 2 paire of dogges, and 1 paire of tonges		5*s.*	
1 joyned bedsteed, 1 fetherbedd, 1 flockbedd, 2 bolsters, 1 pillowe, 1 coverlett, 1 blankett, 2 pillowes, 5 curtains and curtain roddes	4*l.*		
1 bedsteed, 1 olde fetherbedd, 1 bolster, 1 blankett and coverlett, 1 truckle bedsted, and 1 pillowe		46*s.*	8*d.*
2 waynes, 2 olde payre of wheeles with yokes and chaynes and sulloes with a litle plough timber	8*l.*		
Wood and timber	3*l.*		
1 reeke of wheate and 2 stathells	5*l.*		
1 furnas and 2 brasen panns	3*l.*		
2 fates and 10 small treene vessells		25*s.*	
1 malte mill and a yotinge stone		20*s.*	
1 furnas		5*s.*	
1 powdringe stone and 3 powdringe tubbes		20*s.*	
6 brasse pottes, 2 posnettes, and 1 chafer		45*s.*	
3 catherns		6*s.*	
1 morter and 1 pestle		3*s.*	4*d.*
2 little brasse pannes and 1 skillett		5*s.*	
5 broches		6*s.*	

	l.	s.	d.
2 iron rackes, 3 pothangers, 3 dripinge pannes, and 1 iron plate		13*s.*	4*d.*
1 table boorde, 2 tressells, and 1 forme		2*s.*	
1 olde furnas		5*s.*	
12 treene vessells		20*s.*	
2 boordes with 2 frames, 1 forme, 6 joyned stooles and 2 andirons, and 1 little cubbard		30*s.*	
2 carpettes, 6 cushions, 1 table with a frame, 1 cubborde, 1 payre of virginoles, 12 joyned stooles, 1 holberd and 2 bills, 1 paire of andirons, 1 square boorde with a frame, 3 curtaines and curtaine roddes, 1 cubbard clothe, 1 fire shovell, and 2 andirons	5*l.*	16*s.*	0*d.*
1 bedsteed, 1 fetherbedd, 1 bolster, 1 coverlett, 1 blankett, and 1 bedd lye		35*s.*	
1 joyned bedsteede, 1 flockbed, 1 paire of blankettes, 1 pilloe, 1 rugge, 5 curtaines and curtaine roddes	4*l.*		
1 joyned bedsteed, 1 fetherbedd, 2 bolsters, 1 blankett, and 1 coverlett		40*s.*	
2 greate trunckes, 1 presse, and 1 olde truncke		50*s.*	
1 square table, 1 pair of dogges, and 1 warming panne		7*s.*	
3 flockbeddes and 5 paire of sheetes		56*s.*	8*d.*
2 burden bedsteedes		2*s.*	
8 hogges	4*l.*		
2 bedsteedes, 2 flockbeddes, 2 paire of sheetes, 2 coverlettes, and 2 bolsters		40*s.*	
4 ladders		4*s.*	
Total 166*l.* 1*s.* 4*d.*'			

C 239/64 no. 161

159 William Carter

25 Nov. 41 Eliz. I [1598]. *Elegit* by default sued out by Thomas Chafen, gentleman, to whom William acknowledged 400*l.* on 9 Feb. . . . [*MS. torn*] Eliz. I . . . ; upon a writ returnable in oct. of Hil., to which the sheriff of Mdx. has returned that William has not been found.

19 Jan. 41 Eliz. I [1599]. Inquisition at Stratton St. Margaret before Edward Penruddock, esquire, by Francis Kemble, John Spencer, William Morse, Edward Miller, Edward Morse, John Barrett, Robert . . . , John Darrell, Nicholas Morse, John Lamborne, John Edwardes, William Gondye, Ambrose Clyde, John Cuffe, Hercules Cuffe, Aldane . . . , Simon Ryan, and William Waterman.

Seised in his demesne as of fee of a messuage, 2 water-mills, 24 a. of meadow,

8½ a. of pasture in Crecklade *alias* Grakes . . . in the occupation of Thomas Pleydell, gentleman, or his assigns, by the demise of the said William for 20 years, worth 5*l*. yearly and after the term 20*l*. yearly.

C 131/141 no. 5

160 Thomas Brynde, gentleman, of Wanbrough

5 May 41 Eliz. I [1599]. *Extendi facias* returnable in quin. of Trin. next [17 June], for Alexander Staples, gentleman, of Marlebrough, to whom Thomas acknowledged 400*l*. on 14 Feb. 18 Eliz. I [1576] before Christopher Wray, then chief justice of the Queen's Bench, payable at Eas. then next [22 Apr.]; as Alexander had sued out a *capias* to which the sheriff has returned that Thomas is dead.

1 June 41 Eliz. I [1599]. Inquisition at Wanborowe before Edward Penruddock, esquire, by Richard Spencer, William Sadler, William Collet, Nicholas Webb, John Coxe, William West, William Lamborne, Thomas Sinnut, Edward Lovedaye, . . . [*MS. blind*], Richard Warman, William Bristowe, and Robert Webb.

Seised in his demesne as of fee of: 12 a. of meadow in the 'Wythe' in Wanborowe, worth 36*s*. yearly; 20 a. of meadow in 'S . . . ' in Wanborowe (60*s*.); a close of pasture . . . called 'Sangers' of *c*. 1½ a. (20*s*.); a messuage called the 'Moorehowse', closes of pasture called 'Thisleclose' and 'Moreleaze', a meadow called . . . of *c*. 20 a. (10*l*.); a messuage . . . in Marston; a pasture called 'Marstonleaze', 2 closes of pasture in Marston belonging to the tenement . . . of *c*. 20 a., now held by Thomas Morecock (16*l*.); 2 a. of meadow in 'Eastmeade' in Wanborowe . . . ; . . . in 'Eastmeade' of ¼ a. of meadow; ⅓ of a close of pasture called . . . held by Thomas Morecock or his assigns (19*s*.); . . . a tenement held by Richard Reason, 1 a. of meadow in the 'Wythe' . . . ⅓ of the said close of pasture called 'Sawiers' in Wanborowe . . . in a meadow called 'Chinnokes'; a tenement held by William Lewes . . . ; a parcel of the said close of pasture called 'Sawiers' (12*d*.).

C 131/141 no. 13

161 William Shute, citizen and 'imbroderer' of London

4 July 41 Eliz. I [1599]. *Capias* returnable in quin. of Martinmas next [25 Nov.], sued out by Francis Shute, citizen and goldsmith of London, to whom William acknowledged 2,000*l*. on 20 Oct. 40 Eliz. I [1598] before Edmund Anderson, knight, chief justice of the Common Pleas, payable at All Saints then next [1 Nov.]. Like writs to the sheriffs of Lond., Devon, and Kent and to Tobias, bishop of Durham.

3 Aug. [41] Eliz. I [1599]. Inquisition at Calne before Edward Penruddock, esquire, by John Norborne, Benet Allen, and John H . . . [*MS. blind*], gentlemen, Walter Segar, John Felps, John Scott, Robert Scott, Robert Pontinge, Robert Segar, Thomas Goode, John Chilvester, Henry Beare, John Hiscoxe, William Harris, and John Stapleford.

Seised in his demesne as of fee of: the manor of Blakes in Compton Bassett worth 6*l.* yearly; a garden and 4 closes of pasture in Calne and Stock held by John Weare *alias* Browne (60*s.*); a close of pasture called 'Gloverscroft', with 16 a. of arable land, held by William Swaddon (21*s.*); a messuage called 'Scrivens Courte' in Calne held by John Hannam, with 15 a. of land and 12 a. of pasture (30*s.*); a tenement in Calne held by John Hannam, with 7 a. of land and 5 a. of pasture (25*s.* 2*d.*); a tenement in Calne held by Oliver Girdler or his assigns (4*s.*); a cottage in Calne held by Thomas Fooke or his assigns (6*d.*); a close of pasture called 'Little Godwyns' in Quemerford held by Richard Page (3*s.*); a capital messuage in Calne held by Henry Robinson *alias* Peirse, with 4 a. of arable land, [1] a. of land, 1 a. of meadow, and a close of pasture called 'Pertridge Meade' (18*s.* 4*d.*); 3 messuages in Calne held by John Dashe the elder, with 8 a. of land, 2 a. of meadow, and 2 a. of pasture (36*s.*); a tenement in Calne held by James Mylles, with 1 a. of meadow in 'Honygarston' (8*s.*); a piece of land near 'Semiter' in Calne held by Henry Brewer ([8]*s.*); 2 a. of meadow in 'Moore Meade' in Stockley held by John Scott (2*s.* 8*d.*); messuages in Calne held by Isaac Welsted (6*s.*) and Alice Olliffe, widow, (6*s.* 8*d.*); a messuage in Over Segery and Nether Segerey held by Edith Blackmore and William Blackmore, with 50 a. of land, 16 a. of meadow, and 20 a. of pasture (80*s.*); a tenement in Calne held by Godfrey Perry (4*s.*); a messuage in le Devizes held by Alexander Webb (40*s.*); free yearly rent of 6*d.* from [lands] formerly of Thomas Gawen in Stock Strete in Calne parish; a free rent of 6*d.* [from lands] formerly of William Sarvaunt *alias* Rafe in Stock Strete; free rent of [3]*d.* from a close of pasture held by William Swaddon in Stock Strete called the ['Poundclose']; free rent of 6*s.* and 1 lb. cumin from the lands of — [*blank*] Tyndall in Segerey; free yearly rent of 6*s.* 5½*d.* payable to the sacrist of Salisbury cathedral for his prebend in Calne; a similar rent of 6*s.* 5½*d.* payable to Thomas Edwardes, esquire, and his wife Anne for all rents and services.

C 131/142 no. 12

22 Aug. 42 Eliz. I [1600]. *Liberate* returnable in quin. of Mich. next [13 Oct.]; with *capias* against William's body.
Endorsed. The lands were delivered on 3 Oct. 42 Eliz. I [1600]. William has not been found. C 239/66 no. 131

162 George Paige, 'grocer', of Salisbury

13 Oct. 41 Eliz. I [1599]. *Capias* returnable on the morrow of the Purification next [3 Feb.], sued out by Richard Wollaston, citizen and 'grocer' of London, to whom George acknowledged 300*l.* on 30 Nov. 40 Eliz. I [1598] before John Popham, knight, chief justice of the Queen's Bench, payable at St. Thomas then next [21 Dec.].
Endorsed. The sheriff has taken George and put him in the prison at Fisherton Auger.

24 Dec. 42 Eliz. I [1599]. Inquisition at New Salisbury before Walter Vaughan, esquire, by William Beck, Robert Smyth, Robert Roberts, Anthony

Maynard, Richard Barker, Arthur Edmondes, George Churchowse, John Mathewe, Leonard Russell, Robert Withers *alias* Auncel, Edmund Benbury, and Thomas Hill.

No lands or goods in Wilts.

C 239/65 no. 57

163 Henry Gauntlett and Thomas Gauntlett, each 'yoman', of Westwellowe

11 July 42 Eliz. I [1600]. *Capias* returnable on the morrow of All Souls next [3 Nov.], sued out by John Palmer, citizen and clothier of London, to whom Henry and Thomas acknowledged 300*l*. on 17 Apr. 38 Eliz. I [1596] before William Webb, knight, then mayor of the Staple of Westminster, and John Croke, esquire, recorder of London, payable at Whitsun then next [30 May].

The sheriff certifies that Henry and Thomas have not been found and that the lands were delivered to the queen on 24 July 42 Eliz. I [1600].

24 July 42 Eliz. I [1600]. Inquisition at New Salisbury before Walter Vaughan, esquire, by Thomas Tichborne, gentleman, Thomas Cooper, William Good, John Jewell, Thomas Goddyn, Richard Forder, Robert Selwyn, Nicholas Aldridge, Richard Prettye, Thomas Fox, John Pinhorne, and Thomas Adams.

Henry has no goods or lands in Wilts.

Thomas at the time of the inquisition was seised in his demesne as of fee in Westwellowe of: a messuage called 'Pins', now in his own occupation, 2 closes of meadow and pasture of *c*. 10 a. adjoining the messuage, closes of meadow or pasture called 'Pykes' of *c*. 16 a., 'Expringes' and 'Waterlands' of *c*. 7½ a., a tenement and 2½ a. of pasture held by John Crooker, a tenement and 2½ a. of pasture held by Daniel Greenfeild, a meadow called 'Chortridge Meade' of *c*. 6 a. held by Thomas Adams, a tenement and ½ a. of pasture held by Thomas Reade, a tenement and 3 a. of pasture held by Nicholas Hiscockes, a close of pasture held by Thomas Adams of *c*. 12 a., called 'Adams', 4 closes of meadow and pasture called 'Ringston', 'Benacre', 'Expringe Meade', and 'Danyell Ford Meade' held by Thomas Adams and Robert Selwyn, of *c*. 12 a., a close of pasture called 'Feild Close' of *c*. 6 a. held by Simon Webbe, 2 closes of meadow and pasture of *c*. 5 a. held by Maurice Crooker, a tenement and 16 a. of meadow and pasture held by Elizabeth Trett, a piece of pasture of ½ a. in Harebridge, a tenement and 3 a. of pasture held by Andrew Downe, a close of pasture held by Richard Gauntlett of *c*. 12 a., a tenement and ½ a. of pasture held by John Lide, a close of pasture called 'Shutbackes' held by Henry Hutchins of *c*. ½ a., a tenement and 15 a. of land and pasture held by Thomas Blake, a close of pasture called 'Elliottes' held by Thomas Pannell of *c*. 3 a., worth 16*l*. 18*s*. yearly.

C 239/66 no. 125

164 Matthew Grove, gentleman, of Chesenbury

27 Oct. 42 Eliz. I [1600]. *Capias* returnable in oct. of Martinmas next [18

Nov.], sued out by John Maton, 'yoman', of Barwick St. James, to whom Matthew acknowledged 200*l.* on 3 May 30 Eliz. I [1588] before Christopher Wray, knight, then chief justice of the Queen's Bench, payable at Whitsun then next [26 May].
Endorsed. Matthew has not been found.

17 Nov. 43 Eliz. I [1600]. Inquisition at Wilton before Walter Vaughan, esquire, by Richard Redman, Walter Sharpe, Thomas Hayte, Walter Graye, and Robert Boston, gentlemen, William Sharpe, Humphrey Dytton, Stephen Hibberd, John Rowden, Thomas Graye, John Milles, and John Morrys.

Matthew, as assignee of John Maton, of William Flemynge, esquire, and of Francis Flemynge, knight, on the day of the inquisition possessed as his own goods: a messuage called 'the farme' of Chesenbury and 300 a. of land, 10 a. of meadow, 3 a. of pasture, and pasture in common for 600 sheep belonging to the messuage in Chesenburye by virtue of a grant for 99 years from Mich. 38 Hen. VIII [1546] from Thomas Seymour, knight, Lord Seymour of Sudeley, master of the hospital of St. Katherine by the Tower of London, the brethren and sisters to the said Francis, by indenture of 1 Sept. 1 Edw. VI [1547]. The residue of the said term is worth 75*l.* yearly.

22 Nov. 43 Eliz. I [1600]. *Liberate* returnable in oct. of Hil. next [20 Jan.]; with *capias* against Matthew's body.
Endorsed. The lands were delivered on 25 Nov. 43 Eliz. I [1600]. Matthew has not been found.

The writ thus endorsed was delivered to Thomas Snell, esquire, sheriff, by Walter Vaughan, esquire, former sheriff, on his departure from office.

C 239/66 no. 144

165 John Toppe the elder and the younger

. . . [*MS. blind*] 43 Eliz. I [1600]. *Fieri facias* returnable in oct. of Hil. next [20 Jan.], for Roland Lacon, esquire, of Kinlett, Salop., who recovered 412*l.* 16*s.* 4*d.* in Chancery against John Toppe the elder and the younger to be levied from their lands and chattels.

On 9 Feb. 18 Eliz. I [1576], George Blounte, knight, of Kinllett, Salop., James Crofte, knight, comptroller of the queen's household, and Anthony Bourne, esquire, of Saresden, Oxon., at Westminster before Christopher Wray, knight, then chief justice of the Queen's Bench, acknowledged 600*l.* to Henry Ughtred, then esquire, now knight, payable at a date named in the recognizance.

As George, James, and Anthony did not observe the term, Henry laid claim to the following lands in Staffs. In Knightley: the manor and a messuage, 100 a. of land, 40 a. of meadow, and 100 a. of pasture late held by Robert Smithe; a messuage, a garden and a yard, 30 a. of land, 40 a. of meadow, and 60 a. of pasture called 'Knightley Heis' held by Robert Tyllesley; 100 a. of land and 100 a. of pasture in 'Romesmeades' late held by Robert Harecourte *alias* Cooke and William Lawton, esquire.

A messuage and garden, 40 a. of land, 10 a. of meadow, and 20 a. of pasture in Bishopps Offley late held by Thomas Vyse; a messuage and garden, 20 a. of land, 16 a. of meadow, and 20 a. of pasture in Little Onne held by William Hakyn; 4 messuages or cottages, 20 a. of land, 5 a. of meadow, and 20 a. of pasture in Gnowsall held severally by John Payne, Robert Cowper, and Francis Hitchins.

In Waterfall: a messuage, 70 a. of land, 2 a. of meadow, and 6 a. of pasture held by Martin Hall; a messuage, 16 a. of land, 1½ a. of meadow, and 3 a. of pasture held by Robert Owkdenne; a messuage, 15 a. of land, 2 a. of meadow, and 5 a. of pasture held by Richard Plott and Thomas Chesshire; a messuage, 18 a. of land, 2 a. of meadow, and 6 a. of pasture with a messuage, 24 a. of land, 4 a. of meadow, and 10 a. of pasture in Romsore, and a messuage and garden, 30 a. of land, 4 a. of meadow, and 10 a. of pasture in Denson *alias* Denston, held by Thomas Bett.

In Denson *alias* Denstone: a messuage and garden, 15 a. of land, 2 a. of meadow, and 5 a. of pasture held by — [*MS. blank*] Holan, widow; a messuage and garden, 6 a. of land, 1 a. of meadow, and 5 a. of pasture held by Richard Tailor; a messuage and garden, 8 a. of land, 1½ a. of meadow, and 6 a. of pasture held by John Bett.

In Teine: a messuage and garden, 60 a. of land, 30 a. of meadow, and 100 a. of pasture held by Thomas and Edward Witterneis; a messuage and garden, 30 a. of land, 10 a. of meadow, and 100 a. of pasture held by Robert Thacker; a messuage and garden, 15 a. of land, 3 a. of meadow, and 8 a. of pasture held by Edward Phillipps; a messuage, 16 a. of land, 3 a. of meadow, and 10 a. of pasture held by Edward Strongthearme; a messuage, 14 a. of land, 3 a. of meadow, and 7 a. of pasture held by Thomas Saunders; a messuage and garden, 18 a. of land, 5 a. of meadow, and 12 a. of pasture held by Anthony Ralyn and Richard Bucknall; a messuage and garden, 9 a. of land, 1½ a. of meadow, and 6 a. of pasture held by Thomas Hall; a messuage, 10 a. of land, 1½ a. of meadow, and 5 a. of pasture held by — [*MS. blank*] Walker, widow.

In Hopton: a messuage and garden, 100 a. of meadow, 200 a. of pasture held by Richard Foxe; a messuage and garden, 40 a. of land, 20 a. of meadow, and 60 a. of pasture held by Richard Chewnall; a messuage, 30 a. of land, 20 a. of meadow, and 40 a. of pasture held by Francis Lysett and John Mathew; a messuage and garden, 20 a. of land, and 30 a. of pasture held by John Chewnall; a messuage and garden, 20 a. of land, 10 a. of meadow, and 20 a. of pasture held by Humphrey Henne; a messuage and garden, 20 a. of land, 10 a. of meadow, and 20 a. of pasture held by Humphrey Bagnall; a messuage and garden, 30 a. of land, 20 a. of meadow, and 20 a. of pasture held by William Henne; a cottage held by Edward Whithall; a messuage and garden, 30 a. of land, 20 a. of meadow, and 30 a. of pasture held by James Sale; a messuage and garden, 30 a. of land, 20 a. of meadow, and 30 a. of pasture held by John Grime; a messuage and garden, 20 a. of land, 10 a. of meadow, and 20 a. of pasture held by Humphrey Sale; a messuage and garden, 24 a. of land, 20 a. of meadow, and 30 a. of pasture held by John Walker; a messuage and garden, 30 a. of land, 12 a. of meadow, and 4 a. of pasture held by Edward Foxe; a messuage and garden, 22 a. of land, 12 a. of meadow and

20 a. of pasture held by Edward Withall; a messuage and garden, 22 a. of land, 14 a. of meadow, and 300 a. of pasture held by Godfrey Henne and Elizabeth Henne, widow; a messuage and croft of pasture held by Walter Yate; a messuage and garden, 10 a. of land, 6 a. of meadow, and 8 a. of pasture held by John Erpes; divers closes and pasture called 'Hopton Wood' and 'Newfeild' held by John Chetwynde, esquire; closes of pasture called 'the Poole', 'the Lordes Leys', and 'Sale'; 32*s*. 7*d*. rent in Fenton.

The above lands, which Roland Lacon had held in fee, and of which George Blounte, knight, was seised after the recognizance, were acquired by Henry Ughtred by process of Chancery as execution for the debt, except the manor of Alton, Worcs., which also belonged to Blounte after the recognizance.

Because of a plea in Chancery on a writ of *audita querela* in Lacon *v*. Toppe and Toppe, to whom Henry Ughtred had assigned his interest in the lands late delivered to him by the court, it was adjudged that Roland Lacon should be restored to possession of the lands; the sheriff of Staffs. has reported that the rents and profits of the lands since the assignment to the Toppes amount to 412*l*. 16*s*. 4*d*.; the sheriff of Wilts. is to levy that sum from the lands and goods of the Toppes, as they have no goods in Staffs.

Endorsed. The sheriff has levied 412*l*. 16*s*. 4*d*. from the Toppes' goods; later, on a writ of *supersedeas*, he restored the money to them, except 10*l*. which he has retained in accordance with the statute.

4 Jan. 43 Eliz. I [1601]. *Supersedeas* forbidding the sheriff to execute the writ or, if he has done so, charging him to restore to the Toppes all goods taken from them.

C 239/67 no. 23

166 John Berkeley, esquire, of Langley Burrell

24 Oct. 43 Eliz. I [1601]. *Capias* returnable in oct. of Martinmas next [18 Nov.], sued out by William Pyke, gentleman, and his wife Elizabeth, executors of Alexander Staples, gentleman, of Yeatt, Glos., to whom John acknowledged 1,200*l*. on 3 May 30 Eliz. I [1588] before Christopher Wraye, knight, then chief justice of the Queen's Bench, payable at Whitsun then next [26 May]. Like writ to the sheriff of Glos.

Endorsed. John has not been found.

9 Nov. 43 Eliz. I [1601]. Inquisition at Chippenham before Thomas Snell, esquire, by Thomas Rabe, Robert Harris, John Harris, John Baldwyn, Robert Hawkins, Edward Effington, William Jeffery, William Exham, Anthony Butler, Roger Payne, Robert Baker, and Richard Bennett.

At the time of the inquisition John had no lands or goods in Wilts. Since the jury were not charged in the writ to extend the lands and chattels held by John at the time of the recognizance, they have not done so.

C 239/67 no. 137

5 Dec. 44 Eliz. I [1601]. *Capias* returnable in quin. of Hil. next [27 Jan.]; with *extendi facias* for the lands and goods held by John at the time of the

recognizance or afterwards; as it is understood that John held no lands or goods in Wilts.
Endorsed. John has not been found.

23 Jan. 44 Eliz. I [1602]. Inquisition at Chippenham before Henry Baynton, knight, by Ralph Calley, gentleman, Walter Barrett, Thomas Cogswell, John Harrys, John Wastfeild, John Ealy, Robert Baker, William Nowell, John Baylie, Robert Hawkyns, John Newman, William Exam, Thomas Brode, and Richard Terreyll.

On 6 May 30 Eliz. I [1588], seised in his demesne as of fee of the manor of Langley Burrell, worth 80*l.* yearly.

C 239/68 no. 24

167 John Danvers, knight, of Dauntesey, and John Calley, gentleman, of Hilmerton

19 Nov. 44 Eliz. I [1601]. *Capias* returnable in quin. of Hil. next [27 Jan.], sued out by William Tyndall the elder and John Tyndall, esquires, Humphrey Tyndall, doctor of theology, and Francis Tyndall, gentleman, to whom John and John acknowledged 600*l.* on 11 Feb. 26 Eliz. I [1584] before Edmund Anderson, knight, chief justice of the Common Pleas, payable at Eas. then next [19 Apr.]. Like writs to the sheriffs of Glos. and Leics.
Endorsed. John and John are dead.

6 Feb. 44 Eliz. I [1602]. *Extendi facias* for John Calley, returnable in quin. of Eas. next [18 Apr.].
Endorsed. The writ arrived too late to enable the sheriff to execute the whole charge.

C 239/68 no. 2

17 Apr. 44 Eliz. I [1602]. Inquisition at Cricklad' before Henry Baynton, knight, by John Burge, Daniel Sclatter *alias* Champernon, Robert Kemble, Richard Dennys, William Burge, Richard Trinder, Thomas Howse, Charles Taynter, John Walton, Robert Hobbes, Anthony Collywood, John Plover, Richard Butter, Daniel Browne, and William Bathe.

Seised in his demesne as of fee tail of the manor of Cleeve Auncey, worth 9*l.* 10*s.* yearly.

At the time of his death possessed the goods in the attached schedule, worth 323*l.* 10*s.* 7*d.* These goods passed on his death to his relict Martha.

Extract from the register of the Prerogative Court of Canterbury.

'An inventarye indented of all the goodes, chattells, howshoulde stuffe, and utensylls as were in the possession of John Calley, late of Hilmerton in the county of Wiltes., gentleman, deceased, at the tyme of his decease, prised the sixtenth day of Januarye in the fortyeth yere of the raigne of Queene Elizabeth A.D. 1597. George Stratton, William Bonde, Henry Seager, and Robert Thresher.

In the best chamber over the parlor

1 standinge bedstead furnished with 1 fetherbede, 2 boulsters, 2 payre of pillowes, 1 payre

of blankettes, 1 greene rugge coverlett, and 1 other coverlett of tapistrye	7*l.*	16*s.*	8*d.*
1 other bedstead furnished with a canopie, 1 fetherbed, 1 boulster, 1 payre of pillowes, 1 payre of blankettes, 1 red coverlett, 2 lowe stoles, 2 fayre letherne chayres, old wrought cushions, 1 joyned standinge cupboard, 1 litle table, 2 windowe curtayne rodes and curtaynes to the same, 1 cupboard cloth, 1 lardge greate Flanders chest, 1 doz. of bedstaves, and 1 payre of andirons	5*l.*	10*s.*	4*d.*
The wearing apparrell	20*l.*		

In the next little chamber

1 other bedstead furnished with a tester of joyners worke, 1 fetherbede, 2 boulsters, 1 payre of pillowes, 1 old mattris, 1 payre of blankettes, 2 coverlettes, ½ doz. of bedstaves	2*l.*	17*s.*	1*d.*

In the outer chamber over the pantry and closett

1 other bedstede furnished with a tester of joyners worke, 1 fetherbede, 2 boulsters, 1 pillowe, 1 payre of blankettes, 1 rede coverlett, 1 truckle bede of joyners worke furnished, 1 fetherbede, 1 boulster, 1 blankett, 1 coverlette, 1 truncke with locke and keye	3*l.*	3*s.*	10*d.*

In the cockloft over that

1 joyned bedsteade, 1 boulster, 1 fetherbede, 1 blankett, 1 coverlett, 1 tableboard, 2 tressells, 1 chayre stoole, 1 flaskett, 1 cradle, and 6 hampers		25*s.*	10*d.*

In myne owne chamber over the hall

1 bedsteade furnished with a tester of joyners worke, 1 puft flockbede, 1 boulster, 1 payre of pillowes, 1 payre of blankettes, 1 checker rugge, ½ doz. of bedstaves, 1 other joyned bedstead there, 1 other fetherbede, 1 boulster, 1 rugge, 1 blankett, 1 coverlett, 1 truncke, 2 truncke coffers, 1 cypres chest, 1 little flatt coffer, 2 little coffers	3*l.*	10*s.*	8*d.*
1 longe coffer crampt with iron, 1 table boarde with leaves, 1 payre of andirons, 1 fire shovell, 1 payre of tonges, 1 warmynge panne, 1 greate presse of joyners worke, 1 old curtayne and a longe countinge board in studye, 2 deskes with lockes and keyes, 1 standishe, 1 chayre, and the sondrye sortes of bookes	3*l.*	9*s.*	8*d.*

In the maydens chamber within that

2 playne bedsteades of boardes, 2 flockbedes, 2 boulsters, 1 mattresse, 1 quilt, 1 payre of blankettes, 2 old coverlettes, 1 close stole, 1 presse 28*s*. 8*d*.

In the parlor

[1 lardge] Bible, 3 bookes of Common Prayer, 1 [lesser Bible, 1 payre of virginals], 1 greate table board [on a joyners frame], 1 lesser square joyned tableboarde, [12 joyned stooles, 1 joyned forme,] 1 standinge cupboard, [1 leatherne chayre, 1] carpet, 1 cupboard cloth, 1 other fayre carpette, 6 fayre cushions of tapistrye, 1 fayre holberte there trimmed with crimson and goulde and case to yt, 2 fayre Flaunders bills, 1 payre of tables, 1 payre of tonges, 1 fyreshovell, 1 pare of andirons, 3 curteyns and curteyne rodds 6*l*. 2*s*. 10*d*.

In the pantrye

1 fyne coveringe flaskett, 1 save corded up, 1 bason and ewer, 1 fayre standinge beere pott, 6 stone pottes 13*s*. 4*d*.

In the closett

1 small payre of ballaunce and waightes, 8 Venice glasses, 6 gallye pottes, 8 gallye dishes, 5 pewter chamber pottes whereof one old, 1 garnishe of vessell of 6 sortes and 6 of everye sorte, 2 greate payre and 1 little payre of pewter candlestickes, 4 salts and 2 doz. of pewter spoones, 2 chardgers, 2 plates, 1 greate bason, 1 greate bole bason, 6 pewter porringers, 12 fyne plates of alcumine, 1 longe pewter spone, 1 possett bason, 1 stille, 1 limbecke, 6 dozen of trenchers, 1 payre of greate brason candlestickes and a perfumer, 2 little brasse candlestickes, and 2 old basons 4*l*. 8*s*.

In the hall

1 table boarde one a playne frame, 1 longe forme to it, 1 little cupboarde bounde with leaves, 1 old chayre, 1 turkye cushion, 6 greene cushions, 1 other syde boarde one a frame, 6 joyned stooles, 1 payre of andirons, 2 calivers furnished, 1 livery bowe, 2 sheafes of arrowes, and a steelecappe 3*l*. 11*s*. 8*d*.

In the kitchen

1 longe table boarde on two tressells, 1 longe forme to yt, 1 spence of playne boardes, 1 salt

boxe, 1 other planck forme, 4 payre of pothookes, 3 other crockes, 1 crooke and flatt iron bare, 1 payre of rostinge rackes, 5 broaches, 3 trevittes, 1 brasen skymmer, 1 brasen ladle, 1 payre of tonges, 1 fire shovell, 2 iron drippinge pannes — 30*s*.

2 gridirons, 1 brasen bastinge ladle, 1 grater, 2 clevers, 2 choppinge knives and 2 mynsinge knives, 7 brasen pottes, 4 kettles, 3 skillets, 1 fleshforke, 1 chafer, 1 brasen chaffingdishe, 1 litel mustard mill, 1 posnett, and 4 other dripping pannes — 3*l*. 14*s*.

In the larder and whitehowse and lofte over the whitehowse

1 saltinge stone, 2 powdringe tubbes, 1 salt barrell, 1 greate plancke with other spences, 1 cheesepresse, 1 fyne strayner, 3 brasen milke pannes, 10 trynnen kevers for milke, 12 earthen pannes, 1 shelfe for vessell, 9 trayes, 2 churnes, 1 butter printe, 2 creame stobbins, 1 pounde stone, 1 payre of butter skales, 12 cheese vates, 2 drenes, 2 bowles, 1 runninge cowle, 1 lardge malte witche, 1 mault garnerde, 1 greate cheeseracke, 1 other cheeseboard, 2 corne tubbes — 51*s*. 4*d*.

In the wellhowse chamber, brewehouse, and bakehowse

1 standing bedstead, 1 trucklebed, 2 flockbedes, 2 boulsters, 2 blankettes, 1 little tableboard on 2 tressells, 1 furnace, 1 neshinge vate, 1 kever cooler, 1 greate brasse panne, 1 other greate vate, 3 other kevers, 1 longe kever, 2 deepe tubbes, 4 litle coolinge keevers, 1 strayner and other vessell, 2 stickers, 1 litle payle, 1 bowle, 1 tinndishe and cowle and 1 drayne, 1 fayre malt querne, 1 lardge yeatinge stone, 2 kneading keevers, 1 mouldinge board, 1 serse, 1 mealeseave, 1 hereseave, and 1 capon cubbe — 6*l*. 6*s*. 8*d*.

In the outer buttrye

4 hoggesheades, 7 bigger barrells, 7 lesser barrells, 1 other . . . [to sett barrells on, 2 washinge cowles, 1 beere barrell slinge.] — 30*s*.

In the greate maultinge lofte and apple lofte

2 fayre cheeseracks, 1 wynninge sheete, 1 busshell and streeche, 1 maulte seave, 6

smealler seeves . . . 1 greate presse with particions, 1 great oatmeale kipe, 1 coffer for apples, 3 baskettes and noaste heare — 11*s*. 8*d*.

In the stable chamber and stable

2 playne bedsteades, 1 flockbed, 2 boulsters, 2 blankettes, 2 old coverlettes, 1 iron garden-rake, 1 garden hooke, 1 howe for garden, 1 paire of garden sheeres, 1 dungefork for garden — 26*s*. 8*d*.

In and belonging to the waynehowse barne and oxehowses

1 woodbed furnished, 2 corne bedds furnished, 2 dungepottes furnished, 1 little tithecarr furnished, 5 yokes, 8 bowes, 6 ploughe stringes, 2 woodropes, and 1 waynelyne *cum multis aliis* — 9*l*.

In the wardroppe

1 suite of diaper which is 1 tablecloth, 1 cupboard cloth, 1 towell, 1 dossen of napkins, 2 courser diaper napkins, 2 other table clothes, 2 cupboard clothes, 2 towells and 2 dozen of napkins of fyne Normandye canvas, 4 other table clothes, 4 cupboard clothes, 4 towells and 4 dozen napkins, 12 fine payre of sheetes, 14 cooreser payre, 4 other table clothes, 4 cupboard clothes, 4 towells, 2 dozen of napkins, 4 ordinary table clothes and 4 shorter and 2 dozen of napkins, 4 fine payre of pillowbeeres and 6 coorser payre — 20*l*.

the corne in the grounde, 10 pounds, the wheat rycke 28 poundes, the beane reeke 10 pounds, the beanes in the barne 4 pounds, the peaze reeke and the barley mowe 11 pound, the haye at home and abroad 10 pound — 73*l*.

In other safe custodye remayninge in or about the dwelling howse

1 well buckett with an iron chayne to yt, 4 ladders, ploughe stuffe, 2 hammers, 1 payre of pynsers, timber and the wood — 3*l*. 16*s*. 8*d*.

The cattell cum aliis

6 ploughe oxen, 1 steere, 11 kyne and 1 bull, 8 beastes of 2 yeeres, 10 of 1 yeeres [*sic*], 20 sheepe, 3 mares, 2 gueldinges, 3 coltes and 3 pigs, bacon, beefe, butter, and cheese — 114*l*. 10*s*.

In other safe custodye remayninge

2 silver bowles, 9 silver spoones, soe likewise

guilded and marked, 1 bell double silver salt
with a toppe graven on the cover with armes,
1 silver pott graven on the cover with armes,
1 fayre stone pott trymmed with silver 20*l.*

Total 323*l.* 10*s.* 7*d.*

This inventory was exhibited on 15 May 1598 through Anthony Calton in the name of the executors.

Liberate returnable in oct. of Mich. next [6 Oct.].

C 239/68 no. 40

168 Francis Keylewaye, esquire, of Rogborne, Hampshire

29 Apr. 44 Eliz. I [1602]. *Capias* returnable on the morrow of Ascension next [14 May], sued out by Charles Keylwaye, gentleman, of St. Saviour parish, Southworke, Surr., to whom Francis acknowledged 600*l.* on 21 Dec. 40 Eliz. I [1597] before John Popham, knight, chief justice of the Queen's Bench, payable at Christmas then next. Like writ to the sheriff of Hants.
Endorsed. Francis is dead.

C 239/68 no. 73

169 John Stumpe, esquire, of Malmesbury

22 Nov. 45 Eliz. I [1602]. *Capias* returnable in quin. of Martinmas next [25 Nov.], sued out by George Ayliffe, gentleman, of London, to whom John acknowledged 200*l.* on 13 Feb. 39 Eliz. I [1597] before John Popham, knight, chief justice of the Queen's Bench, payable at the Purification then next [2 Feb.].
Endorsed. John is dead.

C 239/69 no. 3 a

170 Thomas Mompesson, of Corton, and Henry Mompesson, of Middle Temple, London, esquires

23 Nov. 45 Eliz. I [1602]. *Capias* returnable in oct. of Hil. next [20 Jan.], sued out by George Ayliffe, gentleman, of Winterborne Ayliffe *alias* Northwinterborne, to whom Thomas and Henry acknowledged 200*l.* on 3 Feb. 42 Eliz. I [1600] before Edmund Anderson, knight, chief justice of the Common Pleas, payable at Eas. then next [23 Mar.]. Like writ to the sheriff of Dors.
Endorsed. Thomas and Henry have not been found.

17 Jan. 45 Eliz. I [1603]. Inquisition at Hyndon before Walter Longe, knight, by George Mervyn, Edmund Pyke, Thomas Harton, Edward Poton, and George Gifford, gentlemen, Thomas Bennett, Robert Wall, William Oburne, William Lewes, Thomas Feltham, John Myles, Augustine Kynge, Thomas Barnard, Robert Farnehill, Anthony Burbage, Humphrey Leare, Thomas Coxe, John Cantlowe, and William Smythe.

Thomas was seised in his demesne as of fee of a capital messuage in Corton *alias* Cortington and lands, meadows, feedings, and pastures belonging, and lands in Sherington, Great Somerford, Calne, and Bachehampton, worth 40*l.* yearly.

Henry had no lands or goods in Wilts.

C 239/69 no. 5

171 James Lovell, gentleman, of Bulforde

5 Feb. 45 Eliz. I [1603]. *Capias* returnable in oct. of the Purification next [9 Feb.], sued out by Richard Hearst, gentleman, of Marlebroughe, to whom James acknowledged 200*l.* on 16 June 33 Eliz. I [1591] before Edmund Anderson, knight, chief justice of the Common Pleas, payable at Midsummer then next. Like writ to the sheriff of Hants.
Endorsed. James has not been found.

8 Feb. 45 Eliz. I [1603]. Inquisition at Wockingham before Walter Longe, knight, by John Coles, John Fulker, John Feltham, John Marshe, William Planner, Ralph Spore, William Bolde, William Hubye, John Merryfield, Henry Collyns, Oliver Hyde, Francis Piggott, Ralph Soper *alias* Gyles, John Lichfield, and John Prince.

Seised in his demesne as of fee of Bulford rectory, worth 70*l.* yearly. On 20 Nov. 36 Eliz. I [1593] seised of a capital messuage or farm and 2 water-mills in Bulford lately held by James Lovell and John Mathewe, worth 100*l.* yearly.

12 Feb. 45 Eliz. I [1603]. *Liberate* returnable in quin. of Eas. next [8 May]; with *capias* against James's body. Like writ to the sheriff of Hants in respect of manors and messuages there worth 20*l.* yearly.
Endorsed. The lands were delivered on 24 Feb. 45 Eliz. I [1603].

C 239/69 no. 20

APPENDIX OF WRITS

CAPIAS

Henricus octavus[1] . . . vicecomiti Wiltes' salutem. Quia Walterus Singleton de Shalborne in comitatu Berk', generosus, filius et heres Thome Singleton de Shalborne in comitatu predicto generosi defuncti, et Nicholaus Thorne de Sonnyng in comitatu Berk', generosus, ultimo die Octobris anno regni nostri tricesimo primo coram Edwardo Mountague, milite, tunc capitali justiciario nostro ad placita, recognoverunt se debere Michaeli Dormer, civi et aldermanno London', ducentas libras sterlingorum quas ei soluisse debuissent in festo natalis domini tunc proximo futuro et eas ei nondum soluerunt nec eorum alter adhuc soluit, ut dicitur, tibi precipimus quod corpora predictorum Walteri et Nicholai, si laici sint, capi et in prisona nostra donec Katherine Dormer vidue et Johanni Dormer executoribus testamenti predicti Michaelis de dictis ducentis libris plene satisfecerint salvo custodiri ac omnia terras et catalla ipsorum Walteri et Nicholai in balliva tua per sacramentum proborum et legalium hominum de eadem balliva tua per quos rei veritas melius sciri poterit juxta verum valorem eorumdem diligenter extendi et appreciari et in manum nostram seisiri facias ut ea prefatis executoribus, quousque sibi de dictis ducentis libris plene satisfactum fuerit, liberari faciamus juxta formam statuti apud Westm' pro hujusmodi debitis recuperandis inde nuper editi et provisi. Et qualiter hoc preceptum nostrum fueris executus scire facias nobis in cancellariam nostram a die Pasche proximo futuro in tres septimanas ubicumque tunc fuerit per litteras tuas sigillatas. Et habeas ibi hoc breve. Mandavimus enim vicecomitibus nostris Oxon' et Berk' quod corpora predictorum Walteri et Nicholai, si laici sint, capi et in prisona nostra salvo custodiri ac omnia terras et catalla ipsorum Walteri et Nicholai in ballivis suis diligenter extendi et appreciari et in manum nostram seisiri faciant in forma predicta. Teste meipso apud Westm' xiij die Februarii anno regni nostri tricesimo septimo.

LIBERATE

Edwardus[2] . . . vicecomiti Wiltes' salutem. Cum Johannes Blount miles de comitatu tuo vicesimo die Octobris proximo preterito coram Willelmo de Walleworth, majore stapule Westm' ad recogniciones debitorum in eadem stapula accipiendas, recognoverit se debere Roberto Pikerell civi et sellario London' centum et viginti libras quas ei soluisse debuit in die sancti Martini tunc proximo sequenti et eas ei nondum soluerit, ut dicitur, [et] tibi preceperimus quod corpus . . . [as *capias*], ac tu nobis retornaveris quod corpus predicti Johannis Blount non est inventus in balliva tua et quod nulla habuit bona seu catalla in comitatu tuo que extendi seu appreciari possint set quod habet apud Beveresbrouk [lands as in extent] quod quidem manerium cum pertinenciis virtute mandati nostri predicti cepisti in manum nostram, tibi precipimus quod eidem Roberto manerium predictum cum pertinenciis, si illud per extentam illam recipere voluerit, sine dilacione liberes habendum sibi et assignatis suis ut liberum tenementum suum quousque dicte centum et viginti libre una cum dampnis suis et misis et expensis suis in hac parte retornabiliter appositis de dicto manerio fuerint levate. Et nichilominus corpus predicti Johannis Blount si laicus sit capias et in prisona nostra salvo custodiri facias donec eidem Roberto de predicto fuerit satisfactum. Et qualiter [as *capias*].

EXTENDI FACIAS

Elizabeth[3] . . . vicecomiti Wiltes' salutem. Cum Edwardus Darrell de Litlecote in comitatu tuo miles nono die Septembris anno regni domini Henrici octavi . . . tricesimo

[1] C 131/116 no. 6. For abstract see 76.
[2] C 131/24 no. 11. For abstract see 18.
[3] C 131/127 no. 1. For abstract see 121.

octavo coram Radulpho Warren, milite, tunc majore stapule Westm' et Radulpho Broke, armigero, tunc recordatore civitatis London' recognoverit se debere Willelmo Essex de Chepynglamborn in comitatu Berk' militi jam defuncto octingentas libras quas eidem Willelmo Essex soluisse debuisset in festo omnium sanctorum tunc proximo futuro et eas ei nondum soluit, ut dicebatur, super quo per breve nostrum tibi nuper preceperimus quod corpus . . . [as *capias*], ad quem diem tu nobis in cancellariam nostram predictam nuper retornaveris quod prenominatus Edwardus Darrell miles mortuus est; tibi igitur precipimus quod omnia terra et tenementa que fuerunt predicti Edwardi die recognicionis debiti predicti seu unquam postea nisi alicui heredi infra etatem existenti jure hereditario descenderunt ac omnia bona et catalla que fuerunt ejusdem Edwardi tempore mortis sue in dicta balliva tua per sacramentum proborum et legalium hominum de eadem balliva tua per quos rei veritas melius sciri poterit juxta verum valorem eorumdem diligenter extendi et appreciari et in manum nostram seisiri facias ut ea prefato administratori quousque sibi de dictis octingentis libris plenarie fuerit satisfactum liberari faciamus juxta formam statuti predicti. Et qualiter [as *capias*].

NON OMITTAS

Ricardus[1] . . . vicecomiti Wiltes' salutem. Cum Robertus Redyng de Nova Sar' vicesimo sexto die Februarii anno regni nostri primo coram Willelmo de Walleworth, majore stapule Westm' ad recogniciones debitorum in eadem stapula accipiendas deputato, recognoverit se debere Ade Fermer civi et cultellario London' quaterviginti libras quas ei soluisse debuit in festo nativitatis sancti Johannis Baptiste tunc proximo sequenti et eas ei nondum soluit, ut dicitur, et tibi preceperimus . . . [as *capias*], ac tu nobis retornaveris quod retornum brevis predicti habere fecisti Thome Hungerford, ballivo libertatis episcopi Sar' qui plenum habet retornum omnium brevium nostrum et execucionem eorumdem, extra quam libertatem nulla execucio inde fieri potuit in balliva tua, qui quidem ballivus nullum inde tibi dedit responsum; tibi precipimus quod non omittas propter libertatem illam quin eam ingrediaris et corpus predicti Roberti, si laicus sit, capias et in prisona nostra donec eidem Ade de predicto debito plene satisfecerit salvo custodiri et omnia terras et catalla ipsius Roberti in balliva tua per sacramentum proborum et legalium hominum de dicta balliva tua, per quos rei veritas melius sciri poterit, diligenter extendi et appreciari et in manum nostram seisiri facias ut ea prefato Ade quousque sibi de predicto debito satisfactum fuerit liberari faciamus juxta formam ordinacionis predicte. Et qualiter [as *capias*].

ELEGIT

Henricus[2] . . . vicecomiti Wiltes' salutem. Cum Henricus Perpoynt, chivaler, Rogerus Bernardeston de Kedyngton in comitatu Suff', armiger, et Robertus Eland de Ratheby, armiger, septimo die Novembris anno regni nostri duodecimo recognoverint se et quemlibet eorum per se insolidum debere Johanni Wynter, Rogero Wynter, Johanni Breghton, et Ade Lovelord viginti et tres libros, sex solidos, et octo denarios quos eis soluisse debuerunt in festo natalis domini quod erat in anno millesimo quadringentesimo tricesimo quarto, sicut per inspeccionem rotulorum cancellarie nostre nobis constat, et eos eis nondum soluerunt, ut dicitur, et per breve nostrum tibi preceperimus quod scire faceres prefatis Henrico, Rogero Bernardeston, et Roberto quod essent coram nobis in cancellaria nostra ad certum diem jam preteritum ubicumque tunc foret, ad ostendendum si quid pro se haberent vel dicere scirent quare prefati Johannes, Rogerus Wynter, Johannes, et Adam execucionem dictorum viginti et trium librarum, sex solidorum, et octo denariorum versus eos habere non deberent juxta formam statuti inde editi et provisi, ac tu nobis retornaveris quod scire fecisti prefato Rogero Bernardeston per Willelmum Smyth et Johannem Randolf, probos et legales homines, quod esset coram nobis in cancellariam predictam ad diem illum ad ostendendum, faciendum, et recipiendum quod breve predictum in se exigebat et requirebat, et quod predicti Henricus et Robertus nichil habuerunt ubi eis scire facere potuisti, ad quem

[1] C 131/28 no. 24. For abstract see 25.
[2] C 131/64 no. 5. For abstract see 46.

diem prefatus Rogerus Bernardeston in cancellaria predicta solempniter vocatus non venit ac iidem Johannes, Rogerus Wynter, Johannes, et Adam juxta statutum inde editum elegerint sibi liberari pro predictis viginti et tribus libris, sex solidis, et octo denariis omnia catalla et medietatem terrarum ipsius Rogeri Bernardeston tenend' juxta formam statuti predicti, tibi precipimus quod omnia catalla ipsius Rogeri Bernardeston ad valenciam viginti et trium librarum, sex solidorum, et octo denariorum per retornabilem appreciacionem eorumdem, exceptis bobus et affris caruce sue, in presencia predicti Rogeri Bernardeston per te inde premuniendi si interesse voluerit faciend' prefatis Johanni Wynter, Rogero Wynter, Johanni Breghton, et Ade Lovelord vel eorum certo attornato facias liberari. Et si catalla illa ad valenciam viginti et trium librarum, sex solidorum, et octo denariorum non sufficiant tunc catalla illa sic minus valencia per retornabilem appreciacionem ac eciam medietatem terre ipsius Rogeri Bernardeston in balliva tua per extentam inde similiter in presencia sua in forma predicta faciend' prefatis Johanni Wynter, Rogero Wynter, Johanni Breghton, et Ade vel suo dicto attornato facias liberari tenend' ut liberum tenementum suum quousque dicti viginti et tres libre, sex solidi, et octo denarii inde fuerint levati. Et de eo quod inde feceris nobis in cancellaria nostra in quindena sancti Michaelis proxima futura ubicumque tunc fuerit sub sigillo tuo distincte et aperte constare facias. Et habeas ibi hoc breve. Teste meipso apud Westm' xviij die Maii anno regni nostri quindecimo.

GLOSSARY

Explanations are given of the modern forms of words whose definitions are not easily obtainable. Definitions of drapery terms are drawn mainly from S. W. Beck, *The Draper's Dictionary*.

ambry (73): cupboard
aune (73): ell (French measure of length)
'*auruefele*' (73): gold thread (Latin *aurifilum*)
'*awndes*', *see aune*
bands, scole wexcke (73):
bat (73): lump, piece
bedstaff (167): staff or stick used in some way about a bed
bedstead, field (156): trestle bedstead
'*bleyte*' (73): bleached, whitened
bolt (73): roll of cloth
bow, livery (167): bow given as livery for servant's use
brander (82): gridiron
brazil (73): reddish dye-stuff from Brazil
broach (73): spit
buckram, paste (73): buckram stiffened with paste
buttons (73): balls (of thread)
caddis (73): kind of yarn used for embroidery, or in making narrow fancy fabrics
camlet (73): fabric of mohair and silk
canvas, vitry (73): light durable canvas originally made at Vitré, Brittany
cloth, Guernsey (73): violet cloth
clout (73): piece of cloth containing a number of pins and needles
cobiron (73): iron on which spit turns
cockloft (167): small upper loft
coser (80, 107): small chest
cotterel (73): trammel over which a pot is hung.
coverlet, list (156): coverlet made up of 'lists' or edgings
cowl, running (167): ? vessel for carrying off liquid
creepers (80): pair of small iron fire dogs placed upon a hearth between the andirons
cupboard, chayrt (107): ? cupboard for maps
dogs, pair of (158): utensils placed on each side of a fireplace to support burning wood
dornick (73): textile fabric originally manufactured at Tournay
dosser (25): ornamental cloth used to cover back of seat
drag (100): harrow
drain (167): kind of funnel
'*eches*' (100): kind of tool
'*fire pike flyse*' (82): *Cf.* pike, fire
forcer (61, 73): casket, chest
fustian, 'apys' (73): fustian from Naples
— , *bevernax* (73):
— , *Geyne* (73): fustian from Genoa
— , *Holmes* (73): fustian from Ulm
ganny bird (107): turkey
garner (167): bin in a mill or granary; partition or 'ark' in a granary
gatherer (25): ? string for re-opening the slats of a louver. *Cf.* vane, closing
gimlet (73): tub
grains (73): a spice
gris (73): grey, or made of grey fur

hales (73): ? tents
haqueton (1): stuffed jacket or jerkin
hats, thrummed (73): hats covered with a pile
heling (80): covering
holland (73): fine linen originally made in Holland
'*ippere*' (1): ? crowbar (O.E. *ypping-iren*)
kever (156, 167): shallow wooden vessel or tub
kimnel (11): vat
kipe (167): basket
lace, British (73): lace from Brittany
lambeau (73): ribbon hanging down from head-dress
lead (73): large pot or cauldron
linite (73): flax prepared for spinning
locks (73): lowest class of wool remnants
'*lore cover*', '*lore pypys*' (73):
'*morwedole*' (5): measure of land
pan, fire (73): chafing dish
pike, fire (82): kind of poker
pillow tie (73): pillow-case
print, butter (167): stamp for impressing design on butter
puke (73): superior kind of woollen cloth
rack (107): forked stick of iron used for supporting cross-bow
ropes, mailing (73): ropes for tying up
rout (147): close or field
sanap (25): cloth to protect the tablecloth
sanders (73): sandalwood
sarplier (73): sack of canvas
sarsenet (73): fine material
say (73): cloth of fine texture akin to serge
searce (167): sieve or strainer
senvy seed (82): mustard
settler (82): vessel in which something is left to settle
silesia (73): sleasy, linen cloth made in Silesia
silk, open (73): a stage through which raw silk passes before it is made up into yarn
sinoper (61): red
sling (167): apparatus to support a barrel while it is being moved
staddle (158): lower part of a stack of corn
'*sticker*' (167):
stillatory (73): still
'*stobbins*', *cream* (167):
stone, pound (167): natural stone weighing 1 lb.
strickle (167): straight piece of wood with which surplus grain is struck off level with the rim of a measure
sullow (156): plough
sultedge (73): coarse apron worn by women in some parts of Wiltshire or kind of coarse sheeting
thrave (80): measure of corn
thread, outnall (73):
tilt (73): awning
'*tithecarr*' (167):
'*trasyll*' (73):
trendle (82): small wheel
truckle (73): castor
tub, bucking (73): washtub
tub, powdering (73, 158, 167): tub in which animal flesh is salted
tucknet (82): smaller net used with the great seine to bring fish to the surface
tunnel (73): kind of funnel

turnsole (73): purple dye
vane, closing (25): ? device for adjusting by wind-power the slats of a louver. *Cf.* gatherer
vat, neshing (167): tub in which some substance is softened
washvat (107): washtub
weight (73): 14 stone (English measure of weight)
weight, pile (73): one of a series of weights fitting one within or upon another to form a solid cone
whitch (167): chest
whitch, bolting (73, 107): chest in which siftings are stored
whitehouse (167): dairy
wool oil (73): oil used for greasing sheep's wool
yoting stone (158, 167): ? shaped and polished stone with lip through which grain is poured

INDEX OF PERSONS AND PLACES

References other than those preceded by 'p.' are to the numbers of entries, not pages. A reference under a personal name to the subject of proceedings is given in bold type. An asterisk denotes that a man is a juror in more than one extent in the same entry. Places not otherwise identified may be presumed to be in Wiltshire.

INDEX OF SUBJECTS

(References are to the numbers of entries, not pages)

WILTSHIRE RECORD SOCIETY

(As at 31 December 1972)

President: PROFESSOR RALPH B. PUGH
Honorary Editor: DOUGLAS A. CROWLEY
Honorary Treasurer: MICHAEL J. LANSDOWN
Honorary Secretary: MRS. NANCY D. STEELE

Committee:

E. J. M. BUXTON
THE COUNTESS BADENI
I. GEOFFREY MOORE
MAURICE G. RATHBONE
MISS ELIZABETH CRITTALL (*co-opted*)
RICHARD E. SANDELL, representing the Wiltshire Archaeological and Natural History Society
BRIGADIER A. R. FORBES, as Secretary and Treasurer of the Wiltshire Archaeological and Natural History Society

Honorary Auditor: G. HYLTON EVANS

PRIVATE MEMBERS

AILESBURY, The Marquess of, D.L., J.P., Sturmy House, Savernake Forest, Marlborough
ALLEN, N., 46 Westland Road, Faringdon, Berks.
ANDERSON, D. M., 64 Winsley Road, Bradford-on-Avon
APPLEGATE, Miss Jean M., 55 Holbrook Lane, Trowbridge
ARCHER, P. J., Cotswold View, 9 Station Road, Highworth
AVERY, Mrs. Susan, 24 Old Hertford Road, Hatfield, Herts.
AWDRY, Mrs. R. W., M.B.E., Haven Court, Cary Park, Babbacombe, Devon

BADENI, The Countess, Norton Manor, Malmesbury
BEATTIE, Prof. J. M., Dept. of History, University of Toronto, Canada
BERRETT, A. M., 65 Mandeville Road, Southgate, London N.14
BIDDULPH, G. M. R., c/o Personnel Records, British Council, 65 Davies Street, London W.1
BIRLEY, N. P., D.S.O., M.C., Hyde Leaze, Hyde Lane, Marlborough
BLAKE, T. N., 16 West Hill Road, London S.W.18
BLUNT, C. E., O.B.E., F.B.A., Ramsbury Hill, Ramsbury, Marlborough
BONNEY, Mrs. H. M., Flint Cottage, Netton, Salisbury
BRICE, G. R., Branchways, Willett Way, Petts Wood, Kent
BRIGGS, M., Glebe Cottage, Middle Woodford, Salisbury
BRIGHT, Sq.-Ldr. Bruce, c/o 1 Westlecot Road, Swindon
BROOKE-LITTLE, J. P., M.V.O., Richmond Herald of Arms, College of Arms, Queen Victoria Street, London E.C.4
BROWN, W. E., The Firs, Beckhampton, Marlborough
BRUGES, Major W. E., 1 Bower Gardens, Salisbury
BUCKERIDGE, J. M., 104 Beacon Road, Loughborough, Leics.
BUCKLAND, L. J., Twelvetrees, Amesbury, Salisbury
BURGE, Miss H. M., The Old Rectory, Huish, Marlborough
BURGE, S. F. M., The Old Rectory, Huish, Marlborough

BURNETT BROWN, Miss Janet M., Lacock Abbey, Chippenham
BUXTON, E. J. M., Cole Park, Malmesbury

CANNING, Capt. J. B., 3902 S Browne' Spokane, Washington, U.S.A.
CAREW-HUNT, Miss P. H., Cowleaze, Edington, Westbury
CARTER, Miss N. M. G., Gatehouse, Cricklade
CLANCHY, M. T., Dept. of History, The University, Glasgow W.2
CLARK, J. W., Manor Farm, Etchilhampton, Devizes
CODRINGTON, Miss N. E., Wroughton House, Swindon
CRITTALL, Miss Elizabeth, 16 Downside Crescent, London N.W.3
CROWLEY, D. A., 333 Cranbrook Road, Ilford, Essex
CUFFE-ADAMS, E. J., Merryfield, St. George's Road, Bickley, Bromley, Kent

DANIELS, C. G., 81 Goffenton Drive, Oldbury Court, Fishponds, Bristol
DIBBEN, A. A., 222 King Street, Hammersmith, London W.6
DOYLE, Leslie, Cheviot, Clay Lane, Wythenshawe, Manchester 23
DYKE, P. J., 35 Buckleigh Avenue, Merton Park, London S.W.20

ECCLES, The Viscount, P.C., K.C.V.O., Dean Farm, Chute, Andover, Hants
EGAN, T. M., Vale Cottage, Stert, Devizes
ELLIS, R. L., 5 Avebury Park, Lovelace Gardens, Surbiton, Surrey
ELRINGTON, C. R., Institute of Historical Research, University of London, Senate House, London W.C.1

FANE, Mrs. Edmund, Boyton Manor, Warminster
FILBY, P. W., Librarian, Maryland Historical Society, 201 West Monument Street, Baltimore, Md. 21201, U.S.A.
FLOWER-ELLIS, J. G. K., Skogshogskolan S104 05 Stockholm 50, Sweden
FORBES, Miss K. G., Bury House, Codford, Warminster
FOY, J. D., 28 Penn Lea Road, Bath, Som.
FRY, Mrs. P. M., 18 Pulteney Street, Bath, Som.
FULLER, Major Sir Gerard, Bt., Neston Park, Corsham

GHEY, J. G., 1 Sandell Court, The Parkway, Bassett, Southampton
GIBBON, Canon Geoffrey, 1 North Grove, London N.6
GIMSON, H. M., Grey Wethers, Stanton St. Bernard, Marlborough
GODDARD, Mrs. G. H., The Boot, Scholard's Lane, Ramsbury, Marlborough
GOULD, C.P. (Correspondent for the U.S.A.), 1200 Old Mill Road, San Marino, California, U.S.A.

HALL, G. D. G., President, Corpus Christi College, Oxford
HALLWORTH, Frederick, Northcote, Westbury Road, Bratton, Westbury
HAM, Chester W., Jr., 187 Rounds Avenue, Providence, Rhode Island, 02907, U.S.A.
HAMILTON, Capt. R., West Dean, Salisbury
HARFIELD, Capt. A. G., 244 Signal Squadron (Air Support), R.A.F. Benson, Oxford
HARFIELD, Mrs. A. G., 244 Signal Squadron (Air Support), R.A.F. Benson, Oxford
HATCHWELL, R. C., The Old Rectory, Little Somerford, Chippenham
HAWKINS, M. J., 121 High Street, Lewes, Sussex
HAYMAN, The Rev. P. E. C., The Vicarage, Rogate, Petersfield, Hants
HOARE, H. P. R., Gasper House, Stourton, Warminster
HOBBS, Miss N., 140 Western Road, Sompting, Lancing, Sussex
HUMPHREYS, Cdr. L. A., R.N. (Rtd.), Elm Lodge, Biddestone, Chippenham
HURSTFIELD, Prof. Joel, 7 Glenilla Road, London N.W.3

JACKSON, R. H., 17 Queens Road, Tisbury, Salisbury
JENNINGS, R. A. U., Newlands, 46 London Road, Salisbury
JEREMY, D. J., Curator, Merrimack Valley Textile Museum, North Andover, Mass. 01845, U.S.A.
JOHN, D. Murray, O.B.E., Town Clerk, Borough of Swindon, Civic Offices, Swindon
JONES, The Rev. Kingsley C., 22 Brookside Road, Fulwood, Preston, Lancs.

KEMPSON, E. G. H., Sun Cottage, Hyde Lane, Marlborough
KOMATSU, Prof. Y., Institute of European Economic History, Waseda University, Tokyo 160, Japan

LANGTON, Sir Henry, D.S.O., D.F.C., D.L., Overtown House, Wroughton, Swindon
LANSDOWN, M. J., 37 Hilperton Road, Trowbridge
LAURENCE, Miss Anne, 29 Sydney Street, Chelsea, London S.W.3
LAURENCE, G. F., 1 Monks Orchard, Petersfield, Hants
LEVER, R. E., Reads Close, Teffont Magna, Salisbury
LITTLE, J. E., The Pantiles, Chapel Lane, Uffington, Berks.
LONDON, Miss V. C. M., Underholt, Westwood Road, Bidston, Birkenhead

MCCULLOUGH, Prof. Edward, Sir George Williams University, 1435 Drummond Street, Montreal 25, Quebec, Canada
MCGOWAN, B., 28 Webbs Way, Burbage, Marlborough
MACKINTOSH, Duncan, C.B.E., Woodfolds, Oaksey, Malmesbury
MANN, Miss J. de L., The Cottage, Bowerhill, Melksham
MARGADALE, The Lord, T. D., Fonthill House, Tisbury
MASTERS, H. A. C., Hossil Lane, Stanton Fitzwarren, Swindon
METHUEN, The Lord, Corsham Court
MILLBOURN, Sir Eric, C.M.G., Conkwell Grange, Limpley Stoke, Bath, Som.
MITTON, A. W. D., The Dungeon, 239 Earl's Court Road, London S.W.5
MOODY, G. C., Montrose, Shaftesbury Road, Wilton, Salisbury
MOORE, I. G., Raycroft, Lacock, Chippenham
MORRIS, Miss Bronwen, 9 Cleveland Gardens, Trowbridge
MORRISON, The Hon. Charles, M.P., Fyfield Manor, Marlborough
MOULTON, A. E., The Hall, Bradford-on-Avon

NAN KIVELL, R. de C., 20 Cork Street, London W.1
NEWALL, R. S., Avon Cottage, Lower Woodford, Salisbury
NORTHAMPTON, Emma, Marchioness of, O.B.E., The Curatage, Horningsham, Warminster

OSBORNE, Major Robert, c/o Lloyds Bank Ltd., Westbury-on-Trym, Bristol

PAFFORD, J. H. P., Hillside, Allington Park, Bridport, Dorset
PASKIN, Lady, Wishford, Salisbury
PERRY, S. H., 117 London Road, Kettering, Northants.
PONTING, K. G., Becketts House, Edington, Westbury
POTHECARY, S. G., 41 Australian Avenue, Salisbury
PUGH, Prof. R. B., 67 Southwood Park, London N.6

RAMSAY, G. D., St. Edmund Hall, Oxford
RANCE, H. F., Butler's Court, Beaconsfield, Bucks.
RATHBONE, M. G., Craigleith, Snarlton Lane, Melksham Forest
RAYBOULD, Miss Frances, 20 Radnor Road, Salisbury
REEVES, Dr. Marjorie E., 38 Norham Road, Oxford
REYNOLDS, A., The White House, Riverfield Road, Staines, Middlesex
ROGERS, K. H., Silverthorne House, East Town, West Ashton, Trowbridge
ROOKE, Mrs. R. E. P., The Ivy, Chippenham
ROOKE, Miss S. F., The Ivy, Chippenham
ROSS, Harry, Leighton Villa, Wellhead Lane, Westbury
RUNDLE, Miss Penelope, 46 St. Andrews Road, Bemerton, Salisbury

SANDELL, R. E., Hillside, 64 Devizes Road, Potterne
SANDQUIST, T. A., Dept. of History, University of Toronto, 5, Canada
SAWYER, L. F. T., 51 Sandridge Road, Melksham
SHADBOLT, Mrs. L. G., Birkhall House, High Kelling, Holt, Norfolk
SHEWRING, D. G., 4 Clifton Street, Treorchy, Rhondda, Glam.
SOMERSET, The Duke of, D. L., Bradley House, Maiden Bradley, Warminster
STEDMAN, A. R., 9 The Green, Aldbourne, Marlborough
STEELE, Mrs. N. D., Milestones, Hatchet Close, Hale, Fordingbridge, Hants
STEVENSON, Miss J. H., Institute of Historical Research, University of London, Senate House, London W.C.1
STEWART, Miss K. P., Moxham Villa, 57 Lower Road, Bemerton, Salisbury
STRATTON, J. M., Manor House Farm, Stockton, Warminster
STYLES, Philip, 21 Castle Lane, Warwick

TANNER, Miss J. M., 155 Shrivenham Road, Swindon

TAYLOR, C. C., Royal Commission on Historical Monuments (England), 13 West End, Whittlesford, Cambridge

TURNER, Miss M., 4 Elm Grove Road, Salisbury

TWINE, S. W., Hopedale, Bremilham Road, Malmesbury

VERNON, Miss T. E., Dyer's Leaze, Lacock, Chippenham

WADE, Miss Elmira M., O.B.E., Bridge Cottage, Lacock, Chippenham

WALKER, Rev. J. G., Buttermere Hill, Churt, Farnham, Surrey

WATKINS, W. T., Carn Ingli, 16 Westbury Road, Warminster

WEINSTOCK, Sir Arnold, Bowden Park, Lacock, Chippenham

WILLAN, Group Capt. F. A., D.L., Bridges, Teffont, Salisbury

WILLIAMS, N. J., 57 Rotherwick Road, Hampstead Garden Suburb, London N.W.11

WILLOUGHBY, R. W. H., Langford Way, Berwick St. James, Salisbury

WILTSHIRE, D. C. S., 17 Macaulay Buildings, Bath, Som.

WILTSHIRE, Julian M., Ashlyns Cottage, Lybury Lane, Redbourn, Herts.

WORTHINGTON, B. S., Vale Lodge, Colnbrook, Bucks.

YOUNG, C. L. R., 25 Staveley Road, Chiswick, London W.4

UNITED KINGDOM INSTITUTIONS

Aberdeen. King's College Library
Aberystwyth. National Library of Wales
,, University College General Library
Allington (S. Wilts.). Bourne Valley Historical Society
Bangor. University College of North Wales
Bath. General Reference Library
Birmingham. Central Public Library
,, University Library, Edgbaston
Bridgwater. Somerset County Library
Brighton. University of Sussex Library, Falmer
Bristol. City of Bristol Library
,, University Library
Cambridge. University Library
Coventry. University of Warwick Library
Devizes. Wiltshire Archaeological and Natural History Society
Dorchester. County of Dorset Library
Edinburgh. National Library of Scotland
,, University Library
Exeter. University Library
Glasgow. University Library
Gloucester. Bristol and Gloucestershire Archaeological Society
Hull. University of Kingston-upon-Hull Library
Leeds. University Library
Leicester. University Library
Liverpool. University Library
London. British Museum
,, College of Arms
London. Guildhall Library
,, Inner Temple Library
,, Institute of Historical Research
,, London Library
,, Public Record Office
,, Royal Historical Society
,, Society of Antiquaries
,, Society of Genealogists
,, University of London Library
,, City of Westminster Public
,, Library
Manchester. Rylands University Library
Marlborough. Adderley Library, Marlborough College
Norwich. University of East Anglia Library
Nottingham. University Library
Oxford. Bodleian Library
,, Exeter College Library
,, New College Library
Reading. Central Library
,, University Library
St. Andrews. University Library
Salisbury. History Dept., College of Sarum St. Michael
,, Diocesan Record Office
,, The Museum
,, City of New Sarum Public Library
,, Royal Commission on Historical Monuments (England), Manor Road
,, Salisbury & South Wilts. College of Further Education

Sheffield. University Library
Southampton. University Library
Swansea. University College of Swansea Library
Swindon. Borough of Swindon Public Library
„ Swindon College Library
Taunton. Somerset Archaeological and Natural History Society
Trowbridge. Wiltshire County Library
„ Wiltshire Record Office, County Hall
„ The Wiltshire Times
York. University of York Library, Heslington

OVERSEAS INSTITUTIONS

AUSTRALIA

Canberra. National Library of Australia
Melbourne. Baillieu Library, University of Melbourne
„ Victoria State Library
St. Lucia, Brisbane. Main Library, University of Queensland
Sydney. Fisher Library, University of Sydney

CANADA

Downsview, Ontario. York Universities Libraries
Kingston, Ontario. Queen's University
London, Ontario. Lawson Memorial Library, University of Western Ontario
Peterborough, Ontario. Dept. of History, Trent University
Toronto, Ontario. University of Toronto Library
Ottawa. Carleton University Library
St. John's, Newfoundland. Memorial University of Newfoundland Library
Vancouver. Main Library, University of British Columbia
Victoria, B.C. McPherson Library, University of Victoria

DENMARK

Copenhagen. The Royal Library

GERMANY

Göttingen. Niedersächsische Staats-und Universitätsbibliothek

REPUBLIC OF IRELAND

Dublin. National Library of Ireland
„ Trinity College Library

JAPAN

Osaka. Institute of Economic History, Kansai University
Sendai. Institute of Economic History, Tohoku University

NEW ZEALAND

Wellington. National Library of New Zealand

SWEDEN

Upsala. Kungl. Universitetets Bibliotek (Royal University Library)

UNITED STATES OF AMERICA

Ann Arbor, Mich. General Library, University of Michigan
Athens, Georgia. University Libraries, University of Georgia
Baltimore, Md. Peabody Institute of the City of Baltimore
Bloomington, Ind. Indiana University Library
Boston, Mass. Public Library of the City of Boston
„ „ New England Historic Genealogical Society
Boulder, Col. University of Colorado Libraries
Buffalo, N.Y. Lockwood Memorial Library, State University of New York at Buffalo
Cambridge, Mass. Harvard Law School Library
„ „ Harvard College Library
Chicago, Ill. University of Chicago Library
„ „ Newberry Library
Cleveland, Ohio. Public Library
De Kalb, Ill. Northern University of Illinois, Swen Franklin Parson Library
East Lansing, Mich. Michigan State University Library
Haverford, Pa. Haverford College Library
Fort Wayne, Ind. Public Library of Fort Wayne and Allen County
Iowa City. State University of Iowa Library
Ithaca, N.Y. Cornell University Library
Las Cruces, New Mexico. New Mexico State University Library
Los Angeles, Cal. Public Library of Los Angeles
„ „ „ University Research Library, University of California

Minneapolis, Ma. Dept. of History, Minnesota University

Newark, Delaware. University of Delaware Library

New Haven, Conn. Yale University Library

New York. Columbia University of the City of New York

,, ,, Public Library, City of New York

Notre Dame, Ind. Notre Dame University Memorial Library

Philadelphia, Pa. Pennsylvania University Library

Princeton, N.J. Princeton University Library

Salt Lake City, Utah. Genealogical Society of the Church of Latter Day Saints

San Marino, Cal. Henry E. Huntingdon Library

Stanford, Cal. Stanford University Library

Urbana, Ill. University of Illinois Library

Washington, D.C. Library of Congress

Winston-Salem, N.C. Wake Forest University Library

LIST OF PUBLICATIONS

The Wiltshire Record Society was founded in 1937, as the Records Branch of the Wiltshire Archaeological and Natural History Society, to promote the publication of the documentary sources for the history of Wiltshire. The annual subscription is £3. In return, a member receives a volume each year. Prospective members should apply to Mrs. N. D. Steele, 41 Castle Road, Salisbury. Many more members are needed.

The following volumes have been published. Price to members £3 and to non-members £4, postage extra. Available from the Hon. Treasurer, Mr. M. J. Lansdown, 37 Hilperton Road, Trowbridge, Wiltshire.

I *Abstract of Feet of Fines relating to Wiltshire for the reigns of Edward I and Edward II.* Edited by R. B. Pugh (1939)

II *Accounts of the Parliamentary Garrisons of Great Chalfield and Malmesbury, 1645–6.* Edited by J. H. P. Pafford (1940). Illustrated

III *Calendar of Antrobus Deeds before 1625.* Edited by R. B. Pugh (1947)

IV *Minutes of Proceedings in Sessions, 1563, 1574–92.* Edited by H. C. Johnson (1949)

V *List of Records of Wiltshire Boroughs before 1836.* Edited by M. G. Rathbone (1951)

VI *The Trowbridge Woollen Industry as illustrated by the Stock Books of John and Thomas Clark, 1804–24.* Edited by R. F. Beckinsale (1951). Illustrated

VII *Guild Stewards' Book of the Borough of Calne, 1561–1688.* Edited by A. W. Mabbs (1953)

VIII *Andrews and Dury's Map of Wiltshire, 1773.* A reduced facsimile in 'atlas' form, with an introduction by Elizabeth Crittall (1952)

IX *Surveys of the Manors of Philip, Earl of Pembroke and Montgomery, 1631–2.* Edited by E. Kerridge (1953)

X *Two Sixteenth Century Taxation Lists, 1545 and 1576.* Edited by G. D. Ramsay (1954)

XI *Wiltshire Quarter Sessions and Assizes, 1736.* Edited by J. P. M. Fowle (1955)

XII *Collectanea.* Edited by N. J. Williams, with a foreword by T. F. T. Plucknett (1956)

XIII *Progress Notes of Warden Woodward for the Wiltshire Estates of New College, 1659–75.* Edited by R. L. Rickard (1957). Illustrated

XIV *Accounts and Surveys of the Wiltshire Lands of Adam de Stratton, 1268–86.* Edited by M. W. Farr (1959)

XV *Tradesmen in Early-Stuart Wiltshire: A Miscellany.* Edited by N. J. Williams (1960)

XVI *Crown Pleas of the Wiltshire Eyre, 1249.* Edited by C. A. F. Meekings (1961)

XVII *Wiltshire Apprentices and their Masters, 1710–60.* Edited by Christabel Dale (1961)

XVIII *Hemingby's Register.* Edited by Helena M. Chew (1963)

XIX *Documents Illustrating the Wiltshire Textile Trades in the Eighteenth Century.* Edited by Julia de L. Mann (1964)

XX *The Diary of Thomas Naish.* Edited by Doreen Slatter (1965). Illustrated

XXI, XXII *The Rolls of Highworth Hundred, 1275–87.* Edited by Brenda Farr (1966, 1968). Map

XXIII *The Earl of Hertford's Lieutenancy Papers, 1603–12.* Edited by W. P. D. Murphy (1969). Illustrated

XXIV *Court Rolls of the Wiltshire Manors of Adam de Stratton.* Edited by R. B. Pugh (1970)

VOLUMES IN PREPARATION

Wiltshire Glebe Terriers, edited by D. A. Crowley; *Salisbury General Entry Books*, edited by Alan Crossley; *The Wiltshire Forest Eyre, 1257*, edited by N. J. Williams; *The Charters of Lacock Abbey*, edited by K. H. Rogers; *Abstract of Feet of Fines relating to Wiltshire for the reign of Edward III*, edited by C. R. Elrington; *The Edington Cartulary*, edited by Janet Stevenson; *Wiltshire Tithe Awards*, edited by R. E. Sandell; *Salisbury Poor in the Early Seventeenth Century*, edited by P. A. Slack; *Wiltshire Clergy of the Seventeenth Century*, edited by Barrie Williams; *Dean Chaundler's Register*, edited by T. C. B. Timmins; *The Bradenstoke Cartulary*, edited by Vera C. M. London.

A leaflet giving fuller details may be obtained from Mrs. Steele.